Adult Dyslexia

A Guide for the Workplace

DEDICATION

This book is dedicated to Shannon and h and f.

ADULT DYSLEXIA
A GUIDE FOR THE WORKPLACE

Gary Fitzgibbon and **Brian O'Connor**
Fitzgibbon Associates, London, UK

JOHN WILEY & SONS, LTD

Other Wiley Editorial Offices

John Wiley & Sons, Inc., 605 Third Avenue, New York, NY 10158-0012, USA

Jossey-Bass, 989 Market Street, San Francisco, CA 94103-1741, USA

Wiley-VCH Verlag GmbH, Pappelallee 3, D-69469 Weinheim, Germany

John Wiley & Sons Australia, Ltd., 33 Park Road, Milton, Queensland 4064, Australia

John Wiley & Sons (Asia) Pte, Ltd., 2 Clementi Loop #02-01, Jin Xing Distripark, Singapore 129809

John Wiley & Sons (Canada), Ltd., 22 Worcester Road, Etobicoke, Ontario M9W 1L1, Canada

British Library Cataloguing in Publication Data

A catalogue record for this book is available from the British Library

ISBN 0-470-84725-5 (cased)
ISBN 0-471-48712-0 (paper)

Typeset in 10/12pt Times by TechBooks, New Delhi, India
Printed and bound in Great Britain by Biddles Ltd., Guildford and King's Lynn
This book is printed on acid-free paper responsibly manufactured from sustainable forestry
in which at least two trees are planted for each one used for paper production.

CONTENTS

ABOUT THE AUTHORS

Gary Fitzgibbon, BA, MSc, PGCE, COccPsychol, is a chartered occupational psychologist with many years' experience of providing a wide range of psychological services to individuals and organisations. Gary developed an interest in adult dyslexia at the end of the 1980s, from which time he has been very active in the field. Although a busy occupational psychologist whose interests lie more in solving practical organisational problems than in academic psychology, Gary has nevertheless given numerous talks and presentations on adult dyslexia, including presentations at international conferences in the UK and the USA; he co-authored the book, *Adult Dyslexia: Assessment, Counselling and Training*, a successful and authoritative work viewed by many as the first significant book on adult dyslexia.

Gary and his colleagues have developed a comprehensive range of exercises and training programmes to enable adult dyslexics to function efficiently in the world of work, and many hundreds of adult dyslexics have found that the training provided by Fitzgibbon Associates, the organisation Gary established in 1980, has been the key to their success in employment. An important element of the work he does in adult dyslexia is the promotion of positive perceptions of adult dyslexia as a condition distinct from child dyslexia and one that requires input from work psychology, in contrast to the more traditional educational psychology emphasis.

In addition to adult dyslexia, Gary is active in other areas of work psychology, including creativity in organisations, retirement psychology, stress risk assesment, stress management, counselling, psychological assessment and memory development. Gary has been interviewed in his areas of interest numerous times for local and national newspapers, magazines, radio and television.

Brian O'Connor, BA, MSc, CQSW, PGDipSocRes, PGCE, is a counsellor and qualified social worker. In addition to substantial practical experience as a social worker, Brian has a background in education where, as a senior lecturer in social work, his responsibilities included training social workers and providing workshops on a range of topics in the general area of disabilities.

In his time in the world of education, Brian was involved with many different client groups, including dyslexic adults and children, offenders, health professionals and managers from the world of business and commerce. He designed and presented many courses on topics related to disabilities in the work environment, and, drawing on his own wide work experience, which, as well as education and social work, includes regular military service, employment in the construction industry, commercial diving, and mechanical and civil engineering, he was responsible for establishing one of the UK's first further education courses aimed at employment rehabilitation for adults with learning disabilities.

Brian developed an interest in adult dyslexia while working as a probation officer in the 1970s; at the end of the 1980s, he started collaborating with Gary Fitzgibbon in the development of programmes for helping adult dyslexics manage their condition in the workplace.

Brian's current interests in the area of adult dyslexia include Internet counselling and psychotherapy, training trainers and strategies for balancing home, social and work commitments. His other active areas of interest include stress management and retirement psychology.

PREFACE

This book is written for employers, psychologists, trainers, human resource personnel and all professional people who have an interest in, or a responsibility for, adult dyslexia in a work-related context. We decided to write this book because, as practitioners with substantial experience of both advising organisations on adult dyslexia issues and providing assessment, counselling and training services to adult dyslexics, we are very aware that the condition is widely misunderstood in the world of work.

Our background of working in commercial, industrial, educational and public service organisations, together with the special expertise we have developed in adult dyslexia, enables us to describe and explain the problems adult dyslexics face in workplaces and to identify possible solutions to those problems. We have seen many examples that confirm that dyslexics can be very successful in the right environment and that they can fail to realise their potential in the wrong environment. In this book we provide practical advice, for both individuals and employers, concerning what constitutes the right environment, how to create it and how organisations can make the psychological transition from a framework that perceives dyslexia as a problem to one that conceptualises it as a solution.

Although aimed at employers and professionals involved in supporting adult dyslexics in (and into) work, this book will also be of interest to adult dyslexics themselves. By improving personal understanding of how dyslexia manifests itself in workplaces, dyslexic people can encourage, work with and assist their colleagues and employers to understand that dyslexics have a wealth of talent to bring to the world of work. Increasing understanding is a key to the process of creating a more efficient and effective work environment, one which, in all probability, will benefit everyone who uses it.

In writing this book, we gratefully acknowledge the encouragement, help and support we have received from many colleagues and friends. We are particularly indebted to Vivienne Young, Dr Tessa Adams, John Emery, Sarah Douglas, Alison Little, Joseph Fitzgibbon and Vanessa Taylor-Brown, as well as the many adult dyslexic clients who agreed to allow us to describe their experiences to illustrate various points we wanted to make. However, it should be noted that throughout the book the names of the adults have been changed to preserve anonimity. Any resemblance to real persons is a co-incidence.

Gary Fitzgibbon and Brian O'Connor
Fitzgibbon Associates, 39–41 North Road, London, UK
Telephone: 020 7609 7809
Websites: www.adultdyslexia.co.uk
www.fitzgibbonassociates.co.uk
Email: fae@fitzgibbonassociates.co.uk

1

ADULT DYSLEXIA: MYTHS, REALITIES AND SUCCESS

INTRODUCTION

The late Professor Leith described dyslexia as the unidentified flying object of modern psychology: until recently, it was an unidentified flying object that was only ever sighted in schools. However, in the last 10–15 years, there have been many sightings in workplaces. Like unidentified flying objects, dyslexia is surrounded by confusion, uncertainty and fear. Many people believe that dyslexia is only weakness and lack of ability, but such beliefs are unfounded; they are myths that have evolved as myths always do when a phenomenon is not well defined. In this opening chapter, as well as examining some of the more persistent myths about dyslexia and discussing possible explanations of their origins, we shall examine why some dyslexics are successful and others, in spite of having considerable potential, are not.

Although this book is concerned with adult dyslexics, this chapter examines how child dyslexics are treated in school and in particular how the education system fails them, and the implications that this failure has for their adulthood. The importance of distinguishing child dyslexia from adult dyslexia is discussed and illustrated, and the appropriateness of different types of training for adult dyslexics is examined. The chapter concludes by looking briefly at what some researchers believe is the key determinant of occupational success for adult dyslexics.

PROBLEMS OF DEFINING DYSLEXIA FOR THE WORKPLACE

There has been such an acceleration of interest in dyslexia over the last 15 years that the word 'dyslexia', which was once a specialist medical term, is now a part of everyday language. However, although the word is well known, dyslexia is not well understood. Most experts, including Miles (2001), agree that the condition has a physical basis, and that in some cases its manifestations have a genetic basis. However, this is far from being an explanation of this complex condition; for example, Frith (1997: p. 17) has observed that 'There may be many different kinds of genes and different kinds of brain conditions interacting with environmental influences that are ultimately responsible for dyslexia.'

There is general agreement that dyslexia causes difficulties in a wide range of behaviours, but there is little agreement about which are the most significant weaknesses and how they arise. As Miles points out, the research findings do not constitute a sound understanding of how the common manifestations of dyslexia result from the condition.

In reality, both the cause of dyslexia and how it produces the behaviours it does produce are poorly understood. In spite of a proliferation of theories, a universally acceptable definition has for decades eluded the efforts of many psychologists, neurologists and other researchers. While many experts consider that a convincing theory and explanation of dyslexia is not far away, it still remains a condition with numerous definitions but no generally agreed best definition.

Of the many definitions that exist, there are very few that make sense in the context of the workplace experience of adult dyslexics. For example, a discrepancy between achievement in literacy and overall ability characterises most of the early definitions of dyslexia, and Thomson & Watkins (1990: p. 3) provide a typical example of this type of 'discrepancy' definition:

> A severe difficulty with the written form of language independent of intellectual, cultural and emotional causation. It is characterised by the individuals' reading, writing and spelling attainments being well below the level expected, based on intelligence and chronological age.

A major problem with this approach is that it does not apply to adult dyslexics who do not exhibit any significant literacy weaknesses, and, as we shall see later, there are many of these people. Discrepancy definitions are useful for describing aspects of child dyslexia, but they are not an appropriate starting point for defining dyslexia in relation to adult dyslexics.

As already noted, there is currently a good deal of work on identifying the neurological causes of dyslexia, and it now seems very likely that evidence from brain research will enable a clear explanation of precisely how the brains of dyslexics differ from the brains of non-dyslexics. There are already explanations focusing on brain differences, but they are usually not entirely appropriate for the workplace. For example, Miles (2001: p. 38) suggests the following theory:

> For neurological reasons (including in some cases, genetic reasons) dyslexics have a weakness in the magnocellular system. As a result of this they are impeded in their ability to process information at speed; and in the case of auditory information the result is a weakness at the phonological level. This weakness creates a wide range of different sequelae (consequences) which vary considerably from one individual to another.

As research progresses, such definitions will become more specific in terms of identifying what are the 'neurological reasons' and the 'genetic reasons', and the academic understanding of dyslexia will therefore be advanced. Such developments are, however, unlikely to influence strategies for helping adult dyslexics to improve their performance in the workplace.

Essentially practical applications and pragmatism are more important in occupational psychology than academic rigour, and the identification of differences in neurological systems that may account for dyslexia are therefore largely irrelevant in the context of occupational psychology. Definitions that explain dyslexia in terms of brain research are not an appropriate starting point for defining dyslexia in relation to helping adult dyslexics in workplaces.

As occupational psychologists working in the field of adult dyslexia we are concerned with empowering dyslexics to take control of their lives. This can be achieved by enabling them to understand their dyslexia and how it leads to the common dyslexic behaviours they experience. With these goals in mind, the natural starting point is a definition of dyslexia that both promotes dyslexic people's understanding of their condition and provides an opportunity for them to identify with the definition, i.e., to attain some insight into, and explanation of, their experiences.

The ideal definition will be one that is valid, brief, and easy to remember, as well as indicating how adult dyslexics should be trained and developed. In addition, it should have clear implications for how workplaces can change to support dyslexic employees. In our experience, a definition that is relevant to adults and workplaces and that meets the criteria listed above can be found by examining how human memory functions in dyslexia. This is a logical approach since measuring a deficit in memory is the diagnostic criterion used by most psychologists in assessing people for dyslexia. For example, in diagnostic assessments involving the Wechsler Adult Intelligence Scale (WAIS), dyslexia is diagnosed by detecting significantly lower scores on subtests that place a heavy load on phonological short-term memory, i.e., arithmetic, digit span and digit symbol.

Memory has been the focus of a good deal of experimental research, and most researchers accept that the condition is characterised by a deficit in the short-term memory system. Some researchers consider short-term memory to be central to understanding dyslexia; for example, Rack (1994: p. 9) argues that 'one of the most reliable and often quoted associated characteristics of developmental dyslexia is an inefficiency in short-term memory.'

McLoughlin, Fitzgibbon & Young (1994), who reviewed most of the main studies on dyslexia and memory, suggest that a weakness in phonological short-term memory can explain all of the most significant behavioural manifestations of dyslexia. They define the condition as simply 'an inefficiency in working memory'.

The term 'working memory' is sometimes used interchangeably with the term 'short-term memory', but they are different systems. Working memory refers to a system of storage and processing of information, in contrast to short-term memory, which refers only to storage of information. The working-memory model of human memory, which was initially proposed by Baddeley & Hitch (1974) and later revised by Baddeley (1986), is a dynamic, limited-capacity system that comprises a master system controlling two slave systems. One of these two slave systems, called the 'sketch-pad', stores visual and spatial information, i.e., pictures. The other slave system, called the 'articulatory loop', stores sound or phonological information, i.e., speech sounds. The articulatory loop is particularly involved in the perception and production of verbal information.

Thomson (2001) acknowledges the working memory as the system that is most relevant to dyslexia. He explains that it is a limited-capacity system which, as well as tracking what we do as we do it, has a role in organising and directing our attention mechanisms. Thomson (p. 6) points out that 'Problems in phonology, written language and attention are all elements of working memory systems.'

Defining dyslexia in terms of an inefficiency in working memory does, then, have considerable potential in terms of explaining the disorder comprehensively. We have found this memory-based definition to be of great utility in designing practical training for improving the dyslexic's work performance. In presenting dyslexia-awareness training, the definition of dyslexia as an inefficiency in working memory leads to almost immediate understanding by employers and employees alike as far as the relationship between dyslexia and the observed dyslexic behaviours is concerned. Furthermore, the definition makes sense to dyslexic people in terms of what they have experienced in their childhood and adulthood, and, as such, it offers them a means of gaining control over their environment, a means which, as we shall see later in this chapter, is a key to their employment success.

The working-memory definition of dyslexia presented above is assumed throughout this book. After the next section, which outlines how dyslexia is detected in schools and the problems that beset its identification, we shall examine how this key weakness in working memory can explain some of the experiences that dyslexics have in their childhood.

APPROPRIATE AND INAPPROPRIATE APPROACHES TO IDENTIFYING DYSLEXIA

Dyslexia should be diagnosed by a chartered psychologist, since this is the only reliable way of obtaining a proper diagnosis. Proper diagnostic procedures involve what are known as 'closed' tests, which are tests that are available only to 'qualifying' chartered psychologists; i.e., test distributors will supply them only to chartered psychologists that have appropriate training and experience. For example, the Wechsler Intelligence Scale for Children (WISC) and the Wechsler Adult Intelligence Scale (WAIS), which are the most commonly used psychometric tests for diagnosing dyslexia in children and adults, respectively, are both 'closed' tests. While some non-psychologists do have unofficial access to these tests, their use by such people is unlikely to yield valid results. These tests require elements of clinical judgement and other psychological skills in order to ensure that their administration, marking and interpretation are valid and meaningful.

The details of how a proper psychological assessment for dyslexia is carried out are not relevant here, since this book is concerned not with diagnosis itself but rather with what happens before and after it. Readers who are interested in issues related to assessment are referred to McLoughlin, Fitzgibbon & Young (1994) and Turner (1997).

In general, what teachers do in schools is a form of dyslexia screening. That is to say, they are carrying out a procedure that should be used to establish whether there is justification for referring a child to a chartered psychologist for diagnostic assessment. It is not uncommon to find so-called diagnostic reports produced by non-psychologists, but these are typically based on inappropriate tests and/or insufficient testing. These reports, particularly if produced by qualified teachers, may be very useful assessments of literacy skills, and, as such, they may be useful information for a psychologist to have when carrying out a diagnostic assessment. Measures of literacy skills are often included in formal assessments, but they are subordinate to measures of cognitive functioning, and without the latter they cannot be used to give a reliable and valid diagnosis of dyslexia.

Some dyslexia specialists have produced their own tests for 'diagnosing' the condition, but these tools usually lack the necessary supporting data, e.g., normative data and data from reliability and validity studies, to make them valid. Although these tests may have an impressive title and seem to measure something relevant (this feature of tests is known as 'face validity'), this is never a guarantee that they are doing what they purport to be doing. In all probability, these informally constructed tests do not measure anything of relevance, and whatever they do measure will, in all probability, be measured in an unreliable fashion. The main problems associated with using such tests are errors that are known as 'false positives' and 'false negatives'. A false positive occurs when someone who is not dyslexic is wrongly identified as being so, and a false negative occurs when someone who is dyslexic is wrongly identified as not being so. Essentially, false positives and false negatives are both likely to occur whenever diagnosis of dyslexia is attempted without proper testing of cognitive functioning. A test that does not come with a technical manual is one that cannot be evaluated, and it should not be used for any purpose, least of all diagnosing complex conditions such as dyslexia. Assessment reports that base a diagnosis on such tests should not be relied upon.

HOW SCHOOLS FAIL DYSLEXIC CHILDREN

In almost all mainstream schools in the United Kingdom, competence in literacy is essential for educational success. The present system makes acquiring such competence difficult for dyslexic children, and when they fail to acquire this competence, they necessarily fail in all academic subjects because of the reliance those subjects have on written communication. Acquiring literacy skills is a very demanding activity that places a heavy load on a person's working memory. Notably, the information to be remembered in learning to spell just a reasonable number of words is enormous. For example, Thomson (2001: p. 130) has observed that the memory demands of spelling include

> Remembering phoneme-grapheme correspondence rules in order to produce the correct output of letters in spelling; remembering letter-by-letter sounds; remembering sounds long enough to blend these in forming words (e.g. c-a-t = cat); being able to correct spelling errors by remembering what the whole word or letter combination looks like; being able to copy spellings from the blackboard without having constantly to look up every 2 seconds or so; and maintaining an auditory or visual image of a spelling or reading pattern long enough for it to be internalised and transferred into other memory systems.

While there is no evidence to suggest that the incidence of dyslexia varies across different cultures, there is evidence of a cultural element in the difficulty that dyslexics experience in acquiring literacy skills. Paulesu et al. (2001) have shown that groups of Italian dyslexics perform better on reading tasks than groups of English and French dyslexics. Paulesu et al. looked at the effect of manipulating one variable across different cultures, namely, the complexity of the language. They found that the more complex the language, the more difficulty dyslexics had in acquiring literacy skills. Their work suggests that as the complexity of a language increases, the demands on memory increase, an effect which means that memory is a factor determining the speed and effectiveness of the acquisition and development of literacy skills. This research has produced results that are consistent with expectations on the basis of dyslexia's being a condition characterised by an inefficiency in phonological working memory.

It is clear, then, that the working-memory inefficiency that characterises dyslexia does make the task of learning to read, write and spell more difficult for dyslexic children than for their non-dyslexic peers. Furthermore, the greater the inefficiency in working memory, the more difficult will be the learning task. Alternatively, we could say that the more dyslexic the person is, the greater the difficulty will be in learning how to read, write and spell. This, however, does not mean that all dyslexics have below-average levels of literacy; there are many other factors operating to determine the end result for any one dyslexic individual. Regardless of how dyslexic people are, they can still overcome their dyslexic difficulties if the environment is right. The next section examines some of the more important factors that can enable dyslexics to overcome the obstacles that the school system places in their path.

FACTORS DETERMINING EDUCATIONAL SUCCESS FOR DYSLEXICS

In spite of the school system, some dyslexic children can learn how to read, write and spell and can achieve academic success. On the basis of the work we have done, we consider that there are three important factors that have a determining influence on whether a dyslexic child achieves success, they are: individual level of ability or aptitude, the motivation and effort the individual makes to acquire literacy skills and the quality of the learning environment to which the child is exposed ('learning environment' refers to both the child's school and the home environment, either one of which can have a determining influence on what the child achieves).

These three factors invariably interact in a complex fashion to determine what happens to individual children as they progress through the school system. Clearly, other factors also play a role; for example, health and individual personality factors affect the individual's educational development. It is therefore very difficult to identify exactly what factor or combination of factors has made what contribution to the person who eventually emerges from the school system. Nevertheless, the three factors referred to above are important, and we believe that there are valuable insights to be gained by examining each of them.

THE ROLE OF ABILITY IN OVERCOMING DYSLEXIC WEAKNESSES

In general, the higher the ability level of dyslexic persons, the easier it will be for them to acquire acceptable levels of literacy. Dyslexia in a high-ability dyslexic will have the effect of disrupting working-memory processes, but if those processes are fundamentally more efficient than average, the effect of dyslexia may be to bring them down to average. Consequently, high-ability dyslexics usually acquire average or above-average levels of literacy, an acquirement which still represents an underperformance in relation to their potential. Although their attained levels might be lower than they should be in relation to their ability level, they are not so low, compared to the class average, that they give their teachers any cause for concern. In a school system such as that which exists in the United Kingdom, where relative as opposed to absolute performance is the focus of attention, the fact that high-ability dyslexics learn to read, write and spell only at a level to match the average will be sufficient not to raise the concern of their teachers.

HOW CHILDREN MAY COMPENSATE FOR FAILURES IN THE SCHOOL SYSTEM

Average or below-average ability dyslexics can succeed in overcoming the difficulties they face in acquiring literacy skills by making above-average efforts. For example, if, on average, a non-dyslexic takes an hour to learn the spellings of a dozen words, a dyslexic might take three hours to learn these spellings. It may require an unusual level of motivation, application and discipline from the dyslexic child to keep up with the rest of the class (working three times longer than everyone else is not easy to do); nevertheless, some dyslexic children have or acquire these strengths. A number of factors might motivate dyslexic children to work much harder than their peers; for example, a desire not to become what they observe their parent(s) to be may be a strong motivator, as the following case history illustrates.

John's Case History

John, a 44-year-old self-employed kitchen designer and installer, had dyslexia-related difficulties throughout his school days. Initially, he received no help from either his teachers or his parents. Fortunately, however, when he was about nine years old, Anna, a concerned teacher who seemed to understand his problems gave him extra tuition. This took place for part of his lunch hour on most days until he finished his primary schooling. She gave John exercises to do at home, which involved reading and comprehension exercises as well as remembering how to spell words. Although John found the exercises monotonous, he was encouraged by the attention he was being given, and he did the exercises almost every night. As a consequence of his efforts, by the time he finished his primary education, he had caught up with the rest of the class.

When John went to secondary school, he started to fall behind again because he no longer had the support and guidance of his primary schoolteacher, and because his new teachers were not so accommodating as she had been. At about this time, John had a long discussion with his father, who tried to convince him to work hard at school. John learnt that his parents had experienced much hardship and had missed opportunities because they had never learnt how to read, write or spell. Although this discovery initially caused John some anxiety, it soon motivated him to take positive action, and he decided to carry on working as he had done in his primary school. Keeping in mind how his efforts would benefit him in the future, John spent hours reading and rereading newspapers, books and magazines as part of a strategy to compensate for his dyslexic weakness. He selected words he didn't know and developed strategies for learning how to spell them.

By assiduously practising his exercises, he successfully compensated for his weaknesses; he acquired the knowledge and skills he needed and subsequently overtook his classmates in most subjects, including English. John continued to be slower than average in learning how to spell new words, but his vocabulary and general knowledge were better than most of his peers. This fact was evident from his performance in public examinations. He obtained more passes and higher grades in his General Certificate of Education O-level examinations than all but one member of his class. John never experienced any difficulties related to literacy after leaving school. He gained employment soon after leaving school, and after some years he became self-employed as a kitchen designer.

John was motivated to apply for specialist dyslexia training as a consequence of a chance conversation with another adult dyslexic, one of his customers, who had completed and benefited considerably from such training. John, who was keen on self-development, decided that such training would be a good investment in his own productivity.

Although severely dyslexic, of only average ability and educated in a secondary school system that failed to provide him with a positive learning experience, John, through his own efforts, acquired above-average levels of literacy and subsequently never had cause in his adulthood to worry about his performance in terms of reading, writing and spelling. Although not very common, there are many dyslexic adults who, like John, are successful because they have been tenacious, hard-working and extremely well motivated.

HOW LEARNING ENVIRONMENTS INFLUENCE DYSLEXIC PERFORMANCE

While, in the case history above, John's success was due very largely to his own efforts, it may be the efforts of 'significant others' that make the difference. The obvious people who can make the difference are teachers and parents. Some dyslexic people owe their success to good teaching, but, as teachers become more and more burdened with paperwork, this is sadly becoming less and less common. Some teachers, either intentionally or unintentionally, make their learning environments 'dyslexia-friendly'. For example, some teachers understand and use multi-sensory methods; they are responsive to, and allow their presentation to be modified by, feedback from the children they teach. Effective teachers are aware of the importance of listening skills, observational learning, demonstrations and visualisation as a method to improve recall. They are aware that active involvement of dyslexic children in a learning process can make learning very effective for both pupils and teacher; dyslexics are very disadvantaged when learning is a passive activity.

There are many ways that teachers can make school learning dyslexia-friendly; for example, it can be of enormous help to dyslexic children if their teachers pace the presentation of material in lessons to suit the children's speed of learning, as opposed to some fixed idea about how fast lessons should progress. Simply breaking units of information down into smaller units, being prepared to repeat a presentation several times when children need to hear it several times and giving them time to process the information may make the difference between their success and failure in the school system. They make little or no progress when information is presented in a rigid and highly inflexible structure. They can effectively give up when the speed at which information is presented makes no allowance for their learning style. Dyslexia-friendly teaching environments are rare, but where they do exist, dyslexic children of average ability can acquire adequate levels of literacy.

THE MYTH OF THE DYSLEXIC'S POOR LITERACY SKILLS

The most misleading and by far the most prevalent misconception is that dyslexic people are unable to read, write or spell adequately. Some people believe that dyslexics cannot perform these skills at all. Others believe that they are incapable of achieving the levels of literacy that are expected of 'normal' educated adults. In each case, people will find ample confirming instances, a fact which has the effect of strengthening their false beliefs. Examples of dyslexic adults with weaknesses in literacy ranging from just below average to very severe can easily be found in abundance. This, for many people, proves that dyslexia is a condition characterised by poor levels of literacy; in reality, however, 'proof' requires more than specific examples.

No matter how many confirming instances are found, the reality is that a single counterexample is enough to disprove the argument. Like the examples that confirm false beliefs that all dyslexics have weaknesses in literacy, examples of the opposite exist in abundance, but they are not as readily identifiable as are their 'opposite numbers'. There are many diagnosed dyslexics whose reading, writing and spelling may be lower than it should be in relation to their intelligence but is nevertheless average. Therefore, they do not stand out in day-to-day situations as do those dyslexics whose literacy skills are weak. Many of these people do, however, stand out in workplaces because of other dyslexic weaknesses, which often undermine their ability to do their jobs efficiently. Our activities in providing adult dyslexia assessment, counselling and training services over the last 10 years have brought us into contact with hundreds of these people. Although many of our clients have had literacy weaknesses, a large percentage of the adult dyslexics we have seen have been people whose reading and spelling were average or above average.

The myth that dyslexia is synonymous with low levels of literacy has persisted for three reasons. First, the school system fails to accommodate dyslexic children, making the acquisition of literacy skills difficult for them. This failing by the school mirrors society's failure to accommodate all of its citizens equally. Essentially, dyslexic children are victims of political decisions to maintain an education system that excludes and disables them when alternative systems exist that would not only end their exclusion but would also be of benefit to all children. Some of the failings of schools are discussed further in Chapter 2; however, for a detailed discussion of how the school system fails children and why it has persisted in spite of its failure, the reader is referred to the book *Why Children Can't Read* by Diane McGuiness (1998).

The second factor that contributes to maintaining the myth that dyslexia is synonymous with reading disorder is to be found in what dyslexia experts do. They largely, and without convincing arguments, promote the myth that dyslexia is simply about poor reading both in how they define the condition and how they provide support for dyslexics. It is not unusual to find definitions of dyslexia that simply fail to recognise that poor reading can result from a number of different causes. For example, a recent report of the working party of the Division of Educational and Child Psychology of the British Psychological Society (1999: p. 20) presented a working definition of dyslexia stating that

> Dyslexia is evident when accurate and fluent word reading and/or spelling develops very incompletely or with great difficulty. This focuses on literacy learning at the 'word level' and implies that the problem is severe and persistent despite appropriate learning opportunities. It provides the basis for a staged process of assessment through teaching.

This definition is so general that it could easily be applied to any child who has poor literacy skills, regardless of their origin. Such contributions simply reinforce false stereotypes and contribute to misunderstandings.

The third factor that makes a major contribution to the false belief that dyslexia is equivalent to not being able to read, write and spell is what happens in schools. The key failing is that the informal screening procedures in schools are particularly vulnerable to 'false negatives' and 'false positives'. Readers may need reminding of how these errors are defined: a false positive occurs when someone who is not dyslexic is wrongly identified as being so, and a false negative occurs when someone who is dyslexic is wrongly identified as not being so.

HOW SCHOOLS IDENTIFY AND FAIL TO IDENTIFY DYSLEXIC CHILDREN

We have seen above that there is a widely held but entirely unfounded belief that dyslexia can be diagnosed on the basis of isolating literacy weaknesses in children. When children do have significant difficulties acquiring literacy skills, they soon attract the attention of teachers. In many cases, the possibility that there might be a condition responsible for the child's failure is either discounted or never considered; teachers, acting in good faith but in error, often label these children as low ability. This leads to some children who are dyslexic falling through the holes in the net of detection and subsequently never receiving any 'support'. Other teachers who are more aware of dyslexia (and again acting in the best interests of the children) often tend to suspect dyslexia in any child who has problems with literacy. The overall effect of these tendencies is that children who are not dyslexic are caught in the net, and children who are dyslexic are, so to speak, left in the sea. False positives, in theory at least, do not represent a major problem, since competent assessment by a chartered psychologist will detect them: 'false negatives' are, however, a more significant problem, since psychologists do not get the opportunity to detect them.

As explained earlier in this chapter, not all dyslexic children display weaknesses in literacy skill development, but they can still display other weaknesses that disrupt their educational progress. Poor memory, disorganisation and poor timekeeping, which are all common dyslexic characteristics, are generally viewed as part of the child's volitional be-haviour; i.e., they are considered to be behaviours over which the child has conscious control. In the absence of literacy weaknesses, they are, understandably, not usually considered to be significant indicators of any underlying condition. Action by teachers, who are likely to be frustrated by the child's puzzling lack of progress, will often be limited to the child's being told to 'try harder'. Dyslexic children who have competence in literacy are often screened out of the pool of children who are referred for psychological assessment. These false neg-atives, unlike the false positives, cannot be detected later in the school system; i.e., what psychologists cannot do is detect dyslexia in those dyslexic children who are never referred for assessment.

The overall effect of the way schools operate their informal screening procedures is that some dyslexics who have poor reading, writing and spelling will be diagnosed, but very few of those who do not exhibit below-average performance in literacy will be detected. This is a fundamental weakness in the system of detecting dyslexia and providing support for dyslexics in schools. Not surprisingly, it is a major cause of the continued inaccurate belief that all dyslexics have literacy weaknesses. Furthermore, what teachers believe and say about dyslexia tends to influence beliefs in the general population regarding the condition. This explains why the general public think dyslexia is a condition that prevents people from acquiring literacy skills and the associated belief that dyslexics are bound to be unsuccessful in education. The evidence to the contrary is rarely presented because successful dyslexics are simply hidden from view; neither their teachers, nor their parents nor the individuals themselves know they are dyslexics. They have fallen through the rather large holes in that net of detection that schools rely on, and many will subsequently never be identified or be identified only late in life.

In describing how schools fail to detect significant numbers of dyslexic children, it is not our intention to suggest that things would be any better if they did detect them. We are only illustrating how a particular widespread myth about the nature of dyslexia has been fuelled by what happens in schools. Given the inappropriateness of what often happens to those dyslexic children who are identified as dyslexic by educational psychologists, a topic discussed further in the next chapter, we feel that to be dyslexic and not to be detected by the education system may sometimes be a blessing in disguise. An efficient dyslexia-screening programme would make little contribution to improving the situation for dyslexic children unless there was associated with it effective interventions to help those identified as dyslexic; however, at present, most interventions are inadequate. As we shall discuss in the next chapter, segregating dyslexic children into special schools or classes is not helpful. Detailed discussion of how the education system could be reformed to accommodate dyslexic children is beyond the scope of this book, but, as stated above, readers interested in this topic are referred to McGuiness (1997).

THE MYTH OF THE DYSLEXIC'S LOW INTELLIGENCE

Predictably, the false beliefs discussed above have led to a widely held view that dyslexics are of low intelligence. The general perception, which is unwittingly promoted by the educational establishment, is that dyslexics are unlikely to get far in terms of academic and occupational achievements. The reality is that successful dyslexics can be found in all walks of life; i.e., dyslexia is not a barrier to occupational success in any field. Furthermore, there is no evidence of any association between dyslexia and intellectual ability. The myth that dyslexics are of low intelligence also has its roots in an educational system that fails dyslexic pupils. Typically, a school's main response when the condition is identified is to provide remedial help in the form of special literacy classes, but this is too easily and too often perceived by peers, as well as some parents and teachers, as indicating low intelligence. The support provided by schools in the form of remedial help, on balance, probably does more damage, because it stigmatises the children, than any good it does by developing them. Apparent confirmation of low ability or stupidity results when remedial classes, which, in any case, are often inappropriate for their needs, prove to be no remedy to the problem. Since all academic subjects require children to read, write and spell, the dyslexic child who has difficulty with these skills will underperform across the board, and this will be seen as yet further evidence of low ability.

Dyslexics' poor performance in all academic subjects often produces considerable negative feedback from their peers, teachers and parents, all of which further undermines their self-esteem, confidence and motivation. Children in this situation who have an interest in and some aptitude for non-academic subjects, such as sports, have a way of building their self-respect. They may be ridiculed for failing in academic subjects, but being good in just one area is enough for them to survive psychologically as individuals. Such people often excel in their area of skill; for example, some adult dyslexics have become professional athletes because at school they had a strong need to prove to others, e.g., their parents, teachers, friends, that they could excel at something. However, not all dyslexic children have talent for sports, art or practical subjects, and for those who do not have an alternative the impact of failure is, more often than not, soul-destroying and psychologically disabling. Often the only thing that such children learn is that they are helpless in the face of their problems. Many of them become victims of a phenomenon known as 'learned helplessness' (Seligman 1975), which is a psychological disorder characterised by strongly held beliefs by victims that no action that they could possibly take to solve the personal problems they face would succeed. People who have developed this condition give up trying to overcome problems because they believe that nothing they do will influence outcomes. They come to believe, falsely, that they are helpless, unable to exercise any control over their environment, when, in fact, they are helpless only because of their false belief that they are helpless.

What disables dyslexic children is not their dyslexia, but society's response to it. The education system is so obsessed with what the dyslexic child cannot do that no consideration is given to what they can do. The concept of identifying and developing dyslexic strengths is not given consideration before the response of implementing remedial classes is implemented. The remedial classes often undermine self-esteem, demotivating the children.

Educators interpret the resultant lack of motivation, uninterest and withdrawal in dyslexic children who have been put in remedial classes as evidence of low ability. The quantity of evidence from different sources conspires to construct a compelling, but entirely false, case for concluding that dyslexic children are of low ability. They are frequently bullied because of the stigma that has been attached to them as a consequence of this false belief. It is not at all surprising to find that so few of these children achieve success, given the considerable psychological barriers that the school system places in their paths.

Educators are predisposed to using reading ability as a measure of intelligence by proxy; consequently, they are led to believe that many dyslexics who are in reality very bright and talented are the opposite. The few dyslexic children who overcome this and the other substantial obstacles are a testimony to the fact that a lack of literacy is not the same as a lack of intelligence. The following extract from an article that appeared in *The Times* (17 January 1998) is evidence that severely dyslexic children with poor literacy skills can be very successful:

> A boy of 14, who is so severely dyslexic that he can barely write, has become the youngest person to win a place at Cambridge [University] this century.
> Alexandra Faludy, who writes at the rate of about two words a minute in a scrawl only he can read, dictated essays about the rationalist argument for God and the influence of Classicism on the work of Andrea Palladio to convince Peterhouse College to admit him to read Theology and History of Art.

This news article draws attention to how success is often largely a function of the support and encouragement that is provided by significant others. That such stories do gain attention from newspapers indicates that such success is rare. However, this is not because talent is rare in dyslexic children but because support for them is rare. In this case the parents gave support, as is so often the case in success stories involving dyslexics. The education system has a lot to learn from such parents!

WHY SUCCESSFUL DYSLEXICS GO UNNOTICED

As we have explained above, many dyslexic children, particularly high-ability dyslexics, but also some of average ability, do not exhibit literacy weaknesses during their schooling. These children may be termed 'literacy-competent' dyslexics. They are the dyslexics who are the least likely to be diagnosed as dyslexic at school, college or university. Many of these people simply never get diagnosed and live their lives completely unaware that the various difficulties they experience are a consequence of dyslexia.

Literacy-competent dyslexics include many successful dyslexics, and the reason why these people fail to make an impact on the way perceptions of dyslexia develop is that they are largely invisible as dyslexics. Successful dyslexics are largely high-ability people, and, as we have seen above, although their dyslexia may well have lowered their performance at school, it was not sufficiently low in absolute terms to attract the attention of teachers. They may have been frustrated by their inability to realise their full potential as children, but very often neither they, nor their teachers, nor their parents considered dyslexia as an explanation of their difficulties. They are bound to go unidentified within an education system that relies on average performance as the benchmark for everyone. As a consequence, their achievements do not feed into the process of perception formation regarding dyslexics that takes place in the minds of teachers, parents and other children.

High-ability dyslexics are almost certainly overrepresented in the population of unidentified dyslexics. Many are very clever and they sometimes develop ingenious coping strategies for the work problems they experience and so go on being unidentified for life. Dyslexics who have developed effective and non-damaging strategies for removing all or most of their dyslexic weaknesses are known as 'compensated dyslexics'. We have found it very useful to distinguish between compensated dyslexics and literacy-competent dyslexics. The former have developed effective strategies for dealing with all the weaknesses that undermine their work performance; the latter have adequate levels of literacy but have not developed strategies for dealing with other areas of weakness, such as organisation and working memory tasks. Others are diagnosed but only after years of struggling with work-related difficulties that may have puzzled them, their families and their employers for years. Once they are diagnosed, the possibilities of disability discrimination are usually sufficient to ensure that most of them will treat their diagnosis as private and confidential. The bright side of dyslexia is largely hidden behind a screen of anxiety and fear created by people's ignorance. It is therefore unsurprising to find that the general perception of dyslexia has evolved without being influenced by the characteristics of the many dyslexics who are very talented and successful.

APPROPRIATE AND INAPPROPRIATE TRAINING FOR ADULT DYSLEXICS

A myth that arises quite logically from those discussed above is that the remedy to dyslexia is intensive training in literacy skills. While this is obviously not a remedy for literacy-competent dyslexics, the important issue is whether it is a remedy for the rest of the dyslexic population. There is a considerable amount of material that details how dyslexics should be taught literacy skills, and an industry has developed around the incorrect assumption that dyslexia is cured if the individual can be taught how to read, write and spell. In assessing the usefulness of what this industry provides, we need first and foremost to distinguish between the relevance of the product, i.e., literacy tuition, to the adult and to the child dyslexic populations.

At school, literacy skills are an important key to academic success; therefore, failure to develop these skills adequately raises concerns—and justifiably so! In adulthood, however, the rules are very different. Poor literacy skills do not absolutely predetermine failure, and competence in those skills does not necessarily secure success. There are many dyslexic adults who, in spite of poor reading, writing and spelling, have achieved success and do not obviously suffer as a result of their condition. There are many other adult dyslexics who have acquired good levels of literacy but who continue to experience significant difficulties in many areas of their lives. There are also dyslexic adults who do have literacy weaknesses but whose work-related difficulties are not products of those literacy weaknesses. There are thus many circumstances where literacy training is simply irrelevant, and Miles (1994: p. 102) has pointed out that

> The emphasis on poor reading diverts attention from the many other needs which, at least in the case of older people with dyslexia, are far more important—the ability to spell, to calculate, to keep appointments, to organise study skills and to retain self respect.

We would go further than Miles and argue that it is not only the emphasis on poor reading that 'diverts attention' from other needs but also the emphasis on literacy generally. There are many adult dyslexics for whom organisational ability and self-respect are the key 'other needs', and for whom reading, writing, spelling and arithmetic are either not difficult or, when they are difficult, not of significance to what they are doing in their lives. Many people offering adult dyslexics training are either unaware of, or choosing to ignore, this reality. While, logically speaking, training for all adults, dyslexics and non-dyslexics alike, should focus on the areas of need, unwittingly, in the context of dyslexia, training in literacy is often implemented regardless of need! Our own anecdotal evidence, based on reports from a large number of our clients, indicates that the enterprise of training dyslexics in literacy skills is largely ineffective. For many well-motivated and able dyslexic individuals, progress in such training is at best a slow and rather laborious process.

Training for adult dyslexics will be successful if it acknowledges adulthood by including the client in the decision-making process regarding the content of the training. Presenting training as personal development, i.e., a trainer working with the client, is more likely to be successful than traditional educational-based presentations, i.e., a teacher providing knowledge. Ideally, some form of 'needs analysis', i.e., an assessment of individual strengths and weaknesses, should guide decisions regarding the content of training. A needs analysis can be carried out in depth by psychometric tests, personality measurement and structured interviews. Alternatively, it can be completed in less depth by, for example, reviewing appraisal documentation and interviewing the person directly. Possible training interventions should be presented to clients for discussion to ensure their relevance, as well as to outline for the client the demands and possible benefits of that training.

Literacy training has a very limited role, and the need for it should be very clearly established before it is implemented. Given that the whole enterprise of adult literacy training is by no means one characterised by success, proponents should carefully consider the needs of the people they are serving before recommending it. It is not helpful to offer a product to people when they do not require it, and it may not work for them anyway!

INFORMATION TECHNOLOGY AS A SOLUTION TO LITERACY WEAKNESSES

In general, as far as training in adult literacy as a strategy for helping dyslexics to improve their work performance is concerned, progress is not commensurate with the efforts made by either the teacher or the student. In reality, even when an adult dyslexic does have literacy weaknesses and is employed in a job that involves a lot of reading and writing, literacy tuition is unlikely to be a practical solution to the problems faced. It is far more realistic to seek solutions in the form of computer hardware and software. There are programs that electronically encode speech sounds into text and text into speech sounds, i.e., voice-activated software and text-to-speech software. This means that adult dyslexics can talk to their computer rather than typing information at the keyboard. Emails and other documents in the computer can be read aloud, and 'hard copy' can be scanned into the computer also for reading aloud. Some software, for example, the Kurzweil 3000 program (Kurzweil Educational Systems), allows simultaneous scanning and reading of documents. There are also many programs that are designed to help dyslexics to organise their ideas into emails, letters, reports and other documents. This technology can very quickly help dyslexic adults gain control of their working life, as the following case history illustrates.

Pamela's Case History

Pamela, a bright 27-year-old freelance television researcher, was keen to gain full-time employment but was unable to do so because of her literacy problems, which were related to her dyslexia. In particular, she experienced work-related problems as a consequence of her slow reading, poor spelling and illegible writing. Although she had produced a number of successful TV programmes, she was able to do so only by spending excessively long hours working on them. She spent much longer than average, compared to peers doing the same job, reading and understanding newspaper articles, journal reports, emails and websites. Her reading was excessively slow, and she needed to reread material several times in order to understand it. She was further disabled by her writing, which included poor spelling and grammar.

Pamela was acutely aware of her literacy weaknesses and avoided applying for any posts that involved reading large quantities of information; this excluded her from professional areas that particularly interested her, notably, history and current affairs. Pamela had tried to improve her skills by attending adult literacy classes and by employing specialist dyslexia tutors, but she had only made incremental progress that had no impact on work performance. After three months of taking adult literacy classes, she eventually gave up. It had become clear to her that the tuition and the amount of work she needed to do between classes were adding to her personal stress level without giving her hope of significant improvement in the foreseeable future. After struggling for several years, Pamela eventually applied for help from the Employment Service under its Access to Work scheme, a special government scheme designed to support disabled people in the workplace by funding or part-funding work related adjustments.

A workplace assessment was completed on Pamela, and it determined that she would benefit from a laptop computer and scanner together with the specialist computer program Naturally Speaking, Professional Edition v5, which is a voice-activated program. This software allowed her to speak to her computer, removing the need for her to use the keyboard, and thus combating the stress of having to spell words. She was also supplied with software that read material aloud, i.e., text-to-speech software, from websites and from documents that she scanned into her computer. Additional software designed to help construct written documents allowed her to organise her thoughts and ideas when writing briefs for programme ideas. After just three days' training in the use of this equipment, she was able to start using the software, and to extract information quickly from written sources and produce more professional-looking reports, briefs, emails, faxes and letters.

In a relatively short time, Pamela, without ever having overcome her reading and writing weaknesses, was feeling considerably less stressed and more in control of her work. In her own words, 'I'm not interested in how I get the work done as long as it's done. I'd rather rely on my computer and stay in work than have to quit just to go back to school and get my writing up to scratch.'

Pamela's experience illustrates how improving literacy is simply not as important in workplaces as it is in schools and colleges. For adults, literacy tuition has an extremely limited role in terms of solving workplace problems arising from dyslexia. When literacy weaknesses in adults are a relevant workplace issue, interventions should be found in computer-based solutions.

Even in schools, literacy tuition is arguably not the complete solution that many think it is. In relation to children, providing remedial help is highly desirable, but there is a strong case for arguing that it should be provided in the context of a complete strategy to help them overcome their dyslexic difficulties. The important elements that are generally left out of interventions to help dyslexic children are cognitive skills training, notably memory development, and life-skills training, notably assertiveness and self-presentational skills. If schools provided classes dealing with these areas, children would probably be better prepared for the world of work.

The extent of adult illiteracy in dyslexics who have received remedial classes at school is very high, suggesting that there is considerable room for improvement in the education system. Many people believe that a complete rethink of what happens in schools is required urgently, a topic that is discussed further in Chapter 2 of this book. In view of the persistent failure of the education system to provide adequate teaching in reading, writing and spelling for dyslexics, it is hard to avoid concluding not only that literacy skills training should be largely restricted to schools but also that in schools it needs to be radically restructured.

A TRAINING PROGRAMME FOR ADULT DYSLEXICS

Relevant training for adult dyslexics will typically involve substantial work in memory development as well as work to improve clients' understanding of, and ability to explain, their dyslexia. Memory training must be tailored to the client's needs but should include exercises to reduce the negative effects of inefficient working memory in a short time scale, and to improve memory functioning comprehensively in the long term. Appropriate memory training might include the use of mnemonics and other well-established tools for improving recall. However, the more important elements of training in memory development are exercises that promote a more efficient use of the working memory, which will most often involve developing visual memory skills. Fitzgibbon (in preparation) outlines how visual memory skills can be developed and used to improve performance in a wide range of behaviours from recalling factual information to making presentations and reducing levels of personal stress.

Improving clients' understanding of dyslexia involves facilitating their insight into the way that their dyslexia operates. This enables them to exercise more control over their performance and consequently be more efficient in dealing with the world of work and work-related activities. Training in how to explain dyslexia in the workplace also increases clients' feelings of control over their environment. An ability to present dyslexia in a positive light enables clients to overcome negative attitudes in the workplace or at the point of selection for work.

In addition to the core training outlined above, clients are likely to have a range of needs in the following areas:

- Managing adult dyslexia, which would typically involve training in interpersonal skills, how to enhance work performance by utilizing personal strengths, and how personal creativity and innovation can result in efficient problem solving in work-related contexts.
- Building confidence for work, which would usually involve exercises for raising awareness of the various factors that determine and influence confidence in a work context and strategies for controlling them.
- Improving verbal communication skills, which would, as a minimum, provide training in listening, talking and communicating information accurately and succinctly. In addition, work to control conversations and information exchange would usually be included.
- Coping with study learning and training, which would focus on developing skills in extracting and storing information from different sources (including other people), as well as skills in thinking and analysis. Strategies for controlling the flow of information provided by others, such as trainers or team members, might also be included.
- Improving self-presentation, which would typically focus on the various aspects of self-presentation that are important in both gaining employment, as in providing personal

information in curricula vitae or job interviews, and performing efficiently in employment, as in interacting with colleagues and supervisors.

- General work-related skills, which would involve training in the development of practical strategies and skills relevant to successful long-term employment. The strategies would need to be relevant to a wide range of work-related tasks, such as report writing, filing, making presentations, note taking, time management and interviewing.
- Career guidance, which would include strategies for finding appropriate work opportunities, identifying career goals and improving employment prospects.
- Managing stress in the workplace, which would include practical techniques for the effective control of stress as well as training in strategies for coping with potentially problematic or stressful aspects of work.

Professionals with a practical and pragmatic approach to skill development are required to deliver specialist programmes for adult dyslexics. This is because a key requirement in training adult dyslexics is helping them to find novel and creative ways of doing the work they are employed to do or that they have aspirations to do. Occupational psychologists are likely to be the best-equipped people to present specialist training, although suitably qualified and experienced professionals who have a background in work, as opposed to education, would also be appropriate.

THE ELUSIVENESS OF ADULT DYSLEXIA

Although 'adult dyslexia' is now a recognised term, the myth that dyslexia is either a purely child-related condition or one that is somehow more important in childhood than in adulthood persists in many people's perceptions. Dyslexia is understandably a cause for concern in children, but it is a lifelong condition that affects the lives of adults very significantly. Dyslexia is less obvious and has attracted less attention in the adult population for a number of reasons. The widely held false belief, discussed above, that it is associated with low intelligence is, for many dyslexic adults, a source of great discomfort and embarrassment, so much so that it discourages many of them from talking openly about their condition to their friends, family and employers.

As well as embarrassment about being labelled as lacking intellectual ability, many adult dyslexics believe, with good cause, that they will be the victims of discrimination, ridicule and unfair treatment in workplaces if they do identify themselves as dyslexic. Interestingly, both of the above factors affect many high-ability successful dyslexics who, in spite of demonstrable achievements, still feel intimidated by people's false beliefs and prejudices, a point we return to in Chapter 6. Consequently, even successful dyslexics who know they are dyslexic are often not prepared to talk openly about their condition. The fact that high-ability dyslexics have well-founded fears of being ridiculed because of their condition and becoming victims of unfair disability discrimination in workplaces is evident from high-profile cases in which dyslexic employees have taken successful legal action against their employers. For example, as this book is being prepared, one such case has been reported in the media. The *Daily Mail* (20 November 2001) reports that a dyslexic banker has won his lawsuit claiming disability discrimination, which was based on the fact that his colleagues ridiculed him in his workplace by calling him by his name in reverse, i.e., *Trebor* instead of *Robert*. Given that this adult dyslexic is seeking damages of £500 000, organisations would be well advised to take action to avoid such outcomes.

Like the compensated dyslexics who conceal their dyslexia with an impressive cloak of competence and talent, adult dyslexics who have pronounced literacy weaknesses can successfully keep their dyslexia a secret by developing strategies for disguising their poor reading, writing and spelling. The reality is that dyslexia persists into adulthood, but the majority of diagnosed adult dyslexics can, and often do, simply hide their dyslexia from public view. The population of adult dyslexics is, then, a largely invisible group made up of diagnosed dyslexics who are hiding their condition and undiagnosed dyslexics whose condition has never been uncovered. This explains why dyslexia is perceived as a childhood condition that largely vanishes in adulthood; it vanishes from sight, but not from society.

ARE ADULT DYSLEXICS MORE THAN CHILD DYSLEXICS GROWN UP?

In spite of the growing acceptance that dyslexia persists into adulthood, adults with this condition are still disadvantaged. This is primarily due to the way they are perceived by the system that exists to serve them; as Patton & Polloway (1992) have observed, most of the help and guidance offered to adult dyslexics treats them as simply child dyslexics grown up. This very common attitude is responsible for maintaining a system that is well meaning but simply does not meet the needs of this group.

The effects of dyslexia change considerably as the individual gets older. The needs of adult dyslexics are significantly different from the needs of child dyslexics. For example, if a child has literacy weaknesses, there is justification in making attempts to improve the child in this area because literacy is a key skill universally important in the school system. However, literacy weaknesses, when they are present in adults with dyslexia, are often largely irrelevant to the individual's occupational success. This point is not well understood, and even adult dyslexics themselves are frequently unaware of the irrelevance of weaknesses they have in literacy. This is illustrated in the following case history.

Alex's Case History

Alex, a 22-year-old university graduate with a first-class honours degree in mathematics, started specialist training in memory development three months after graduating, seeking specialist training for his dyslexia. He was convinced that he would not be able to gain employment because his spelling was weak, he read very slowly and his handwriting was largely illegible. He was particularly concerned about his inability to complete application forms. It transpired that in the weeks after graduating he had made exploratory calls to a number of organisations to seek employment with them. Having had no success in this initiative, he gave up and decided that he would need to improve his literacy in order to gain employment.

Being aware that he had a short-term memory weakness, he sought memory training as a logical first step to embarking on a college course to improve his reading and spelling. Shortly before and after graduating, Alex had made efforts to gain employment by making telephone calls to a number of organisations; he had, however, failed to impress potential employers because his ability to communicate verbally was considerably undermined by his poor ability to track what others said and his inability to structure what he wanted to say to them.

Alex followed a programme focused on developing his memory skills generally and the use of memory strategies to support and develop verbal communication and self-presentation skills. Within less than three months, without ever having focused his attention on reading, writing or spelling, Alex gained employment as an actuary. Once he was able to communicate effectively, he gained employment rapidly because his mathematical skills were in high demand. His new employer accepted his dyslexia and his weak literacy skills, taking the view that neither had an impact on his ability to do his job. Alex is now well established in his field; he is a respected actuary who enjoys a rich professional, social and cultural life. He has no particular concerns about his weaknesses in literacy.

In the above case history, the perception that literacy was important operated as a barrier to Alex's employment success and personal happiness. It is the perception of the importance of reading, writing and spelling, as opposed to any objective importance, which is frequently the barrier to advancement for adults. When perceptions are distorting reality, more benefit can be achieved by an intervention designed to correct the false perception than one that simply reinforces false beliefs. This could be achieved by focusing purely on the issue of matching job demands with personal abilities and skills and disregarding assumptions about the importance of literacy skills.

For adult dyslexics who have literacy weaknesses, the question of whether or not a particular approach to teaching literacy will have a beneficial effect is not as important as the question of whether or not adults need to bother trying to improve their literacy skills in the first place. Unhelpfully, literacy skills are considered by some to be an absolute requirement for full membership of a civilised society. Many commentators fail to appreciate that, although reading is important in school, alternative methods of accessing information and expressing individual feelings, ideas and thoughts do exist and are valid. Attitudes to competence in reading, writing and spelling are often dogmatic. For example, Pumfrey & Reason (1991) assert that for the literate to suggest to the illiterate that literacy is unimportant is like Marie Antoinette telling the masses to eat cake if they lack bread. They argue that not to be literate is to be seriously and progressively disadvantaged, both materially and in terms of access to cultural enrichment. This is not entirely accurate and does not take account of the very substantial successes, artistic creativity and other cultural enrichments that many adult dyslexics with poor levels of literacy achieve.

As occupational psychologists, we are consulted on matters concerning work and how to be successful in work; matters of cultural enrichment do not arise as issues for our clients, but we have not observed any systematic deprivation in this area. As far as work is concerned, we have seen many people over the years who, in spite of severe difficulties with aspects of literacy, have reached the highest points in their respective professions. It is very common for writers to assume that literacy skills are of paramount importance and that poor levels of competence in literacy in some way undermine the significance of what the individual has achieved. The evidence that poor literacy does not necessarily represent a barrier to occupational success exists in abundance. We have also seen many clients who have been held back in their careers because false assumptions about the importance of acquiring literacy skills have led them to focus on developing such skills when they would have been more productively occupied in developing other skills. For example, if scientists can't spell, having secretaries to spell words for them is a far better solution to their literacy problems than receiving tuition in literacy. There is no doubt in our minds that adult dyslexics who have literacy weaknesses can achieve success without ever needing to focus on overcoming this weakness.

It can be very damaging for adult dyslexics to be given the message that, because of a weakness, they must necessarily be deprived of some aspect of living; the misunderstanding can anger even those who have proved the assertion false. To explore the extent of this phenomenon, we asked 10 of our clients, all of whom identified themselves as successful in their careers, interested in cultural activities and very weak in terms of literacy, to comment on the assertion made by Pumfrey & Reason (1991: p. 3) that 'in Western industrial societies, not to be literate is to be seriously and progressively disadvantaged, both materially and in terms of access to cultural enrichment'. Only one person could agree to a limited extent with the expressed sentiment. The other nine were unanimous in rejecting it as a valid description of what they had experienced in their lives. Most of them commented that their dyslexia was the reason for their success; their comments focused on how it had made them work harder and find different ways of doing things, and had thus improved their creativity. Interestingly, they mostly felt a sense of annoyance that they were thought of as being deprived. This purely anecdotal evidence is consistent with what we have heard from our clients over the years that literacy weaknesses are not insurmountable barriers to success.

To be fair to Pumfrey & Reason, their focus is children and they quite rightly emphasise the importance for children of learning to read, write and spell. The problem is that little thought is given to the differences between what children need and what adults need before statements that are relevant to children are generalised to adults. Whereas children need education and knowledge, adults, in general, need employment.

DISTINGUISHING ADULT DYSLEXIA FROM CHILD DYSLEXIA

As discussed in the previous section, much of what is said about dyslexia applies to children, but not adults. This situation arises because the two conditions have not been sufficiently, if at all, distinguished. Explanations of adult dyslexia and interventions for adult dyslexics are in general simply the product of extrapolating to adults and the world of work what has been developed for children in schools and students in colleges. Whatever the merits of the research on childhood dyslexia may be, it is, for the most part, irrelevant to adults. Adult dyslexia should be seen as distinct from childhood dyslexia, and explanations of adult dyslexia should emphasize this difference. Adult dyslexia, like child dyslexia, can be defined as an inefficiency in working memory; however, in adults, this basic memory difference that distinguishes dyslexics from non-dyslexics has been modified and influenced by educational and environmental childhood experiences and the development of conscious and unconscious cognitive-behavioural strategies that operate in an adult context.

The educational experiences refer to the sum total of positive and negative learning experiences from a person's primary and secondary schooling. These experiences are important because they largely determine people's motivation and their observable personality disposition. The 'observable personality disposition' is distinct from the genetic personality type; for example, a potentially extraverted child who has been ridiculed at school may become an introverted adult with low self-esteem and low confidence. Another child of similar make-up who is encouraged and given constructive criticism may become an extraverted adult, confident, self-assured and outgoing.

The 'cognitive-behavioural strategies' referred to are ideas, thoughts and behaviours that dyslexics develop, either consciously or unconsciously, to help them cope with the problems that their dyslexia presents. For example, some dyslexics develop very good visual memory capabilities without ever intending to do this (unconscious behaviour). Others consciously write down every important task that they need to do (conscious behaviour). These strategies are important because they represent the extent to which people are controlling their own lives and thereby determining their success. The quantity and quality of these behaviours determine the degree to which dyslexia disrupts a person's life.

The key difference between children and adult dyslexics is that the factors described above are operating in an adult context or environment. Individuals are no longer the legal responsibility of their parents or guardians and have a greater decision-making role. Children are exposed to a much more homogeneous, controlled and restricted environment than are adults after they leave school. Individuals are highly dependent in schools, and they have little choice about being there. After leaving school, people need to be much more independent, and they have opportunities to exercise greater degrees of choice concerning what they do and what they do not do. Environmental demands for children are more or less restricted to attending a school and following specific directions from a teacher.

Environmental demands after leaving school vary enormously, and people are expected to complete a wide range of tasks originating from their employer, their family, their friends and organisations with whom they interact. Adult life experiences show a much greater variety than school experiences. For example, dyslexic adults who are married and have children are likely to be subject to a different set of demands than those who are single and without children. The former may be under considerable pressure to be more organised, to manage their lives more efficiently and to accommodate the needs of others. The latter may be free of all of these pressures. One dyslexic may have a potentially very stressful job that involves meeting deadlines and working in a busy open-plan space. Another may have a potentially stress-free job, working in a small, private office under no particular pressure. The number of variables determining the experiences of adults is clearly enormous.

Distinguishing adult dyslexics from child dyslexics has many practical benefits, not least of which is that adults appreciate that they are being treated as adults with a distinct set of issues, and not simply as older children.

WHAT DETERMINES SUCCESS IN THE WORKPLACE FOR DYSLEXICS

Although dyslexic adults can be found working effectively at the highest levels in many occupational areas, the perception of dyslexia as the cause of occupational failure persists. Even the knowledge that some very successful people are dyslexic has not significantly altered the view held by many people, dyslexic and non-dyslexic alike, that dyslexia is a condition that should be hidden, denied, treated, or conquered.

Successful dyslexics are often viewed as people who achieved their good results in spite of their dyslexia. In reality, however, many successful dyslexics are successful because of their dyslexia. Many others could achieve success by seeing their condition not as the enemy to be vanquished but as an ally to be worked with.

The industry that has grown up to service the adult dyslexic population has not made it easy for most of these people to develop a positive attitude to their dyslexia. On the contrary, the language adopted by dyslexic specialists is all too often one of compensation rather than development. Most of the available training or, more accurately, 'tuition' for adults gives far too much attention to dyslexic weaknesses and far too little attention to dyslexic strengths.

While it would obviously be both absurd and misleading to argue that every dyslexic has the potential to become a brilliant artist, scientist or entrepreneur, it is equally obvious that every dyslexic, like every non-dyslexic, has potential, which can be either realised or suppressed. A key to releasing this potential is specialist training and development, such as that outlined above, which focuses on increasing the individual's sense of control and independence.

Acknowledging that dyslexic people can be found working in every area of employment is important because it establishes that the condition is not an insurmountable barrier to success in employment. There are many people, employed and unemployed, who experience severe employment-related difficulties because of their dyslexia. These difficulties would be very much reduced if employers and dyslexics themselves understood the condition better and appreciated how it can be managed and how appropriate training (see below) combined with other workplace adjustments (see Chapter 4) can make it a positive force.

THE IMPORTANCE OF GAINING CONTROL

Essentially, what determines success for dyslexics is high levels of actual and self-perceived control over their environment. Gerber et al. (1992) demonstrated the importance of the concept of control in a study that examined two groups of adult dyslexics. The two groups were distinguished in terms of their employment success; i.e., the authors compared a successful group and an unsuccessful group. They identified the ability of individuals to take control of their lives as the major factor determining success. They found 'taking control' to be made up of two elements: internal decisions and external manifestations. As well as expressing a desire to succeed and being goal orientated, internal decisions involve reframing, which is accepting and understanding the difficulties that exist and acting to neutralise them. The external manifestations are persistence, the development of skills, the use of support networks and finding a comfortable working environment. The following case history illustrates how important the concept of taking control is to achieving employment success.

Alison's Case History

Alison, a 26-year-old insurance clerk, had worked in the same company for eight years and was growing steadily more dissatisfied with her work. She had originally joined the company on a part-time basis while studying for General Certificate of Education A-levels in history and law. Although she took the A levels twice, she failed them on both occasions. Failing these examinations undermined her confidence and convinced her that she had little or no ability. Although encouraged to try again by her sister, who was already at university, she gave up her goal of studying law, accepting instead the full-time post that her employer offered her.

After Alison had worked full time for 6 years, her line manager raised the possibility that she might be dyslexic in an annual appraisal, and subsequently he organised a psychological assessment for her, which diagnosed her as dyslexic. She became depressed, believing that the diagnosis was both a confirmation of her lack of ability and the reason why she could never be successful. Twelve months after the diagnosis, with the support and encouragement of her sister, she attended a specialist-training programme. She acquired and developed skills in memory development, verbal communication, understanding dyslexia, learning and stress management.

The training Alison received led her to 'reframe'; i.e., she re-examined personal information, looked for rational explanations for her failures and reassessed her conclusions about her past experiences. She examined her educational history in detail to gain insights into the reasons for her failure, and she constructed a plan for dealing with weaknesses. Most importantly, she identified her poor memory as the cause of most of her educational difficulties. She came to realise that, although she attended classes regularly and did all the required reading, she was never able to retain information easily. She gained insights that revealed to her that her lack of confidence in her ability ever to do a degree was in a large part due to her teachers not supporting her in her learning. In particular, she realised that her inability to express herself when asking questions in class was a function of her dyslexia, but that her teachers had interpreted this as her lack of ability. She reasoned that their messages to her that she was a failure contributed to her failure. She learned how to neutralise each of these threats by memory strategies, verbal communication skills and clear explanations of her dyslexia that she ensured that she could present competently to her teachers.

Alison reinstated her goal of studying law at university, ignoring the advice in her assessment report that law would not be the best choice of subject for her to study. She enrolled in an evening A-level course, planning carefully how she would manage her studies. She discussed her dyslexia openly with the college where she was studying, explaining what her needs were and how they could support her. Applying her memory strategies to her studies, she was soon recognised by her teachers and fellow students as someone who remembered a lot more than average, so much so that many of her classmates asked her for help to improve their recall of information. She very rapidly regained her confidence and desire to succeed, and at the end of the year was one of the strongest students in the class. She passed her A-levels with good grades and was successful in gaining a place at a university, studying law and commerce. By the time she started her degree studies, she was convinced that her dyslexia would be the reason for her success rather than the cause of her failure—a complete reframing.

This case history is important because it illustrates that many factors that may be seen as independent of one another are in fact closely interconnected. For example, poor memory adversely affected on Alison's performance, causing significant others to make inaccurate assessments of her ability. The negative evaluations made by her teachers served to undermine her self-esteem. The lack of both confidence and feelings of self-worth negatively affected her motivation to achieve a goal. The case history illustrates the importance of people having self-knowledge and understanding of their condition; i.e., it emphasises how knowledge of what causes problems can lead to solutions. Finally, the case history highlights the role others can play in determining that an individual succeeds rather than fails. Over the last decade we have seen many examples of individuals who, like Alison, succeeded because they took control of their lives in the way Gerber et al. (1992) described. A key goal of this book is to enable others to do the same.

2

HOW SOCIETY CAN DISABLE OR EMPOWER ADULT DYSLEXICS

INTRODUCTION

The issue of whether or not dyslexia is a disability is an emotive one. Some dyslexic people accept that it is a disability, but others find the idea totally unacceptable. United Kingdom law recognises dyslexia as a disability in a number of separate pieces of legislation, most importantly, the Disability Discrimination Act of 1995, but individual cases are judged according to how they fit the legal definition. In other words, it is not the case that every dyslexic is automatically disabled; whether they are or not is for a judge or chairman of an employment tribunal to decide. The World Health Organisation's definition of disability is equally open to interpretation. The World Health Organisation distinguishes between disability and impairment, the latter referring to a psychological or anatomical disorder, while disability is defined as the impact of the disorder on everyday living. Again, in this definition, some dyslexics will be disabled and some will not. Disability is not a fact about an individual; it is the product of a relationship between the individual and the society to which the individual belongs.

This chapter examines how disabilities are created by society and how society can be changed to reduce or eliminate disabilities. After examining the effect that different relationships between individuals and society have on disability generally, we examine dyslexia as a special case. The importance of experts on dyslexia understanding how society can disable dyslexics is discussed, and an argument for occupational psychologists becoming more actively involved in the field of adult dyslexia is presented, together with comments on how employers stand to benefit from their expertise.

APPROACHES TO UNDERSTANDING DISABILITY

Beliefs about disability in society are the product of a number of influences. Medical science, advances in genetics, the political climate, economic factors and religious convictions all make a contribution. Consequently, explanations and perceptions of disability vary across national boundaries. Furthermore, as the influence of the various factors listed above change, so do the perceptions of disability within individual nations.

The way society views disability at any one time determines the extent to which disabled people are included or excluded from its various functions. In North America and the United Kingdom, as well as most of the rest of Europe and the developed world, definitions of disability have been dominated by the equation of disability with illness and personal tragedy. This outcome is largely due to the impact of medical science and religious beliefs, with the latter exercising significant influence over the former. Most, if not all, world religions reinforce the idea that there are physical and psychological 'norms' from which disabled people deviate. This belief determines a general perception of disabled people as victims of a personal tragedy. Medical science confirms this to be the case by classifying disabilities as illnesses or disorders for which treatments need to be developed.

Based on the strong message from medical science to the effect that disability is an illness, the common-sense explanation of it as a personal tragedy has evolved and become pervasive. This conceptualisation is known as the medical model of disability. It is one of two important and conflicting approaches to defining disability. The other, which is discussed later in the chapter, is known as the social model of disability.

THE EFFECT OF THE MEDICAL MODEL OF DISABILITY

The medical model is the older of the two models that influence contemporary policy making in the area of disability. The medical model conceptualises disability as the impact that people's physical, mental or cognitive impairment has on their relationship with society. It promotes the belief that disability is an individual matter upon which society has no causal effect. It implies that disabled people must overcome the problems arising from their impairment by learning how to accommodate the demands of the social and physical environment that surrounds them. In the medical model view, the disabled person is, as a consequence of some physical or mental deficit, abnormal. Society's role is simply to provide support—for example, in the form of state benefits.

As observed above, the underlying assumption of the medical definition is that there is a set of desirable and fixed norms within society and that disabled people, because they deviate from these, can never achieve full citizenship. The effect of these assumptions is to separate the disabled from the non-disabled, i.e., the rest of society. By creating this division in society, the medical model promotes the exclusion of disabled people from all the key elements of society.

AN ALTERNATIVE TO THE MEDICAL MODEL

In challenging the medical model of disability, activists draw attention to the fact that society's norms can and do change, and that, as they change, so too does the level of disability experienced by those who have impairments. Drake (1999: p. 11), for example, argues that

> Medical definitions . . . fail to take sufficient account of the fact that as environmental circumstances vary, so the consequences of impairment become more or less acute. In a world perfectly suited to a disabled person, although the physiological impairment still remains, he or she is no longer disabled.

The social model of disability promotes the belief that disability is the product of environmental and social structures that exclude people who have physical, intellectual or cognitive impairments. Rejecting the medical-model view that disability is inherent in individuals who, because of their differences, have special needs, advocates of the social model argue that the problems associated with people's impairments could be solved if society changed to accommodate their needs. Within this model, disability is conceptualised as the product of society's failure to modify its existing institutions, laws, values and norms to take account of the needs of all people who have psychological and physical impairments. Drake (1999) argues that disabling social conditions could be eliminated if there was the will to do this within society. He rejects the view that disability is the consequence of personal misfortune, arguing instead that the problem of disability is one that has its origins in the exercise of power. Drake (p. 14) considers that 'the successful assertion of one definition (of disability) over the other depends on which set of antagonists is the more powerful in any particular time and place.'

Drake (p. 14) believes that a social-model perspective requires the non-disabled majority to cede power to the disabled minority, but he believes this is unlikely to happen in 'a state that believes that people are rendered incapable through personal impairments'. He clearly identifies a medical model of normalisation as an obstacle to enabling people who have impairments to become full citizens of their communities.

HOW MODELS OF DISABILITY DETERMINE LIFE EXPERIENCES

The two models of disability discussed above not only represent very different ways of understanding disability but also determine policy making on disability at all levels. The model that has the upper hand governs the course of action that countries, national organisations and institutions adopt in managing disability and in dealing with disabled people. Traditional disability policy in the United Kingdom, which is a typical example of a social welfare policy of disability, is a direct product of medical definitions. It can be characterised by the effect it has of separating disabled people from non-disabled people. This separation, which is known as 'social exclusion', is achieved on different levels. In physical, economic and occupational terms, social exclusion is the direct product of the segregation of disabled people from non-disabled people. It is implemented first in schools, e.g., by streaming children into special education, and later in employment, notably by excluding disabled adults from employment.

The effect of removing disabled people from mainstream education is to make them less effective in their interactions in the real world. Separated from others and stigmatised by a label that many people see as indicating low intelligence, many fail to learn and develop fully the full range of skills required for social interaction. They are often shunned when they do come into contact with others, who, because of strong negative stereotyping, will normally retreat from the label the disable bear before ever examining the person behind it.

Dyslexic people's lack of social skills and inexperience in social interactions often translate in their adulthood into an inability to gain and retain employment. The effect of being excluded from employment is to undermine their self-respect and confidence. In addition, it reduces their economic and political power, which makes them ineffective as agents of change in society. The provision of state benefits allows them to survive, but they are denied the dignities and influence that non-disabled people are afforded through the access they have to the world of work. On the psychological level, social exclusion, as well as stripping disabled people of their dignity and undermining their self-esteem and confidence, creates a negative social environment, one where a group of people are characterised by what they cannot do instead of what they can do.

THE CIVIL RIGHTS APPROACH TO DISABILITY POLITICS

Social welfare policy on disability is currently confronted by the civil rights approach to formulating disability policy. This approach, which has its foundations in the social model described above, directly challenges the social welfare orientation. It questions the validity of creating alternative societies for disabled people, and it promotes the view that the state has a responsibility to accommodate all of its citizens equally. Civil rights policy focuses on inclusion instead of exclusion; its supporters argue that mainstream social institutions need to be reformed to include disabled people. In a nutshell, the difference between the social welfare approach and the civil rights approach is that while the former excludes people from the mainstream, the latter seeks to return them to it.

Advocates of the civil rights approach present arguments that undermine the theoretical basis of the social welfare approach, but, at the same time, they recognise that it needs to be dismantled carefully. They argue for selective reforms, in recognition of the fact that many disabled people are almost totally reliant on provisions that have been made for them by the state. While seeking an end to segregated schooling and inflexible employment practices, which make disabled people so reliant on state benefits, they argue for those state benefits to be preserved. Although some may view this as an inconsistency in the position held by civil rights activists (what could be a more obvious form of charity than giving people money?), it is nevertheless a logical position to hold. While there already has been recognition by the United Kingdom government that segregation in schools should be brought to an end, it will obviously take time for the positive effects of this and the ending of inflexible employment practices to be felt by disabled people. During the time it takes to restructure, society state benefits are the only means of survival for many disabled people.

As well as 'educating' society about a different, arguably more constructive, way of dealing with disability issues, the advocates of a civil rights approach have focused their attention on creating legislative changes in line with their arguments. The history of the civil rights disability movement is a testimony to the fact that education, which changes people's views, must work in tandem with legislation, which changes their behaviour. This is very clear in the United States, where change has resulted from strong legislation in the form of the Americans with Disabilities Act of 1990. Legislative changes that are now forcing countries in the European Union to accept the responsibilities they arguably should never have relinquished in the first place are the visible rewards of the civil rights activists on this side of the Atlantic. The details of how disability anti-discrimination legislation has evolved in the United Kingdom and the rest of Europe are the subject of the next chapter. We shall now look at how, while general movement from a medical model of understanding disability is well under way, dyslexia and hidden disability generally risk being left behind.

THE ORIGIN AND PERSISTENCE OF THE MEDICAL MODEL OF DYSLEXIA

The process of framing dyslexia within a medical model starts at school when a child's failure to learn how to read is interpreted by teachers and educational psychologists as evidence that there is something wrong with the child. An extremely common label used to describe the child's failing is 'dyslexia'. Once the label is invoked, it is used as the explanation for that child's difficulties as if they in some way resided in the child's personality and intellect. The child is deemed to be abnormal and interventions are introduced to change the child. The goal of these interventions is to make children fit into the education system that they have been brought into. After children are diagnosed as dyslexic, they lose their identity as individuals. Their teachers' and peer perceptions (often parent perceptions as well) become a function of the adjective 'dyslexic'. Teachers and other pupils change the way they think of the 'dyslexic' child. Beliefs concerning what the child can and cannot do are no longer based on a common-sense appraisal of the child's ability; instead, they are determined by the unfounded beliefs, half-truths and negative stereotypes that plague dyslexic people, the more significant of which were discussed in Chapter 1.

The change in the perceptions and thoughts of significant others isolates such children psychologically from the social world they existed in before being identified as dyslexic. Dyslexic children are often ignored by most of their teachers, are ridiculed by other children and may even be rejected by their parents. The psychological and social isolation has the effect of disrupting the normal development of the child's self-esteem and self-image. It undermines the development of normal social relations, interpersonal skills and confidence. These negative outcomes often lead to emotional and mood-state disorders, including depression, anxiety and lack of trust. All of these negative outcomes, the products of bad decisions by the education system, are interpreted by that system as part of the dyslexic syndrome. The education system assumes that the child can and should be changed without exploring how the system could change and what the benefits of such a change would be.

Diane McGuiness (1998), whose work was referred to in Chapter 1, has challenged the dominant medical-model orientation that determines what happens to disabled children in our schools. She has argued that children's failure at school is more likely to be a consequence of an organisational impairment than disability. McGuiness believes that inadequate training of teachers, ineffective methods of instruction and inappropriate political interference all serve to disable some unfortunate children. She presents a compelling case for looking for deficits in the system as opposed to deficits in the child, and her view is therefore very firmly within the social model of dyslexia. McGuiness argues that schools need to make fundamental changes in the way they function. They need to embrace a system that both recognises individual differences and accommodates different needs. Rather contentiously, she suggests that dyslexia is a myth created by the system to cover its flaws and preserve its continuity. Although the idea that dyslexia does not exist is abhorrent to many people, particularly adult dyslexics, McGuiness is correct in one important sense. Concerned as she is with the failure of children to learn to read, write and spell, she correctly concludes that the reason cited by educationalists as the cause of their failure in this enterprise, namely, dyslexia, is a myth. It is a myth that the explanation for their failure to benefit from the school system can be found in the effect of some hidden impairment that disables them. It is a myth that dyslexia is a condition that makes it difficult or impossible for those who have the condition to perform educationally as well as their non-dyslexic peers. The educational problems that dyslexics experience are not part of their condition but artefacts of the school environment that surrounds them. Dyslexia is real—the myth is that it is the reason why dyslexic children fail. Most dyslexic children who fail to acquire literacy skills are the victims of gross incompetence, which is widespread throughout the educational system, and largely a result of government complacency about the problems that exist. The British Dyslexia Association recently drew attention to the lack of adequate provision in schools when its spokesperson was quoted in *The Times* (9 April 2001) as saying that 'more than 70% of schools have no teachers qualified to teach dyslexic pupils even though up to one in ten children suffers from some form of dyslexia.'

What is significant about this statement is that it implies that what is needed is some teachers to be qualified to teach dyslexic children. This reinforces the social welfare policy of segregation; i.e., it suggests that the solution lies in creating a two-tier system of education, with dyslexics using one method and non-dyslexics using another. The more enlightened approach is to change the way teachers are trained so that all teachers are qualified to teach dyslexic children, a change which would not only solve the problem of dyslexic failure but also improve the product, i.e., education, for all the consumers.

Many different educational theorists and practitioners have presented evidence that the education system is failing dyslexic children. For example, recent research presented to the British Dyslexia Association's 2001 conference in York showed how dyslexic children can acquire reading skills in a relatively short period of time if given the appropriate intensive tuition. As *The Times* (18 April 2001) reported,

> The results of a study at Florida State University suggest that children aged between eight and ten can achieve spectacular advances in reading ability but only if they follow an individual teaching programme that is rarely offered in British and American schools. Daily specialised lessons, taught on a one to one basis for two months, can improve reading skills to average levels.

The same article reported that Dr Torgesen, the researcher from Florida State University, believes that his work demonstrates the need for a 'profound rethink' of how dyslexic children should be taught. Dr Torgesen's work demonstrates that dyslexic children could be kept in the mainstream by being given special programmes lasting just a couple of months. This remedy is not as radical as that advocated by McGuiness, i.e., an overhaul of the entire system, but it is probably more practical. Certainly, segregation for a couple of months of a child's schooling would be unlikely to have the impact that segregation for the duration of a child's schooling has. It is likely to be a very long time before any significant changes take place, and, as McGuiness (1998: p. 372) has observed, 'Until then, parents and teachers are left holding the baby while they and other taxpayers foot the bill for a system that hasn't worked for over a hundred years.'

HOW ORGANISATIONS SOMETIMES DISABLE DYSLEXIC ADULTS

The attitude that failure to complete a task is a failure of the person doing the task, which is so characteristic of schools, is often found in workplaces. When employees fail to complete their duties to a sufficiently high standard, they are usually identified as having a deficit, either in skills or knowledge. This leads to action by, or directed at, the employees. Remedies often include having the employees work longer hours or redo tasks, or, in extreme but not uncommon cases, termination of their employment. However, it is often a failure of the organisation, not the individual, that is the cause of a dyslexic's poor work performance.

Consider what often happens in organisations when dyslexics are given instructions about work tasks. Rather than being given a written list of instructions that they can read and reread as required (or have read to them by voice-activated software), their line manager tells them orally what is required of them. The line manager assumes that employees can remember what they are being told, usually because the line manager knows how much other workers can remember. In general, however, as was discussed in Chapter 1, dyslexic employees cannot retain as much information as their non-dyslexic peers can. They remember less of what they are told by their supervisors and managers; consequently, they may not be equipped to perform all of their duties. They may be potentially more able to do the tasks required of them than are their colleagues, but they appear to be incompetent because they do not know what they are supposed to do. Although some readers may think that the obvious solution is for the dyslexic employees to ask their line manager to give the instructions again, there is no reason to suppose that they will remember instructions given orally the second or third time they hear them. If readers think that the dyslexic employee should ask for the instructions in writing, the reality is that this too may not be a solution.

Communication in workplaces that takes no account of dyslexic needs is just one of the many work-based systems that disable dyslexic people. In general, dyslexic people are severely disadvantaged when any key work system or procedure fails to accommodate the way their memory functions; such failures are common features of work environments. Some readers may be inclined to assume that the type of failure referred to above affects low-ability dyslexics, but not high-ability dyslexics, but this is not the case. As the following case history illustrates, even very high-ability dyslexics can be severely disabled by inefficient work systems.

Mike's Case History

Mike, a 27-year-old business systems analyst with a postgraduate degree and published work to his credit, decided to leave an academic post to take up a position with a firm of management consultants. Although he had never experienced any particular work-related difficulties in his university post, he experienced a number of problems very early in his new employment. The most significant problem was that he found it difficult to work in an open-plan office. He had a great deal of difficulty dealing with interruptions, often finding that, if he was interrupted while completing a task, he needed to start the task again because he could not remember what he had been doing before the interruption. As a strategy to combat this difficulty, he often refused to allow people to interrupt him, ignoring their questions, waving his hand to indicate that he did not want to be interrupted, and avoiding eye contact. Although this strategy allowed him to complete his work tasks efficiently, his colleagues soon identified him as an unpleasant person who lacked social skills and was unwilling to work as a team player. He discovered this information, to his surprise, in his first performance appraisal, which took place six months after he had taken up the post.

His appraisal included specific reference to his poor memory for names, and his appraiser emphasised the importance of his knowing the names of his colleagues. An additional problem highlighted was his inattentiveness, apparently evidenced by his difficulties remembering instructions given orally by his line manager. His manager typically gave instructions and "important snippets" of information about clients in brief face-to-face meetings and telephone calls, most of which Mike would forget before he could write them down. Although he had made several requests for his manager to give him instructions and other important information in writing, these requests had never resulted in any changes.

As time went by, Mike was given less and less to do and was becoming sidelined, while his colleagues were establishing themselves as high-powered employees. He was eventually reprimanded for poor performance and considered himself likely to lose his job. Fortunately, his employer was keen to avoid losing him and agreed to have a psychologist investigate whether there was any condition that might explain Mike's difficulties. He was subsequently diagnosed as dyslexic, and the employer commissioned a workplace assessment, which showed how his condition was responsible for his underperformance.

On the basis of advice provided in the workplace assessment report, Mike's employer made a number of changes in the physical work environment, e.g., introducing screens and moving Mike's desk to a position where he was less vulnerable to disruptions. The employer also introduced new procedures; e.g., Mike's line manager agreed to use a tape recorder to supply Mike with taped instructions and information. Furthermore, his employer allowed him to attend a specialist-training programme to improve his memory. Not only did Mike's performance improve significantly but also his employer acknowledged that certain of the changes introduced were general improvements that would benefit all employees.

It is worth noting that this case history illustrates how a direct negative effect of dyslexia, such as a difficulty working with distractions, can produce additional negative effects, such as being judged to be anti-social because of strategies used to overcome an obstacle. This is a particularly interesting case history because after Mike was diagnosed and the adjustments were in place, his line manager confided to him that he, too, was dyslexic. Mike's reasonable requests for his line manager to do things differently were not met because the line manager himself was disabled by his employer's, albeit unknowing, failure to accommodate his dyslexic needs. Unlike Mike, who had no literacy difficulties, his line manager, whom we will call Max, was a very poor speller. Max hid his difficulty by avoiding writing anything down; he had developed effective memory strategies and always gave instructions orally, usually at length. Thus, Mike's initial difficulties were in part a product of another dyslexic's difficulties, a situation that is not as uncommon as readers may think.

In some situations, Mike would have lost his job; in this case, the organisation removed his disability by introducing changes to accommodate him; i.e., the employer's actions were within a social model of disability. The alternative medical-model thinking would have made Mike himself responsible for overcoming his dyslexia-related problems. When dyslexic employees are placed in the situation of finding their own solutions to the problems they face, they often fail, simply because the tasks are too great. Failure has the effect of creating anxiety and stress that, in turn, affect work performance. To make matters worse, failure often results in blame, which increases further the employees' levels of stress and anxiety; this can lead to physical illness and absence from work. It is illogical and counter-productive for an employer to burden employees with problems that they are unable to solve, when the employer could solve those problems with relative ease, but this is exactly what happens in many cases with predictable results, i.e., a lowering of work performance and subsequent loss of productivity to the employer. Employers have a lot to gain from finding the best solution to the problem, not just the most convenient one. Mike's case history is an example of how making changes to work systems represents a better solution than changing people. The latter is costly both in the talent lost and the time it takes to find and train new people.

Organisations disable employees when they make the assumption that an employee's poor performance is entirely due to individual failings; they enable employees when they consider the extent to which such failings are due to organisational procedures, processes and structures. There are sound commercial reasons for organisations adopting a social model of disability and changing to accommodate their dyslexic employees. The obvious logic of expecting employers to be responsible for making changes is that they have the power and the resources while the employees usually have neither. Organisations could remedy many system failures by restructuring their systems to accommodate all their employees, enabling them to do the work they have been employed to do. This would create a level playing field for dyslexics, but all too often no 'levelling' takes place. While the level playing field is happening more and more in the context of visible disabilities, particularly as the civil rights approach gains ground, it is not happening for dyslexics—the next section looks at the reasons for this.

WHY ORGANISATIONS FAIL TO SUPPORT DYSLEXICS IN THE WORKPLACE

The workforce in the United Kingdom includes a substantial number of dyslexic people; although estimates of incidence vary considerably, a very conservative estimate is that 10% of the workforce are dyslexic. Given the loss that is likely to result if they are not properly equipped to do their jobs effectively, the question arises of why employers have not made better provision for dyslexic people in the workplace. The answer is most likely that there is a lack of appropriate expertise to tell them what they should do in some key areas where dyslexics are disadvantaged. The available expertise has unwittingly promoted the belief that the inefficiencies in work systems that disable adult dyslexics are largely restricted to one discrete area, i.e., learning and literacy, when, in fact, they are pervasive throughout the entire work environment.

Employers need to restructure all their work practices, procedures and processes, including the employees performing the tasks, the tools that they are given to perform the tasks, the physical, psychological and social environments in which the tasks are to be completed, the organisational culture and the human-resource factors. Providing expert guidance to organisations requires detailed understanding of all these areas, as well as a comprehensive understanding of adult dyslexia as distinct from child dyslexia. Experts need to understand the psychology of work, as distinct from the psychology of education, and the needs of adult dyslexics in work, as distinct from the needs of child dyslexics in schools. However, advice from professionals who have expertise in one area, but not both areas, will necessarily be rather narrow in scope and poor in quality. At present because the field of adult dyslexia is still relatively new, this combined expertise is still quite rare.

Most adult dyslexia experts are educationalists, educational or child psychologists, or academics whose main field of expertise is child dyslexia. Their training has not included workplace psychology, so they are left to extrapolate from what they do know, i.e., solutions to educational problems, to what they do not know, i.e., solutions to workplace problems. Such extrapolation would only be appropriate if there were a great deal of similarity between workplaces and educational places. The important question is how similar they are. The next section provides the answer to this question.

DIFFERENCES BETWEEN WORKPLACES AND EDUCATION PLACES

The world of work is very different from the world of education, physically, psychologically and functionally; correspondingly, the patterns of needs for dyslexics functioning in the two environments are also very different. University classrooms and lecture theatres, where students listen to 'experts' elucidating theories, stand in stark contrast to offices and meeting rooms where workers carry out tasks that will be evaluated by their line manager, customers and/or co-workers. Students' relationships with their personal tutors are largely characterised by pastoral concern; mistakes, misunderstandings, poor performance and poor understanding are typically treated significantly differently by personal tutors in universities than they are by supervisors in workplaces. Whereas a university tutor is likely to exploit errors as learning experiences, line managers are likely to record them on annual appraisal forms. This, for an employee, can often translate into financial penalties arising from lack of promotion and, in some cases, job loss.

Group dynamics in the two environments can be distinguished in several dimensions. In workplaces people attending meetings may have been working together for very long periods of time, they are often in relationships of mutual dependence with one another, they may have strong expectations of each other, and they may be involved in complex and demanding tasks. In education students attending tutorials do not generally have the same range or quality of experience. The tasks that they are involved in tend to be well defined, sometimes contrived as part of a structured learning experience, and typically the consequences of errors are not as significant as they may be in workplaces.

Even if we examine the area that one would expect to be very similar across the two environments, i.e., education and learning, we find significant differences. Furnham (1997) identifies some important ways in which learning in work is distinguished from learning in education. Using the training of managers to illustrate his points, he argues that:

- The main concern of education is with 'understanding processes, procedures and principles'. In contrast, training in work is 'nearly always practical and concrete'.
- Education is context independent insofar as the process is not usually linked to a specific organisation. Training tends to be context specific; i.e., what takes place in training often relates directly, sometimes exclusively, to the organisation where the employee works.
- In terms of time scales, education is more relaxed than training. The latter requires trainers to be up-to-date, topical and fast. In contrast, education often relies on old material.
- Deadlines are not as important in education as they are in training, and teachers are much more tolerant of students' failure to complete tasks than trainers are when their trainees fail in the same way.
- Students are required to find the resources they need to complete tasks; for example, they may need to surf the net or use the library. Trainees expect to be given all they need by the trainer.
- Teachers tend to be cautious and concerned about theories and academic points, while trainers are more likely to be pragmatic and enthusiastic, and they often rely on persuading people to believe something rather than proving it.
- Teaching tends to be a verbal process, at best supplemented by transparencies and other visual aids. In contrast, training is based on activities, models, visual aids and demonstrations; in short, it is designed to be far more memorable.

Although Furnham focuses on factors related to the training of managers, the points he makes apply generally, a fact we can testify to on the basis of both our own personal experience of working in the two environments and from what we have learnt from our clients.

Educational expertise is being brought to bear on problems that adult dyslexics face in workplaces on the tacit assumption that what applies in the world of education applies to a significant degree in the world of work. But, as we have illustrated above, this assumption is false; the pattern of difficulties dyslexics experience in educational establishments does not mirror the pattern of difficulties they experience in the workplace. University life for students has much in common with what they experienced in school but has little in common with working life.

The attitude of experts advising organisations has been that the knowledge base needs only minor adjustments to make it relevant. In reality, however, the knowledge base that has its origins in educational experiences is largely irrelevant to the workplace, and, as opposed to a simple modification of the rules, an entirely new set of rules needs to be developed. Those studying adult dyslexia whose expertise is solely or mainly in education are understandably concerned with issues of literacy, education and learning. While these areas have some relevance in the workplace, they are only a part of the story. The failure by some dyslexia experts to make this clear is likely to lead employers to underestimate greatly the extent to which they need to change their workplace to accommodate dyslexic employees. The real risk is that, by failing to outline the full extent to which organisational processes disable dyslexic people, the 'experts' will reinforce the false belief that dyslexia is nothing more than a learning difficulty that the individual must overcome.

MEDICALISING DYSLEXIA IN WORKPLACES

A major problem with the fact that an educational model has come to dominate the area of adult dyslexia in workplaces is that medical-model thinking has been imported with the educational expertise. Schools, colleges and universities are considerably behind work organisations in terms of changing in response to pressures from the civil rights movement. Places of education are conservative and slow to respond to change, and they are less likely to accommodate disability than are workplaces. This is implicitly acknowledged in United Kingdom disability anti-discrimination legislation, which has placed fewer demands on schools, colleges and universities than on businesses. Furnham's distinctions outlined above between learning in schools and in workplaces also highlight how schools and colleges are less dyslexia-friendly than workplaces. The medical model goes unchallenged in educational establishments, and therefore it has come to exercise considerable influence on what educational experts and academics do in organisations.

The dominant influence of the medical model in the thinking of many dyslexia experts is very evident in the literature on adult dyslexia. Most books on the subject outline interventions that require significant efforts on the part of dyslexic employees but little on the part of their employers. Typically, the recommended solution for dyslexic adults faced with problems at work is for them to acquire and develop a range of skills and strategies that enable them to fit into their job. Given how recent an innovation it is for the social model to exercise influence over perceptions of disability, it is not surprising that most of what was written about adult dyslexia before the year 2000 was written from a medical-model perspective. It is, however, surprising and perhaps depressing to find that some books published in the last two years reinforce the view that dyslexic individuals, as opposed to the society they live in, should shoulder the burden of change necessary to make them full members of that society. Sadly, the bulk of the available guidance from dyslexia experts to employers tends to reinforce the belief that remedies require the dyslexic to accommodate the organisation, as opposed to the organisation accommodating the dyslexic. Furthermore, the language used to describe dyslexia all too often conveys to readers the idea that the problems dyslexics have are problems they can solve themselves.

The problems that dyslexics face are more often organisational problems than individual ones. Many of the organisational failures that disable dyslexic employees require organisational policy changes, but those writing on adult dyslexia and employment rarely make this point. For example, many authors writing on adult dyslexia discuss how the social model is the desirable framework within which to work but nevertheless fail to promote it in the advice they give. When they do acknowledge that employers should accommodate the needs of dyslexic employees, they often fail to emphasise the issues sufficiently. Comments made by experts on adult dyslexia often undermine the social model by saying too much about the employee's responsibilities and too little about those of the employer.

Some authors do not appear to understand the social model, while others who are aware of it and do consider alternatives to the medical model do not go far enough. For example, Reid & Kirk (2001) discuss the alternative models of disability, using the term 'individual model' in preference to 'medical model'. They highlight the fact that both employers and employees have a responsibility to change in order to reduce the debilitating effects of workplaces. However, their discussion is neither as thorough nor as detailed in relation to what employers should do as it is in relation to defining the employee's responsibilities.

Most dyslexia experts advising organisations do not consider the human-resource functions of workplaces, such as recruitment, selection, induction, appraisal, training and development, and organisational change. Weaknesses in these key processes significantly disable dyslexic employees and far outweigh the disabling effects of literacy-related issues in the workplace. Experts, however, tend to say little or nothing about how employers could restructure these key procedures to ensure that people with dyslexia are not disadvantaged and excluded from the opportunities that the employers are supposed to provide. Again, this probably reflects the core expertise, i.e., education related, of most of the dyslexia experts writing on the subject.

Stress in relation to dyslexia is one of the few non-literacy-based workplace issues that dyslexia experts do sometimes examine. In the case of dyslexics, perhaps unsurprisingly, most of the analysis of stress and dyslexia appears to be governed by a medical-model orientation. For example, ascriptions such as those of Reid & Kirk (2001) of 'those who may be vulnerable to perceived work stress, such as dyslexic people', encourage perceptions of dyslexics as frail and damaged individuals who become stressed because of their individual failings, when it would be more constructive to acknowledge that most people would become stressed if they were placed in the situation that many dyslexics find themselves in when they gain employment, i.e., being asked to do a job without being given all the tools they need to do the job. How organisations unwittingly fail to give dyslexic people all they need to perform their duties is discussed further in Chapter 4, but the important point here is that assuming that stress is the consequence of individual dyslexic weakness without looking at alternative explanations of how organisational failures make it a particular issue for dyslexic employees reinforces the medical-model thinking that serves to exclude dyslexics from workplaces. In occupational psychology, stress is more often portrayed as an organisational construct than the consequence of individual vulnerability; dyslexia experts advising organisations about stress may find this approach enlightening.

The reality is that many dyslexic people who gain employment are, at the start of their employment, no more susceptible to stress than are other employees. Stress is a dyslexic issue because organisations create stressful environments for dyslexic people, and therefore, unsurprisingly, this group are frequently victims of stress and burnout. Explanations of stress from a social model of dyslexia would identify system failure as the source of stress, not inherent weaknesses in dyslexic employees.

Reid & Kirk (2001) are quite correct in suggesting that employers should promote a positive climate within the workplace, but what employers need is clarification of what constitutes a positive climate. They need details of practical methods of producing one; without this, they are unlikely to take any action. Perhaps more significantly, organisations need to be made aware of how and why stress is a particular issue for dyslexics. They need to know how to recognise it in the context of dyslexic employees and what they can do to remove the health risks it poses to those employees. These issues are discussed in some detail in Chapters 4 and 6.

In arguing that interventions in the context of employment and adult dyslexia should move towards a social model, the intention is not to deny that individuals have a responsibility to improve their situation. The employer and employee must both take action if they are each to be successful, but, historically, the employer's responsibilities have been left out of the equation. This needs to be corrected, and if it is to be corrected, a considerable effort needs to be made to emphasize the employer's role. Employers themselves would welcome accurate guidance and advice on how they can best accommodate dyslexics. Most employers are fully aware that they have nothing to lose and everything to gain from taking such action. One approach advocated by some writers to this problem of getting employers to act involves advising employees to approach their line managers or supervisors directly to give them guidance on workplace changes. For example, Bartlett & Moody (2000: p. 89) advise dyslexic employees who cannot follow verbal instructions to 'ask people to produce written instructions for them as back-up'. In acknowledging that 'written instructions [are] hampered by dyslexia', they also advise employees to 'be assertive and ask their employers to produce clearer instructions—for example with spaces, a large typeface, key words in bold and clearly numbered sections'. Continuing with advice to the employee, they suggest that if confusion about what is required has not been resolved after the above requests, the employee should 'muster the confidence to go back and ask for clarification and explanations'.

All of this well-meaning guidance is, in principle, good advice, but what Bartlett & Moody require of employees is arguably expecting too much of them. These authors themselves observe (p. 173) that 'low confidence hinders dyslexic people in many ways. They can find themselves unable to perform even the most basic tasks because they doubt their own ability.' The dyslexics who fit this description are unlikely to find it easy to approach their line managers and make all the requests suggested above. Even those dyslexics whose confidence is not particularly lacking might shy away from such action because of how it could undermine their working relationship with their line manager.

It is highly desirable to empower dyslexic employees to be agents of change in the workplace, and it is within a social-model orientation of dyslexia that dyslexics themselves should take control of the change process. However, expert advice on how they can achieve this control needs to take account of workplace dynamics and of how changes come about. Bartlett & Moody's (2000) suggestions have a number of significant flaws. Even if line managers comply with requests from employees, the action they take is unlikely to translate into policy. Focusing on changing workplaces in this way, to borrow a metaphor from Zola (1972), is like waiting downstream to pull people out of the river when one could prevent them from falling in by going upstream. Ensuring that decision makers and those responsible for disability policy understand the social model of dyslexia and how they can create socially inclusive work environments is equivalent to going upstream to make sure dyslexics do not fall in the river in the first place!

Another objection to the strategy of directing employees to tell line managers what to do is that the latter may not respond positively. It is not difficult to imagine a line manager interpreting requests from an employee for 'special' treatment as unreasonable. Line managers faced with requests from employees to write instructions down and then to clarify further what they have written might easily consider that the employees were being awkward. We have seen that such requests can thus undermine working relationships. A further disadvantage is that line managers who do respond may see their action as a favour granted, i.e., a form of charity, with all the reciprocal expectations this implies.

Potentially good advice, such as the elements identified by Bartlett & Moody (2000), will, more often than not, be lost if due consideration is not given to who should be given the advice and how it should be packaged. Rather than suggesting that employees should react to events as they happen, the advice might be that employees, perhaps through their trade union or personnel representative, raise the issue of reasonable adjustment as an area that needs attention and for which there needs to be a policy statement of some form. In the context of very small employers, this might translate into making time to discuss the whole issue of reasonable adjustment with a business partner or the owner of the business. The important point is that encouraging dyslexic employees to raise the issue as an ongoing concern and responsibility of the employer is empowering them to promote a social model of dyslexia within the workplace; it is empowering them to dismantle disability at work.

HOW TO IMPROVE SUPPORT FOR ADULT DYSLEXICS AT WORK

Explanations and arguments that focus attention on organisational responsibilities increase the likelihood that employers will eventually understand and assume those responsibilities. Neither employers nor employees are helped as much as they could be because the medical model of dyslexia so dominates the thinking of dyslexia experts that they consistently, albeit inadvertently, fail to challenge it. Presenting explanations, arguments and advice that are significantly unbalanced in favour of the medical model sends completely the wrong message to employers. When advice to dyslexic employees is specific and emphatic, and advice to employers is general and mentioned without emphasis, both sides can be forgiven for assuming that dyslexia is fundamentally the individual's problem. The persistence of attitudes that are the product of medical-model thinking is such that, in order to promote a social model, it is necessary to emphasise the responsibilities of employers much more than those of the employees; yet, in practice, exactly the opposite happens. The absence of a strong emphasis on what employers should do is responsible for maintaining perceptions of dyslexia as a personal tragedy that the individual must overcome. At the same time, it causes organisations to miss opportunities to make adjustments, in some cases very simple adjustments, which would benefit both sides.

Dyslexics need to be accommodated in ways that do not undermine their rights, compromise their work relationships or frame them as damaged people vulnerable to stress. Advice and guidance should encourage employers to accept that the changes that they need to make to accommodate dyslexic employees are not charitable acts but are their responsibility within a society that values diversity and seeks to eradicate social exclusion. There is a pressing need for available expertise to be expanded and upgraded. Experts should have the appropriate skills, including a detailed and comprehensive understanding of workplace psychology. They should have an appreciation of how to introduce interventions in a social-model framework, and they may benefit from reflecting on how, as Campbell (2001) has forcefully argued, the social model is the key tool for achieving the social inclusion of disabled people.

Advice to employers about workplace changes to accommodate dyslexic employees needs to take account of organisational culture, workplace dynamics and, importantly, the differences already discussed between workplaces and educational places. Suggested changes should be practical and acceptable to the employer. They should not risk disrupting relationships between the dyslexic employees and their co-workers, managers or supervisors. Advice that fails to give due consideration to these issues is unlikely to improve the situation.

WHO SHOULD ADVISE ORGANISATIONS ON ADULT DYSLEXIA ISSUES?

The following four key areas are where organisations need professional services from experts in the field of adult dyslexia:

- psychological assessment services to diagnose the condition
- workplace assessments to identify specific adjustments for known dyslexic employees
- dyslexia awareness training for managers, trainers and supervisors (including how to recognise dyslexia in employees and what to do when the condition is suspected)
- advice and guidance on how to modify procedures, processes and systems in the workplace (including aspects of the physical, psychological and social environment) in order to create workplaces that accommodate dyslexic employees.

When these services are provided by appropriately qualified and experienced professionals, organisations will be able to accommodate dyslexic employees. If, however, the services are provided by consultants who lack the necessary expertise, the result will at best have no impact and at worst will create more problems than it solves.

It is obvious that any professional offering services to organisations needs to understand the difference between adult dyslexia and dyslexia in childhood. The key differences between child and adult dyslexia, which were discussed in Chapter 1, need to be understood in the context of their implications for people in workplaces. In particular, an awareness of the full range of dyslexic symptoms is important; for example, understanding the role of working memory can provide insights into, and suggest solutions to, many work-related problems. People providing services should be aware not only of dyslexic weaknesses but also dyslexic strengths. The latter are important because they often determine key dyslexic behaviours; for example, it is important to be aware of dyslexics' ingenuity in developing strategies for both overcoming their difficulties and hiding them. Without such insights, practitioners will have little to offer the many high-ability dyslexics who have very successfully developed strategies for hiding their difficulties from public scrutiny. These are the basic requirements in all four areas listed above; additional expertise and skills are required as detailed below.

Psychological assessment involves information gathering and report writing. The information is gathered in a number of ways, but it notably involves the administration of psychological tests. Report writing involves the interpretation of psychological test scores and the synthesis of this information with interview and other data. As noted in Chapter 1, the psychological tests are 'closed' tests, such as the Wechsler Adult Intelligence Scale, that are available only to chartered psychologists. The administration, marking and interpretation all require the skills of a chartered psychologist who is familiar both with how adult dyslexia manifests itself in behaviours and with how adult dyslexics can disguise dyslexic symptoms by coping strategies.

Workplace assessments can be carried out in a number of ways, none of which generally require the administration of psychological tests. They usually involve assessment of work-related strengths and weaknesses, analysis of work environments and the identification of workplace adjustments. This is an activity that should be completed by either a qualified occupational psychologist or a trained professional under the guidance of one.

Dyslexia awareness training should be tailored to the needs of the audience, and therefore the content and detail will vary. However, it should always involve explaining adult dyslexia and making the explanation relevant to the work context. It is therefore essential that the trainer is familiar with workplaces, as opposed to schools and colleges. The trainer should understand and be able to explain in clear language a working definition of adult dyslexia. It should be one that can offer some explanation of typical workplace dyslexia-related symptoms. In many cases, the audience will need to know the implications of disability anti-discrimination legislation; therefore, trainers should be familiar and up to date with such legislation. They should be able to explain what is required of employers under such legislation. Here once again either a qualified occupational psychologist or a trained professional under the guidance of one is the most obvious and desirable person for the job.

In terms of guidance on how to adapt workplaces to accommodate dyslexics generally, the benefits of which adaptation are discussed in a later chapter, consultants need to have the ability and skill to

- identify what needs to change and what in practical terms can be changed
- explain to employers and employees the intended effects of recommended changes
- advise employers on how recommended changes should be implemented.

Chartered occupational psychologists have the appropriate skills, as do appropriately qualified and experienced human-resource personnel. If the latter are employed by the organisation and are suitably experienced, they will be in a good position to design programmes for introducing adjustments, ideally working with occupational psychologists.

The activities listed above are currently carried out by a range of people, from fully qualified and experienced chartered occupational psychologists and educational psychologists to people who have no qualifications but who have appointed themselves experts in the field. The latter group include people who are themselves dyslexics, and who claim that their condition qualifies them to provide professional services. While it is an additional benefit for a suitably qualified psychologist to be dyslexic—for example, it may provide insights that would otherwise not be as clear—being dyslexic itself cannot be deemed an appropriate qualification. We believe it is absurd to argue that simply being dyslexic makes someone skilled in the areas outlined above, and that it is counter-productive for them to provide services to organisations.

Adult dyslexia is not recognised as a distinct field that has a natural home in any one area of psychology. Although clinical and occupational psychologists work with adult dyslexics the condition has found temporary accommodation in the field of educational psychology. This is because educational psychologists deal with child dyslexia and historically, and rather unfortunately, adult and child dyslexics have been seen as requiring more or less the same type of support and guidance. This is by no means an ideal arrangement, and it is not one that benefits either adult dyslexics themselves or their employers. There is a pressing need for adult dyslexia to be recognised as an area distinct from child dyslexia, and one that requires the attention of psychologists who have training and experience that is relevant to the problems that adult dyslexics face.

Adult dyslexia is an important workplace issue that directly affects a large proportion of the workforce; as such, it is an area that occupational psychology needs to recognise as relevant to the discipline. Perhaps because it is still a relatively new area, it has not yet attracted the attention of many occupational psychologists, and at present it is either not covered or inadequately covered by professional training courses in occupational psychology. The result of the rather piecemeal fashion that characterises adult dyslexia services at present is that employers receive a service the quality of which is more a matter of chance than guaranteed by a professional society.

Employers can, however, significantly improve their protection from inappropriate and poor quality services by ensuring that any trainers or consultants that they instruct are chartered occupational psychologists or the equivalent, or professionals working under their supervision. Such action would guarantee at least that professionally qualified people with relevant psychological knowledge and skills and an understanding of workplaces were providing advice. Furthermore, all chartered psychologists are subject to a code of ethics, which, in theory, should prevent them from claiming expertise in adult dyslexia when they do not have it. The British Psychological Society publishes a list of chartered psychologists each year; i.e., 'The Register of Chartered Psychologists', copies of which are available in most libraries or directly from the British Psychological Society, the head office of which is in Leicester (see the Appendix).

DISABILITY ISSUES IN EUROPE

There are nearly 40 million disabled citizens living within the European Union, including a very large number of diagnosed and undiagnosed dyslexic adults. In spite of this very large group of affected people, disability issues have historically not occupied a particularly high profile within the European Union, and in spite of very obvious unfair discrimination, particularly in workplaces, the plight of disabled people has been ignored until relatively recently.

In general, the experience of disabled people in Europe is one of exclusion from the workforce, assessment on the basis of what they cannot do as opposed to what they can do, and lack of legal protection from unfair discrimination. The European Disability Forum, which was founded in 1996 and is the major disability organisation representing the interests of all disabled people throughout Europe, has described the position of disabled people within the European Union as follows:

> Disabled people are the least utilised group in the workforce. . . . Various official estimates suggest that people with disabilities are at least two to three times more likely to be unemployed and be so for longer periods than the rest of the working population. Unemployment does not necessarily represent a corresponding lack of ability or merit. There is a tendency on the part of employers and prospective employers to look more at the disability rather than the actual ability of the person in question. (http:/www.edf-feph.org/en/Campaign/European%20of . . ./EDDP-2000-infonote.htm)

It is easy to understand why disabled people are 'virtually invisible in the workplace', given how little support this group has received on a political level to combat unfair discrimination in employment. Disability was not recognised by the European Union as a legitimate area of interest until the early 1980s, and it was only recognised then because disability activists, armed with the fact that United Nations initiatives had raised the profile of disability issues globally, forced the European Union to move on the issue. The United Nation's considerable contributions to this field, i.e., the Declaration on the Rights of Disabled Persons in 1975, the International Year of the Disabled in 1981 and the Decade of Disabled Persons from 1983 to 1992, gave disability groups the leverage they needed to ensure that disability issues generally, and integration issues related to disabled people in particular, were included and remained firmly on the European Union's agenda from the early 1980s onwards.

Progress towards overcoming the many barriers that societies put in front of disabled people was achieved because disability groups co-ordinated and combined their efforts across national boundaries. They became a powerful force lobbying European Union politicians to take positive action to advance the civil rights of disabled people. The various measures that the European Union was forced to take led to significant changes in terms of both law and policy affecting disabled people in the European Union. The journey to full European citizenship for disabled people, i.e., the removal of discrimination in all areas, is by no means over, but it has started and a number of significant landmarks have already been passed. The formulation of the European Active Social Policy in the early 1990s introduced a new way of thinking about disability within the European Union. It led to policy documents that made specific references to disability for the first time in the Union's history.

A United Kingdom White Paper on the Future of Social Policy in 1994 was the first official recognition that disabled people need to have their fundamental right to equal opportunities built in to European Union policies. This was a significant step forward because it made full civil rights for disabled people a real possibility and a goal that disability activists could pursue, one that they have consistently pursued ever since.

In 1996, the European Union firmly committed itself to the civil rights-based perspective on disability. Once again, this was largely a response to pressure from disability activists, who used another United Nations development, i.e., the adoption of the 'Standard Rules for the Equalisation of Opportunities for Persons with Disabilities' (Resolution 48/96), to force change. The adoption of a rights-based approach within the European Union was a significant point in the history of the disability movement, and, since 1997, there have been many positive and very significant changes in policy and laws affecting disabled people across the European Union.

The overall outcome of the developments mentioned above is that equal opportunities for disabled people and the elimination of all forms of disability discrimination are becoming tangible possibilities. Disability rights are now being recognised across the European Union as of equal importance to the corresponding goals in other areas where unfair discrimination is an issue, notably gender, sexual orientation and race discrimination. The convincing evidence for this and for the fact that the European Union is committed to a civil rights perspective on disability is the passing of laws making discrimination on the grounds of disability illegal. As we shall see when we examine these laws in the next chapter, they do not affect all groups of disabled people in the same way, and dyslexics in particular can find accessing justice more difficult in practice than in theory.

3

DISABILITY ANTI-DISCRIMINATION LEGISLATION

INTRODUCTION

Disabled people do not comprise a self-contained community distinguished by social class, age, gender, social group or political affiliation. However, as we have seen in the previous chapter, they have one experience in common; whatever society they are ostensibly a part of, they have been excluded from it. We discussed in Chapter 2 how social exclusion is the result of implementing policies of segregation of the disabled from the non-disabled in both education and employment, and how the exclusion is reinforced by people's prejudices, fears, ignorance and false beliefs about the nature and implications of disability. In this chapter, we examine how legislation in the United Kingdom and the European Union is developing to combat these negative forces. We shall look at how employment prospects for disabled people have been improved in the United Kingdom as a consequence of anti-discrimination legislation respecting disability and how future developments in that legislation are likely to create further improvements in the workplace.

Although none of the disability anti-discrimination laws referred to in this chapter identify separate categories of disability, people with different types of disability will find that they are faced with different problems when they seek to assert their rights under the law. Notably, people with hidden disabilities generally experience considerably more difficulty finding legal remedies to alleged acts of disability discrimination than people with visible disabilities. This is because the laws as they stand adopt a medical-model approach to disability, making it necessary for individuals to establish a clear link between their impairment and the needs they have as a result of it. Clearly, this is an easier task in the context of visible disabilities than it is in the context of hidden disabilities. Similarly, in terms of hidden disabilities, the needs of people that have well-defined and accepted medical conditions, such as diabetes, HIV and heart conditions, are easier to specify and therefore easier to fulfil than the needs of people with less well-defined conditions such as dyslexia.

This book is concerned with the plight of adult dyslexics, a category of disabled people that represent a sizeable proportion of all disabled people, and how they as a group can overcome the obstacles that they face in employment. Consequently, in discussing current and soon to be implemented United Kingdom legislation relating to disability generally, the main concern of this chapter is how the legislation affects people with dyslexia, as well as their employers, potential employers, work colleagues, supervisors, trainers and managers.

The adoption of disability anti-discrimination legislation is the most compelling evidence that national policies on disability are moving towards a civil rights perspective. There is now primary legislation in the United States of America, Canada, Ireland, Sweden and the United Kingdom, as well as in a number of European countries outside the European Union and other countries, which makes discrimination against people with disabilities illegal. Our focus of concern in this chapter is the workplace implications of United Kingdom anti-discrimination legislation and how it will need to change to take account of European Union disability anti-discrimination legislation.

In 1990, the United States of America introduced disability anti-discrimination legislation that is generally recognised as a benchmark for measuring anti-discrimination legislation worldwide. It influenced considerably the United Kingdom laws that were introduced six years after the United States of America had theirs in place, and the European law that was passed in 2000. We shall therefore start this chapter by briefly outlining the legislation that operates in the United States of America.

DISABILITY ANTI-DISCRIMINATION LEGISLATION IN THE UNITED STATES OF AMERICA

The first significant piece of anti-discrimination law dealing with disability was the Americans with Disabilities Act 1990, which defines discrimination as the denial of equal jobs or benefits to a qualified individual because of a known disability. The Americans with Disabilities Act represents an attempt to remove barriers that prevent people with disabilities from entering the workforce and to protect this group from the adverse impact of false beliefs and prejudice about disability that are widespread and often unchallenged in workplaces. The act defines disability broadly so that a wide range of groups is included.

A key part of the Americans with Disabilities Act is the concept of reasonable accommodation. This provision obliges employers to make appropriate changes in the workplace to accommodate the known physical or mental limitations of an individual with a disability. The philosophy that motivated the Americans with Disabilities Act is that workplaces should change as much as they can to allow people with disabilities full access to employment. The only exception to this full-access rule is when the employer can show that such changes would be unreasonable, i.e., when they would impose an 'undue burden' on the employer. It would, for example, be an undue burden if employers could show that a suggested change was outside their financial resources.

Importantly, the employer is obliged to investigate all (internal and external) available funding possibilities for financing reasonable accommodation before the claim of 'undue burden' can be considered. In other words, the Americans with Disabilities Act obliges employers to investigate possible changes to essential job tasks that would allow a disabled person to do the job. Such changes once identified must be implemented if they are not unrealistic in terms of the impact they have on the employer. Employers in the United States of America who fail to do this before concluding that a person with a disability is unable to do the job may be acting unlawfully. Whether or not they are acting unlawfully is difficult for either employers or employees to determine without the benefit of appropriate legal opinion, reflecting the fact that key terms used in the act are not clearly defined. The

American employment-law specialists Casey et al. (n.d.) summarise the situation as follows:

> The Americans with Disabilities Act is a new and not clearly defined area of the law. Employers must make "reasonable accommodations" for employees' disabilities but what constitutes "reasonable" and what constitutes "disability" are litigated nearly every day. Obvious physical disabilities seem to fit the description, but less obvious are mental disabilities such as ... dyslexia.

These problems and other structural defects in the legislation significantly dilute its power to protect people who experience disability discrimination. As the last sentence of the above summary implies, it is people with hidden disabilities such as dyslexia that suffer most from the lack of clear legal definitions. Dyslexics are particularly disadvantaged because, as well as sharing all the difficulties that other people with hidden disabilities experience, they have a condition the definition of which has eluded experts for decades. Until relatively recently, the existence of dyslexia was widely questioned, and even today there are many who doubt that it is a 'real' condition. Not surprisingly, therefore, dyslexics have an uphill struggle when they find themselves in litigation against their employers, although, as we shall see later in this chapter, the hill is rather steeper in the United Kingdom than in the United States of America.

Despite its shortcomings, the Americans with Disabilities Act is a landmark development in disability anti-discrimination legislation, which has been used as a model for legislation in other countries, including the United Kingdom. Unfortunately, however, although influenced by the Americans with Disabilities Act, the equivalent United Kingdom legislation did not overcome the weaknesses of the American laws. On the contrary, in many ways, the legislation introduced in the United Kingdom not only duplicated weaknesses in the American anti-discrimination legislation but also added to them.

Many observers believe that the United Kingdom's current legislation is a watered-down version of the Americans with Disabilities Act, which is not a particularly strong weapon in the fight against disability discrimination. For example, Lord Lester (1994), a prominent civil liberties lawyer, reflected widespread disappointment with the provisions of the United Kingdom's first piece of anti-discrimination legislation concerning disability when he observed that the Disability Discrimination Act is 'riddled with vague, slippery and elusive exceptions, making is so full of holes that it is more like a colander than a binding code'. In the next section we shall examine this legislation and some of the reasons that have led people such as Lord Lester to be so dismissive of it.

DISABILITY ANTI-DISCRIMINATION LEGISLATION IN THE UNITED KINGDOM

In the United Kingdom, discrimination against disabled people in certain employment contexts was made unlawful by the Disability Discrimination Act of 1995. This legislation defines 'disability' as 'a physical or mental impairment which has a substantial and long-term adverse effect on a person's ability to carry out normal day-to-day activities'.

This definition is one of the main weaknesses of the act. It is a rather confusing definition that can be understood only by further defining its component parts.

'A physical or mental impairment' is not well defined, and there is no exhaustive list of qualifying impairments that can be consulted for reference purposes. Therefore, whenever a dispute arises concerning whether or not the Disability Discrimination Act covers an individual's condition, it is ultimately up to the courts to decide. Mental impairments are obviously more difficult to specify than are physical impairments, and, further clouding the issue, the Act distinguishes between severities of conditions. As far as dyslexia is concerned, the courts in general accept that it is a mental impairment, but it is covered by the act only if it is sufficiently severe and affects 'normal day-to-day activities'.

Normal day-to-day activities are defined as those activities that most people carry out on a regular, daily basis and that involve one or more of a number of broad categories that are listed in the act. The category that is relevant to dyslexia is 'memory, or ability to concentrate, learn or understand'. Since dyslexia can be characterised by a failure in short-term memory that affects concentration, learning and comprehension of material, it affects a large number of 'normal day-to-day activities'. A further layer of complexity is added because, to come under the terms of the act, the disruption of normal day-to-day activities must have a 'substantial effect', which means 'more than minor or trivial' as opposed to 'very large' effect. In principle, establishing this for a dyslexic adult is not too difficult, since examples normally abound. For example, day-to-day activities that often take dyslexics significantly longer to complete include shopping, travelling on public transport, following directions, giving and taking messages, following instructions, dealing with bill payments and completing forms of various kinds.

The final component of the definition is 'long term'; impairments are covered by the act if they

- have lasted at least 12 months, or
- are likely to last 12 months, or
- are likely to last for the rest of the life of the person affected.

Developmental dyslexia, being a life-long condition, is clearly a long-term impairment; however, the situation may not be as clear for acquired dyslexia, i.e., dyslexia that results from a head injury, although most psychologists would expect this condition to be for life.

This cumbersome and very narrow definition of disability within the Disability Discrimination Act has been the focus of much disparaging comment. Criticism has focused on both the narrowness and the nature of the definition. The definition of disability in the act focuses purely on the characteristics of the individual and does not take account of the way society, because of prejudice, unwarranted fears, stereotypes and ignorance, discriminates against people. The act assumes that the degree of disability is related to the degree of impairment; a very severe dyslexic is more disabled than a mild dyslexic. This is a very strong medical model orientation; i.e., the underlying belief system is that dyslexics' difficulties are located in the individuals, not the environment they live in. This feature of the legislation makes it a very ineffective tool for combating discrimination in the workplace.

As it stands, the Disability Discrimination Act provides some dyslexic adults with some protection from unfair discrimination in work and employment, but, illogically, it does not afford others the same protection. To illustrate this point, we can consider how the law could deal quite differently with two people subject to the same mistreatment at work. Let us assume that two people each have a psychological assessment report, completed by a chartered psychologist, confirming the fact that they are both dyslexic. Both of them are employed and both inform their employers about their dyslexia. They each experience a marked change in the way they are treated by their respective employers, and, eventually, both decide to take legal action against their employer under the Disability Discrimination

Act. Although these two people have been mistreated by their respective employers in an identical way, one could win the case and the other lose if the employment tribunal ruled that the dyslexia was not severe enough to be covered by the act. Although common sense dictates that if one employer has acted improperly, then so has the other, the law punishes only one. Both people are victims of disability discrimination, but one is denied a legal remedy.

There is simply no logic to making a distinction between severe and mild dyslexia when the context is employment discrimination. The premise that the less severe the disability, the less likely the person is to suffer unfair discrimination is false. All dyslexics are likely to suffer discrimination by people who hold strongly negative views about this condition. It is common sense that if employers are likely to discriminate against dyslexic job applicants or employees, they will do so without matching the extent of discrimination to the severity of the condition. In reality, although dyslexic adults may not be severely disabled by their condition, they can be severely disabled by adverse employment decisions that arise from the very fact that they have the condition. Common sense dictates that if such discrimination is ever wrong, it is wrong all the time. To make it legal some of the time, which is precisely what the Disability Discrimination Act does, is unjust. The concept of 'common sense', a concept that was supposed to have an important influence in the drafting of the Disability Discrimination Act, is arguably more apparent in the act by its absence than by any obvious influence it has exercised. This situation is accurately summarised in a paper entitled 'A Critical Analysis of the Disability Discrimination Act', which includes the following observation:

> Far from achieving the government's stated goal of mirroring a common sense understanding of disability, the Act's definition is actually very complex and counter-intuitive. The definition of disability is focused on a person's medical impairment. This definition will not cover all disabled people. Disabled people support a definition which recognises that discrimination is based on stigma and social restrictions and which recognises that it is the experience of discrimination which is the issue, not the degree of impairment.

Fundamentally, what makes the Disability Discrimination Act a weak weapon against discrimination is the fact that it is based on an unyielding medical model of disability. No concessions are made in recognition of the fact that discrimination is not a function of what a physical or mental impairment does to an individual but of what other people do to the individual who has the impairment.

Defenders of the legislation as it stands argue that the justification for adopting a medical-model orientation is that the alternative, i.e., adopting a social model, would have entailed that the legislation cover people who are not disabled as well as those who are, but this, in fact, is precisely what would have made the legislation more powerful, fair and effective. Employees who are treated poorly in their workplaces because their employers believe them to be dyslexic should be protected by the law regardless of whether they are dyslexic or not. The Sex Discrimination Act was intended primarily to combat unfair discrimination against women, but it applies equally to men. The Race Relations Act was intended primarily to combat discrimination against non-whites, but it protects white people as much as non-white people. If the whole population are given equal protection against sex discrimination and race discrimination, it stands to reason that the same should apply to disability discrimination, which is the case in the United States of America, but not in the United Kingdom.

It is lamentable that many dyslexic adults and other disabled people seeking protection from unfair discrimination under the law would, for no reason that could logically be upheld, be far more likely to find themselves protected in the United States of America than they would in the United Kingdom.

EMPLOYERS NOT COVERED BY THE DISABILITY DISCRIMINATION ACT OF 1995

Further inflating the numbers of people who are afforded no remedy to acts of unfair discrimination as a consequence of their disability, the Disability Discrimination Act makes significant groups immune from its provisions. Currently, the police, the armed forces, the prison service and certain other employers, most notably all employers with fewer than 15 employees, are not covered by the act. The net effect of these exclusions is that, for a very large number of disabled people, the Disability Discrimination Act, in its present form, is a meaningless piece of legislation. As we shall see later in this chapter, the situation is soon to change.

WHEN DISABILITY DISCRIMINATION IS JUSTIFIED

It is perhaps surprising to find that legislation designed to combat disability discrimination has a provision that makes the discrimination legal, but this is the case with the Disability Discrimination Act, wherein Section 5(4) reads, 'failure to comply with a section 6 duty [i.e., the duty of the employer to make reasonable adjustment] is justified if, but only if, the reason for the failure is both material to the circumstances of the particular case and substantial.'

Neither of the two older pieces of domestic anti-discrimination legislation has an equivalent provision for legally justifying direct discrimination, nor does the Americans with Disabilities Act. These three pieces of legislation were well established when the Disability Discrimination Act was being drafted and were obvious models to use for deciding the content of the new legislation. Why, then, did the government feel it necessary to include a provision to make disability discrimination legal?

The government's argument for including a justification of discrimination is that disabled people are different from other groups who are subject to discrimination, because disability can be relevant to a person's ability to perform a job. This is an unconvincing position to adopt for two reasons. First, the implication that race and gender are never relevant to a person's ability to perform a job is inconsistent with the Race Relations Act of 1976 and the Sex Discrimination Act of 1975, each of which has provisions for race and gender, respectively, to be an occupational qualification for employment. Second, and more significantly, the logical and more equitable route is to restrict legal rights to disabled people who have the skills and abilities to do the job, and this is how the Americans with Disabilities Act deals with this issue. The latter alternative puts disabled people in the same position as non-disabled people; i.e., employees from either group would have no case against an employer whose employment decisions were based on objective judgements about the employee's ability or lack of it.

Constructing disability anti-discrimination legislation that justifies discrimination on the grounds of disability is counter-productive. The Disability Discrimination Act should have been drafted so that employers are not in any way prevented from making sensible employment decisions based on objective assessments of applicants' competence to do the job for which they are applying. The clumsy attempt of United Kingdom legislators to deal with the issue of disabled people lacking appropriate qualifications by introducing the concept of 'justifiable discrimination' serves only to create confusion among those people trying to understand the act. More importantly, however, on a psychological level, by communicating to employers that discrimination against disabled people is sometimes acceptable, the act reinforces the false belief that disabled people are in some way inferior to non-disabled people. United Kingdom law should present a clear and unequivocal statement that the concepts of fair and unfair discrimination apply to everyone equally, regardless of any physical or mental impairment. By failing to do this in the single case of disability discrimination, the legislation itself contributes to disability.

THE RESPONSIBILITIES OF EMPLOYERS IN THE UNITED KINGDOM UNDER THE DISABILITY DISCRIMINATION ACT OF 1995

As with the Americans with Disabilities Act and all anti-discrimination legislation affecting disabled people, a key element of the Disability Discrimination Act is the obligation it places on employers to make 'reasonable adjustment' for their disabled employees. Section 6 of the Disability Discrimination Act deals with this concept; in particular, it specifies that

> Where (a) any arrangement made by or on behalf of an employer, or (b) any physical feature of premises occupied by the employer, places the disabled person concerned at a substantial disadvantage in comparison with persons who are not disabled, it is the duty of the employer to take such steps as it is reasonable, in all the circumstances of the case, for him to have to take in order to prevent the arrangements or feature having that effect. Disability Discrimination Act (1995), Section 6(1)

This means that all employers covered by the act are under a legal obligation to identify and introduce appropriate changes, known as reasonable adjustments, to their work environment in order to create a level playing field for any disabled people they employ and any others who apply for vacant posts. The work environment includes human-resource functions such as recruitment, selection, appraisal, promotion, training and development.

As we saw in terms of the Americans with Disabilities Act, the key word is 'reasonable'; i.e., employers are not obliged to make adjustments that represent an unreasonable burden in any way. Again, as with the Americans with Disabilities Act, exactly what constitutes reasonable and unreasonable is not well defined within the terms of the act. The Disability Discrimination Act specifies that, in determining whether adjustments are reasonable, all the circumstances must be taken into account, e.g., financial resources, practicality and the extent of likely disruption caused by introducing adjustments, from which it is clear that the word 'reasonable' can be defined only in context. Within broad guidelines, employers and employees are left to determine for themselves what the word 'reasonable' means. If they cannot agree and arbitration fails, it becomes a matter for the courts.

This whole problem of defining 'reasonable' is an area where dyslexics are more disadvantaged than any other group. While identifying adjustments will be more difficult in the context of hidden disabilities generally, compared to visible disabilities, there are two important complicating factors that operate in the context of dyslexia that make the identification particularly difficult.

First, there is a very wide range of possible workplace manifestations of dyslexia, most of which will not be apparent to either the employee or the employer. Readers interested in what the possible manifestations of dyslexia are should consult Tables 4.1, 4.2 and 4.3 in Chapter 4.

Second, as we have discussed in Chapter 2, expert opinion on adult dyslexia is dominated by what applies to educational establishments, in spite of the fact that workplaces are very different from educational places. Adjustments recommended by consultants will very probably focus almost exclusively on literacy.

Dyslexia is a condition that many employers feel they understand (more often than not, wrongly!); they expect solutions to dyslexic problems to focus on reading, writing and spelling, and usually that is what they do focus on.

This translates into a major problem for many dyslexic adults because they have significant work-related problems that are simply ignored, albeit unintentionally. The widespread misunderstanding that dyslexia is purely about needing support with literacy may result in employers feeling that they have made reasonable adjustments by providing literacy-based adjustments when, in fact, those adjustments may have a neutral or very little effect on the employee. In a sense the employer has made a reasonable adjustment, but not a relevant one.

The courts themselves have an insufficient understanding of the issues outlined above, and they often labour under the same false belief held by most employers. As a consequence, articulate dyslexics who were aware that they needed a range of non-literacy-based adjustments and argued their case before an employment tribunal would have an uphill struggle to convince them that what was being requested was reasonable. The proper enforcement of the legal responsibilities that employers owe to their dyslexic employees depends to some extent on the awareness of dyslexia of those who sit on employment tribunals hearing cases of alleged discrimination. However, the Disability Rights Commission consider that awareness is lacking in the whole field of disability—so much so, that they believe it would be beneficial to have a special court to deal with disability cases.

> It could be argued that, given the general lack of expertise on disability matters in the County Courts, all cases under the Disability Discrimination Act should come under a single Tribunal service. . . . while there might be attractions in principle in such an approach, there seemed little prospect of it becoming a reality in the foreseeable future.

Given the extent to which dyslexia is misunderstood within the field of disability generally, it is logical to conclude that dyslexics are very likely to suffer most as a consequence of the 'general lack of expertise on disability matters'.

REASONABLE ADJUSTMENT: CONCESSIONS FOR SMALL EMPLOYERS

Defining 'reasonable' in the context of the employer's resources obviously implies that less is expected of smaller employers who are covered by the Disability Discrimination Act than larger organisations. Small employers do, however, need to exercise caution before assuming that they have a defence in the claim of unreasonable burden. It is important for small employers to understand that they do have a legal obligation to consider all available resources, internal and external, before concluding that possible adjustments are unreasonable. In particular, small employers need to consider Section 6(4), sub-section *e*, of the Disability Discrimination Act, which specifies that 'the availability to the employer of financial or other assistance with respect to taking the step' must be considered when determining whether it is reasonable to take the step, i.e., to make the adjustment.

In relation to this requirement of employers to examine all sources of help and finance when making reasonable adjustments, one source of assistance that should be considered by employers in the United Kingdom is the government's Access to Work scheme, which is operated by the Employment Service. Access to Work is designed to help disabled people, including dyslexics, gain and retain employment by funding or part-funding adjustments. This can include but is not restricted to workplace assessments, specialist training for employees, provision of support workers and the purchase of computer hardware, such as laptop computers, and computer software, such as voice-activated programs.

Access to Work has helped many dyslexic adults, from the self-employed to employees of large multinational corporations, to overcome dyslexia-related difficulties and succeed in their chosen area of work. Any employer, large or small, who has a dyslexic employee can make an application for assistance under the Access to Work scheme. Either the employer or the employee can make such an application by contacting a Disability Employment Adviser in a local jobcentre. It is important for small employers, excluding those with fewer than 15 employees, to be aware that if they fail to consider Access to Work before deciding that an adjustment is unreasonable, they risk falling foul of the Disability Discrimination Act.

Aggrieved employees who take their employer to an employment tribunal have a strong case if that tribunal determines that an application under Access to Work should have been made but was not. Disregarding legal requirements for the moment, however, making an Access to Work application is simply common sense because it helps improve an employee's efficiency. This not only benefits all employers but is also a benefit that frequently increases in significance as the size of the employer decreases.

Although small employers have most to gain by what is available through Access to Work, they rarely take advantage of it. As we shall see later in this chapter, the evidence suggests that they are not aware of the scheme rather than being aware of it and choosing not to use it. Our anecdotal evidence, based on over a decade of experience of providing adult dyslexia services to many large and small firms, is that, while the majority of the former are aware of the services that they can access through the government's Employment Service, a large proportion of employers and employees in small firms are unaware. Over the years, we have met very many more small employers who were unaware of the Access to Work scheme than who were aware of it. We have had many clients who have left employment with small employers because of difficulties that probably could have been solved had they, or their employers, been aware of and used the Access to Work scheme.

Our experience as psychologists actively involved in providing adult dyslexia services to organisations is that when small firms are aware of the Access to Work scheme they have learned of it by word of mouth rather than by any proactive initiatives by the government. Communication about government provisions to facilitate the social inclusiveness of disabled people would probably have a major positive impact on their plight, yet such communication remains abysmally ineffective—so much so that it is hard to believe that there is within government any honest intention to publicise the provisions that they have put in place to help disabled people gain and retain employment. If disabled people are to be integrated into society, there needs to be both legislation and communication; however, while the former is being attended to, the latter is considerably lacking.

BURDEN OF PROOF WITHIN THE DISABILITY DISCRIMINATION ACT OF 1995

In addition to the problems of defining disability and reasonable adjustment, which, as we have seen, serve to reduce the overall effectiveness of the Disability Discrimination Act, there are further flaws in the legislation. One particular aspect, the burden of proof, serves to undermine significantly its effectiveness as a tool for combating disability discrimination in workplaces.

At present, under the provisions of the Disability Discrimination Act, when allegations of discrimination are made, it is, except in one exception, the employees who must prove that they have been unfairly discriminated against. The exception is when unsuccessful job applicants allege that their failure to be employed was due to discrimination on the grounds of disability. In this case, the Disability Discrimination Act acknowledges that all the relevant information rests with employers and for this reason obliges them to prove that the applicant's failure was not a consequence of disability (or, if it was, that such a decision was justifiable in the context of the concordance between the skills of the applicant and essential job functions).

In reality, the argument to justify the reversal of the burden of proof in Section 11 of the Disability Discrimination Act applies generally. It would have been far more logical to make a reversal of the burden of proof the norm in the Disability Discrimination Act rather than the exception. The fact that such a large number of cases of disability discrimination, i.e., more than four out of five, heard by employment tribunals result in victory for the employer strongly suggests that the system is inequitable and weighted in favour of the employer. The favourable conditions for the employer largely arise because employees simply cannot get hold of the incriminating evidence that often does exist, sometimes in abundance. There is a 'questions procedure' that applicants can use to gain access to information from their employer and which involves sending a standard questionnaire, which is available from jobcentres, to the employer. This, however, does not provide an effective remedy to the problem of gaining access to all the relevant information in situations where employers withhold key information. Employers defending themselves against allegations of disability discrimination are obviously unlikely to provide anything more than the minimum required amount of information to satisfy the employment tribunal. Key information, typically in the form of conversations, memos, minutes of meetings and emails, all of which might enable employees to win their case, is likely to exist, but very often the employees will simply not know of it, nor is the questions procedure likely to unearth it.

Obviously, an employee who does not know that incriminating information exists cannot make a request for it to be supplied. Since there is no provision within the Disability Discrimination Act requiring the parties involved in an action to produce lists of all relevant documents they have (or have had), employers can, if so inclined, simply withhold any information that they consider to be incriminating. This disabling effect of not being able to access the information is likely to be more significant for employees in junior posts. Such employees are obviously less likely than more senior employees to know what documents exist, what meetings have taken place and who has said what to whom. At the same time, junior employees are generally more exposed to discrimination and more damaged by it than more senior ones. Therefore, perhaps unsurprisingly, not only is the legislation weighted against employees but also it is particularly impotent in relation to helping those who are the most likely to be victims of disability discrimination.

In addition to documents, the witnesses to alleged adverse employment actions or decisions are often the key to presenting a strong case in court. Witnesses will usually be colleagues or former colleagues of the employee making the complaint. For a number of reasons, these individuals are likely to be very reluctant to give evidence against their employer. The possibility of being treated poorly themselves by the employer would be a real fear for many potential witnesses. Although, in theory, those victimised by employers for giving evidence against them in an employment tribunal have a legal remedy, this is not going to convince people that they will not suffer in some way in their employment by giving evidence.

In addition to the natural inclination of employees not to get involved, adult dyslexics frequently find recruiting witnesses particularly difficult because of the relationship problems that tend to develop in workplaces between them and their colleagues. Our own experience of helping adult dyslexic employees to overcome work-related problems is that very often their dyslexia-related difficulties have already alienated their managers and co-workers. For example, people in workplaces often interpret poor performance in a dyslexic employee as the result of laziness or incompetence. Negative evaluations of dyslexic employees by other workers often translates into a general feeling that any action taken by the employer, such as official warnings or even termination of employment, is justified. The combined effect of not wanting to get involved and feelings of hostility towards the dyslexic employee is that the dyslexic employee's work colleagues are often most unlikely to act as witnesses.

An additional factor that conspires to undermine the dyslexic employee's case when taking an employer to an employment tribunal is the lack of proper legal representation. Whereas the employer will usually appoint a lawyer who specialises in such cases, most employees will not have this luxury because of a lack of funds. Although, in theory, the employment tribunal will be sympathetic to individuals representing themselves against legal counsel representing the other side, such self-representation is by no means as effective as being represented by properly qualified and experienced counsel. Even if the professionals hearing employment tribunal cases were more aware of the obstacles facing dyslexic applicants, the support they could provide would do nothing to help the applicant in the preparation of the case before the hearing. Dyslexic applicants can seek support from organisations such as the Disability Rights Commission, an organisation that provides a very good service to disabled people, but not all who make such an application receive help since the commission cannot accept every case.

While disabled individuals representing themselves at an employment tribunal face a very stressful and demanding task, dyslexics have an added burden by virtue of their disability. Verbal communication problems generally, together with impaired memory functioning and difficulty organising information (including papers and documents), all typical but not widely recognised dyslexic characteristics, make the task of preparing a case for, and answering questions in, the employment tribunal a considerably more difficult one for a dyslexic than for a non-dyslexic. In cases when the employer is represented by counsel, as is usually the case, dyslexics will find the task of proving their case rather futile. In all respects, the burden of proof, as it stands at present, is inequitable. It represents an extremely formidable barrier to employees who have genuine grievances in achieving a fair result in disputes. The reality is that many dyslexic employees who feel they have been poorly treated are faced with either taking on the very demanding and stressful task of preparing and presenting a case knowing the odds are stacked against them, or simply accepting that they have no remedy in law. The burden of proof is probably the most significant obstacle on the dyslexic person's road to justice and almost certainly explains why, as mentioned above, only one in five cases results in success for the employee.

THE LIKELIHOOD OF RESOLVING DYSLEXIA DISCRIMINATION CASES OUT OF COURT

Given how stressful court cases are for employees and how costly they can be for the employer, it is obviously in everyone's best interest to resolve disputes without going to an employment tribunal. Discussions to resolve disputes outside an employment tribunal normally take place on two levels. The first level is discussion with the employer directly, which may be in the context of a formal grievance procedure, and the next level is by using the Advisory, Conciliation and Arbitration Service (ACAS). In both situations, as in court cases, the very nature of difficulties that dyslexics face with memory and verbal communication can disadvantage them significantly in negotiations. For example, dyslexics who in verbal exchanges tend either to talk excessively or interrupt others, both quite common dyslexic behaviours, are likely to meet with hostile responses from their employer. If they fail to overcome these tendencies in delicate negotiations with their employer, such talks are likely to harden the resolve of the employer.

Although hostility will not usually be an issue in negotiations with the Advisory, Conciliation and Arbitration Service, dyslexic weaknesses can still undermine what should be a constructive attempt to resolve the dispute out of court. An inability either to follow negotiations closely or to express arguments effectively when trying to settle disputes using the Advisory, Conciliation and Arbitration Service is obviously a major disadvantage and one that makes it less likely for dyslexics to resolve their disputes out of court than their disabled peers who are not dyslexic. Obviously, appropriate training to deal with disputes involving dyslexics would in all probability, if it were made available to Arbitration, Conciliation and Advisory Service negotiators, increase successful outcomes.

A TIMETABLE FOR CHANGE IN THE DISABILITY DISCRIMINATION ACT OF 1995

The above discussion paints a rather bleak picture for adult dyslexics, but the situation is changing for the better. While the Disability Discrimination Act is generally acknowledged to be a rather ineffective tool for dismantling disability discrimination, it is soon to be improved. Developments in certain provisions of the Disability Discrimination Act will make it a more powerful instrument for providing legal remedies to acts of disability discrimination, but precisely how much more powerful remains to be seen.

Although changes to the Disability Discrimination Act are discussed later in this chapter, the precise nature of the changes will not be known until the government's Department of Work and Pensions produce an official paper on the subject, which is not due until the end of 2001 at the earliest. What is known at this time is that some of the changes are following a European Agenda and must be adopted into United Kingdom law by 2006. Other changes are following a domestic political agenda and will be adopted into the legislation by 2004. The earlier date for some of the legislation to be in place represents the successful work by the Disability Rights Commission and the, now disbanded, Disability Rights Task Force.

The Disability Rights Commission continues to work to persuade the United Kingdom government to adopt into the Disability Discrimination Act all the new provisions arising from European legislation as soon as possible, and not to wait until 2006. There is, however, no indication that the government will respond positively to this pressure. Sadly, it seems unlikely that the full provisions of the European Anti-Discrimination Legislation will be adopted into the Disability Discrimination Act before the European deadline of 2006. What is certain is that when it is eventually in place the new law will contribute to making working life more equitable for disabled people. We shall now look in some detail at what the European disability anti-discrimination legislation requires of member states, including the United Kingdom.

DISABILITY ANTI-DISCRIMINATION LEGISLATION IN THE EUROPEAN UNION

The Framework Directive on Equal Treatment in Employment and Occupation became part of European law on 27 November 2000. This law is generally referred to as the 'Framework Directive', and that is how it will be referred to in the rest of this chapter. The Framework Directive, which evolved from the non-discrimination clause of the Amsterdam Treaty, i.e., Article 13, is the first piece of legislation to be introduced by the European Union that outlaws discrimination against disabled people across all member states. It represents a firm commitment to fight discrimination in all countries of the European Union, and it presents disabled people with the possibility of achieving recognition as full citizens of Europe.

The Framework Directive applies to private and public companies and public authorities, and it makes illegal both direct and indirect discrimination against, and harassment of, disabled people. The Disability Discrimination Act and the Americans with Disabilities Act influenced the development of the Framework Directive; understandably, therefore, it has much in common with these laws. Nevertheless, the Framework Directive has gone further than the Disability Discrimination Act, and there are some important features of the European law that must be adopted into the United Kingdom legislation. Like all disability anti-discrimination legislation, a primary source of the Framework Directive's potency in combating employment discrimination, which is arguably the most invidious form of discrimination, is the fact that it states unequivocally that employers have a legal obligation to make 'reasonable accommodation' (the equivalent term in the Disability Discrimination Act is 'reasonable adjustment').

The Framework Directive gives examples of reasonable accommodation that are similar to those in the Disability Discrimination Act. It provides that employers are exempt when the measures imply that the employer would experience a disproportionate burden. Like the Disability Discrimination Act, the formula for determining disproportionate burden involves taking account of all the circumstances, including financial costs, of making the suggested changes in the context of the scale and resources of the employer and the employer's eligibility for public subsidies. This provision will have little impact on the United Kingdom since it is already in place there. In other countries in the European Union, however, it has the potential to create substantial change for disabled people. For disabled citizens of the United Kingdom (and other citizens of European Union member states), this change provides some comfort to those who wish to work in different European Union countries in that, wherever they go, they have some chance of being protected from disability discrimination, at least from 2006 onwards.

The Framework Directive has not imposed a definition of disability on member states, leaving each one to formulate its own definition. There is therefore the possibility that countries will choose rather narrow definitions and so exclude some, possibly many, disabled people from legal protection from discrimination. It seems likely, however, that after 2006, the deadline by which all European Union member states must have adopted the provisions of the Framework Directive into their domestic laws, the obligations that employers in different countries have to make reasonable adjustments will vary considerably because of variations in the way their definitions of disability have been formulated. There may be potential here for legal challenges from disabled people who feel that their free movement across member state borders is restricted because of variations in employment opportunities arising from differing definitions of disability.

Although there are many similarities between the Framework Directive and the Disability Discrimination Act, a fact which means that there will be less change in the United Kingdom than most other member states, implementation of this Directive will require United Kingdom law to be amended in a number of significant ways.

IMMINENT CHANGES TO UNITED KINGDOM DISABILITY ANTI-DISCRIMINATION LEGISLATION

The Framework Directive introduces two particularly important changes in United Kingdom disability legislation that are very significant for dyslexic employees and their employers.

The Framework Directive extends protection from disability discrimination to groups not currently covered by the Disability Discrimination Act. Although there are areas of employment where there is some ambiguity, the new law will very drastically reduce the numbers of employers who have immunity from the provisions of the updated version of the Disability Discrimination Act. Practically all employers and, most notably, all small employers will be covered. The only significant employer that is explicitly identified as not being covered by the act is the armed forces.

The fact that large employers, such as the prison service, who are currently not covered by disability legislation, will become subject to the provisions of the new law may not be as significant as it appears at first sight, at least in relation to dyslexic employees. Our experience of providing adult dyslexia services, including workplace assessments, training and consultancy services, to large employers that are not currently covered by the Disability Discrimination Act, including the armed forces, suggests that, while changes in the law will have an effect, very significant improvements will not arise. This is because, unlike small employers, these large organisations are already aware that dyslexia is a disability, and although they are not under a legal obligation to do so, many are already actively involved in helping dyslexic employees overcome their difficulties. They are aware of and make use of the Access to Work scheme, and, in general, they are prepared to make reasonable adjustments regardless of the fact that they are not legally obliged to do so.

One possible effect of the extension of the law to cover large organisations is that dyslexic employees who have for some reason not identified themselves to their employer may be more prepared to make their condition known. They will then be more likely to have reasonable adjustments identified and implemented, representing a gain for both sides.

THE IMPACT ON SMALL EMPLOYERS OF INTENDED LEGISLATION CHANGES IN THE UNITED KINGDOM

While there is some doubt about the full impact of extending the umbrella of disability anti-discrimination legislation to cover large organisations, there is very little doubt that the European requirement to extend cover to *all* small employers will have a very considerable impact on small employers.

In theory, small employers could experience a considerable adverse impact from this change, since they are likely to be far less equipped to meet the legal requirements of disability anti-discrimination legislation, particularly in terms of making reasonable adjustments. Unlike larger employers, many small employers simply do not have personnel specialists with expertise in equal opportunities and disability issues; they are even less likely to have access to expertise on dyslexia. Consequently, small employers could find that they are very much in the firing line. For example, sophisticated and well-informed dyslexic employees who feel aggrieved because of their treatment may well decide to take legal action to remedy the problem.

To avoid falling foul of the law, small employers will need to become much more aware of disability issues, including dyslexia and its manifestations, and they will need to be aware of their legal responsibilities under the Disability Discrimination Act. Disability awareness training can help employers to avoid becoming casualties of legislation through ignorance; however, employers should be mindful that dyslexia is a particularly complex hidden disability that may require awareness training in its own right—i.e., general awareness training may not cover the important issues. Accessing such training could prove to be an important element of a strategy of self-defence and small employers should be mindful of this. Such training should include advice about current and soon to be introduced legal obligations, particularly the concept of reasonable adjustment. In addition to seeking specialist training, small employers would be well advised to take full advantage of government help and guidance, notably that which is available from the government through their employment service; in particular, they need to be fully aware of the Access to Work scheme that was referred to above.

Although small employers have always had the option of applying for Access to Work funding to help dyslexic employees, as we discussed earlier in this book, they tend, in general, not to do so. Research suggests that the reason for this is simply that they are unaware of the available services. The British survey Jobs Worth: Disability in Small Business, which was launched in September 2000, and which surveyed 1100 small businesses to identify their attitudes to employing people with disabilities, found that four out of every five of the employers surveyed did not know that they could receive information, guidance and advice from the United Kingdom government's Employment Service.

Our experience is consistent with the finding of the Jobs Worth survey regarding the lack of awareness of small employers about the Access to Work scheme. However, our experience is not consistent with the report's findings in relation to the disability attitudes of small employers, i.e., that a large proportion of small employers appear to think positively about employing disabled people; we have found that this is not the case generally. Our experience of providing services to small businesses is that most of them do not have awareness of disability and do not think positively about employing disabled people. One possible explanation for the discrepancy between our experience and the results of the survey is that the employers surveyed in the Jobs Worth survey were not representative of all small businesses. If, for example, the sample of small businesses that was surveyed excluded all those small employers who had negative attitudes towards disability, it would not be representative of all small businesses. The Jobs Worth survey report, Goss (2000, p. 7) itself suggests this might be the case: 'Many of the 200 small businesses contacted during the telephone survey commented that the survey and information on disability employment issues was not relevant to their company and, as a result, they were unwilling to participate.'

As a further distortion of the reality of what small businesses think about disability, there is the possibility that the Jobs Worth survey results were influenced by a failure to take account of the well-documented tendency of people to give socially desirable responses when surveyed; i.e., people incline to respond to questions with what they perceive to be the desirable response (Aiken, 1985). For example, employers who are asked whether they would be prepared to employ a disabled person might well say they would, when in reality they would not, because they think that being prepared to employ disabled people is socially desirable. The key point is that the survey referred to above may have overestimated the degree to which small employers in the United Kingdom are prepared to deal with disabled job applicants without discriminating against them because of their disabilities. If this is indeed the case, there is the risk that the full extent of the needs of small employers, in relation to disability awareness training, will be underestimated.

In summary, we have noted in our work that many small employers have both little disability awareness and little knowledge of schemes that would help them if they employed a disabled person. Furthermore, it seems likely that a significant number of small employers harbour the belief that there is no business case for employing disabled people, some believing that to employ a disabled person is to take an unnecessary risk. The implication of this is that, rather than legislation, what is needed is better communication. This is one of the key points made in the Jobs Worth survey, which concludes that the government's Employment Service has failed to communicate information to small employers about the services they offer to encourage the employment of disabled people.

Given that imminent changes in the law are likely to have the greatest impact on small employers, to underestimate their needs in terms of education about disability and disability anti-discrimination legislation is to invite conflict between what the law requires and what small employers do. Although (to borrow the motto of the Disability Rights Commission) the argument of force can be used to ensure that small employers meet their legal obligations, it would be far more desirable to use the force of argument first, i.e., to explain to small employers the business case for employing disabled people. Action based on education rather than legislation is more likely to produce and maintain a better working environment for all concerned. At this point in time, however, it seems distinctly likely that the force of argument is unlikely to be given the attention it needs. Since, as we have already observed, awareness of dyslexia is particularly lacking, dyslexic adults in particular may well find that the only way to benefit from the new law is to use it.

A widespread lack of understanding by small employers about what disabled people have to offer, together with some degree of unfounded belief that disabled employees cost employers more than non-disabled employees do, is currently the most likely explanation why small employers are not actively encouraging applications from disabled people when in many cases they represent the best available option. Small firms would almost certainly respond very favourably if they were aware of the business case for employing disabled people (see Chapter 4). The lack of communication probably contributes considerably to the high levels of unemployment of disabled people generally and dyslexic people in particular. Given the obvious need that exists for small employers to be made aware of the government's provisions for disabled people in employment and the fact that there have been no significant national campaigns by the government to raise such awareness, it is difficult to avoid the conclusion, which we have already hinted at above, that short-term cost-saving considerations by the government's Employment Service, rather than political oversight, is responsible for the lack of communication.

There is a pressing need for an awareness-raising campaign so that small businesses know what is available to help them if they already have disabled employees or if they wish to employ people with disabilities. Without improved awareness, the new legislation, no matter how strong it is, is unlikely to result in a significant increase in the numbers of people with disabilities moving into employment. Unless employers' awareness is increased before new European laws are in place, small employers stand to be in breach of European law without realising it. Although ignorance is, of course, no defence, it is impractical to expect small employers to seek out the information they need to comply with every piece of changing legislation. Small employers are often just not able to resource such activity, a fact widely recognised; for example, the Jobs Worth survey (p. 10) reports that, 'whilst being the fastest growing sector of British industry in recent years, small business is also increasingly burdened by regulation and red tape'.

The report goes on to cite the findings of a survey, completed in 1999, which reported that a business with 10–14 employees could expect to spend 31 hours a month complying with government regulations. The regulation and red tape represent major obstacles to success for many small businesses, and additional requirements may well put some small employers out of business. The government need to act if this is to be avoided; furthermore, the Framework Directive makes it their legal responsibility to act. Article 12 (Dissemination of Information) of the Framework Directive makes member state governments responsible for making employers aware of their responsibilities under the new provisions. It remains to be seen whether or not the government respond to this requirement competently, although, in view of the apparent general lack of awareness of employers in the United Kingdom regarding the full implications of the current legislation, there is little reason for optimism. If the government fail to adopt a more efficient method of disseminating information than was used to make people aware of the provisions of the current laws, small employers are likely to be exposed to unnecessary litigation. If small employers operate without understanding what their legal responsibilities are, some of them will inevitably find disabled people taking legal action against them and winning.

Although the time limit imposed by the European Union on member states for adopting into the Disability Discrimination Act the relevant provisions of the Framework Directive is 2006, some changes to United Kingdom law are, as mentioned above, following a domestic political agenda. Notably, extending the Disability Discrimination Act to cover small employers and other employers currently not covered was a recommendation made by the Disability Rights Task Force and subsequently accepted by the government for implementation in 2004. Small employers are therefore due to start feeling the impact of legislation in just two years' time!

POTENTIAL DISADVANTAGES FOR DYSLEXICS OF GOVERNMENT FAILURE TO EDUCATE SMALL EMPLOYERS

Our experience of working with adult dyslexics over the last decade has been that self-employment and working for small employers is more attractive to dyslexic people than other types of employment. The reasons that we have heard most often cited by our clients for this preference is that it provides a better chance that they will be able to work in the way that suits them. This is obviously the case in the context of self-employment and, in relation to small employers, it is probably true because there is usually more opportunity, compared to the situation with larger employers, for people to negotiate how the work can be done. Being able to discuss alternative procedures that are acceptable for achieving work objectives and the possibility of closer involvement with the whole process of work activity are definite advantages for dyslexics. There are other differences between large and small employers that seem to favour dyslexics being employed by the latter. For example, in terms of either office- or factory-based employment, working spaces that are occupied by a small number of employees, as we shall see in Chapter 4, are more attractive to dyslexics than the open-plan workspaces of larger organisations.

It is therefore distinctly likely that dyslexics, more so than other disabled groups, are losing out on opportunities as a consequence of the failure by government to educate small employers. Since over half of all vacant posts in this country are with small employers, the number of opportunities being lost is likely to be very large. The arguments for improving communication are compelling; furthermore, in terms of the social model of disability, it could be argued that poor communication is significantly disabling dyslexic people.

THE POSSIBLE EFFECTS OF REVERSING THE BURDEN OF PROOF IN DISABILITY ANTI-DISCRIMINATION LEGISLATION

Another element of the Framework Directive that will produce a very significant change in all member states, including the United Kingdom, and that is arguably the most radical element of the directive, is that it reverses the burden of proof. The Framework Directive specifies that if persons consider themselves to have been discriminated against and can establish some facts that allow presumption of the existence of direct or indirect discrimination, it lies with the employer to prove that the principle of equal treatment has not been violated. Effectively, this makes employers accused of discrimination guilty until proven innocent.

Reversing the burden of proof removes many of the obstacles that people with disabilities face when they seek legal remedies for genuine unfair discrimination in the workplace. Since the employer will need to prove that they have not violated the principle of equal treatment, the employees will no longer be in the largely no-win situation of needing to prove their case without having adequate access to the information they need in order to do so. Employers who genuinely do not violate the principle, who have good systems for ensuring it is not violated and who have given some thought to how they can demonstrate this will, in general, be able to prove their innocence.

Employers who do violate the principle of equal treatment will have some difficulty proving the opposite and therefore it is logical to assume that employers will not wish to go to an employment tribunal hearing. It is therefore highly likely that reversing the burden of proof will result in more cases being resolved out of court. They will be resolved faster and should cost less even if a financial settlement is agreed; i.e., at present, even though employers who go to an employment tribunal tend to win, it is nevertheless an expensive exercise for them. Thus, the burden of proof change could result in more favourable outcomes for both sides without going to court. In all respects, once the Framework Directive's provision regarding the burden of proof has been adopted into United Kingdom law, those employees who do have a genuine grievance and decide to assert their rights will have a more realistic chance of achieving a just outcome.

COMBATING MALICIOUS ALLEGATIONS OF DISABILITY DISCRIMINATION

Reversing the burden of proof has inevitably been interpreted by some people as a threat to employers and particularly small employers. There are concerns that it will encourage disabled people who have grievances with their employers that are unrelated to their disability to abuse the law by alleging disability discrimination. Such malicious actions are a problem in all anti-discrimination legislation, and they can be very damaging to small employers, but there is no evidence to suggest that they will become a significant problem when the new laws are in place. Although fears about increases in the numbers of malicious actions after the reversal of the burden of proof may be unfounded, safeguards need to be built in to any new legislation so that unscrupulous people who make malicious allegations are not allowed to hold back the progress of justice for disabled people.

The 'pre-hearing review' that currently exists in the United Kingdom represents an attempt to derail legal actions that have little substance. It allows employers facing allegations of discrimination to seek an initial judgement, by the employment tribunal chairman, on the strength of the case. If chairmen decide that the case is weak, they can rule that applicants can proceed to a full hearing of the employment tribunal only after paying into the court a deposit, currently up to a maximum of £100, which they forfeit in the event that they proceed to a full hearing and lose the case. This provides some, albeit rather limited, protection from malicious allegations, but in reality employers themselves can take more effective measures.

Having a written policy on equal opportunities, including specific references to disability and preferably specific references to dyslexia, is probably the most basic step employers can take to ensure that they do not discriminate against people on the grounds of disability. In addition to a written policy, employers who attempt to eradicate disability discrimination in their physical and social environments, as well as in their human-resource management processes and procedures, are reducing substantially the risk of falling foul of the law. This particularly important area for ensuring that dyslexics are not subject to discrimination is discussed in detail in Chapter 4.

When employers make the efforts mentioned above, they make it difficult for someone who is intending to make malicious allegations to establish a prima facie case of discrimination. Taking this type of precautionary action is arguably more important for small employers than large employers because the former are far more likely to be damaged by a single malicious allegation, particularly if it goes to a full employment tribunal.

HOW SMALL EMPLOYERS CAN REDUCE THE LIKELIHOOD OF LITIGATION

While people who are predisposed to make malicious allegations may well be attracted to do so by a system that requires the other side to do most of the work, there is no reason to suppose that the new provision in relation to the burden of proof will be greeted with a flood of such actions. Genuine grievances are potentially a far more significant problem for employers than malicious allegations, particularly for small employers, and most employees go to court because they have a genuine grievance. Given the findings of the Jobs Worth Survey, outlined above, and the related comments suggesting it has underestimated the need of small employers for disability awareness training, it seems highly likely that small employers will be exposed to legal actions from people who have been the victims of unintended discrimination. This problem is most likely to manifest itself in situations where a small employer inadvertently discriminates against a well-informed employee with a hidden disability, such as dyslexia, and the employee decides to take action because of that injustice.

Clearly, small employers will be in a better position to defend themselves and to prove that they have not violated the principle of equal treatment if they can demonstrate that they are aware of, and willing to accept, their responsibilities under the law. Employers who can show that they have taken all reasonable steps to make their workplaces disability friendly, including evidence of discussions with disabled employees and experts in disability issues regarding reasonable accommodations, will be in a much stronger position to defend themselves than other employers who do not take such action. For example, small employers are in a very strong position to defend themselves against allegations of disability discrimination from a dyslexic person if they can show that they

- had a written policy on equal opportunities, which refers to dyslexia explicitly, and which was explained to all employees
- had detailed discussions at an early stage with dyslexic employees about their needs in relation to their dyslexia
- contacted the local jobcentre Disability Employment Adviser for advice on how to support the affected employee
- fully co-operated in the process of completing any workplace assessment recommended by the Disability Employment Adviser
- explored all the recommendations in any workplace assessment report that was completed
- acted quickly to ensure that all agreed reasonable adjustments were put in place

- monitored the effects of those reasonable adjustments and maintained a dialogue with the affected employee and outside experts, such as the Disability Employment Adviser, to ensure the reasonable adjustments introduced were having the desired effect
- took appropriate steps to ensure that all staff had appropriate dyslexia awareness
- Implemented appropriate disciplinary procedures against any member of staff exhibiting dyslexia discrimination (NB: In relation to the actions of staff generally, employers do have a responsibility for acts of discrimination carried out by them against others, and they have a legal responsibility to take reasonable action to prevent such behaviour).

Perhaps it is more important than being in a strong position to construct a defence that employers who meet the above criteria are very unlikely to need a defence because their employees would not be inclined to take legal action in the first place. This applies equally to all employers, not just to small employers. Larger employers would, however, be well advised to carry out additional actions, which are detailed in Chapter 4.

It is important to emphasise that taking the actions listed above does not cause the employer any great financial sacrifices. Access to Work exists in part to assist employers, particularly small employers and self-employed people, with any costs involved in supporting disabled people in work. Furthermore, much of what is recommended above and the related information presented in Chapter 4 serve to improve workplace efficiency and therefore can produce benefits in the long term.

GRIEVANCE PROCEDURES AS STRATEGIES FOR AVOIDING LITIGATION

Whatever actions are taken by employers to reduce the likelihood of direct and indirect disability discrimination, they cannot guarantee that a disabled employee will never feel badly treated. However, most disputes need not lead to an employment tribunal, and they are much less likely to do so if employers have appropriate mechanisms in place. Efficient internal procedures for employees to express their grievances, and for genuine grievances to be remedied without the need to go to law, are probably the most effective way of preventing disputes and grievances from escalating into legal wrangles. Employees who have a genuine grievance will obviously look for remedies in the courts if none exist within their employment. It is very much in the employer's interests to establish an objective and fair complaints or grievance procedure, since this will reduce significantly the likelihood of a grievance's becoming a legal action. A recent development, in the form of an employment bill introduced in the House of Commons on 7 November 2001, includes a provision that parties in a dispute must exhaust a formal conciliation procedure before they can proceed to a full hearing. While this should have the effect of reducing the number of cases that do go to a full hearing, it would be desirable for both sides if employers had a mechanism for solving disputes without needing to bring in independent conciliators.

While the law does not require employers to establish mechanisms for resolving employee grievances, it does require any that are established to be non-discriminatory, but once again this is only a common-sense requirement. To ensure that a grievance procedure does not discriminate unfairly against dyslexic employees, the employer should construct it with a view to making it easy to understand, easy to use, objective, equitable and effective. It is of particular importance that it is flexible in terms of how information is presented by employees who wish to use the procedure. For example, allowing employees to present a tape recording of their grievance or to be represented by another person, such as a friend, would make the procedure more flexible than one that demanded written submissions.

ADDITIONAL CHANGES IN UNITED KINGDOM LEGISLATION OF RELEVANCE TO ADULT DYSLEXICS

In addition to reversing the burden of proof and extending the coverage of the Disability Discrimination Act to include previously immune groups, the Framework Directive is likely to lead to other changes in the United Kingdom legislation. The Disability Discrimination Act's requirement that a disability last at least 12 months is likely to be challenged on the grounds that it is inconsistent with the European Directive. This will remove an unnecessary and illogical restriction, a change which, as mentioned earlier, may have implications for acquired dyslexics.

The Disability Discrimination Act's concept of the justification of discrimination and the current provisions for allowing a justification of failure to make reasonable accommodation in certain situations should be repealed, although this is by no means certain. This will increase the protection that disabled people, including adult dyslexics, have under the law and bring the Disability Discrimination Act more into line with the other two pieces of current anti-discrimination legislation in force in the United Kingdom, i.e., the Race Relations Act and the Sex Discrimination Act.

The Disability Discrimination Act will be amended to include a provision for dealing with indirect discrimination; i.e., it will force employers to ensure that they are not inadvertently discriminating against disabled people by, for example, having some requirement in the workplace that, although intended for all employees, particularly disadvantages persons with a given disability. Although this will strengthen the protection offered to disabled people, it is an important change, not so much because of the increased protection it offers as because it makes the duties of employers explicit and therefore reinforces the fact that disability discrimination is as wrong as other forms of discrimination. This provision brings the Disability Discrimination Act more into line with the Race Relations Act and Sex Discrimination Act.

Another aspect of the Framework Directive that will affect current practices in the United Kingdom is the requirement that any provisions contrary to equal treatment principles in employment contracts or other internal rules by employers have to be declared null or be amended. These general provisions will lead to legal challenges in many areas, as disabled people come to realise that they are facing unnecessary obstacles to their progress in employment and can legally challenge them. For example, at present, most organisations include on application forms a requirement that applicants state whether or not they are disabled. Employers are not allowed to discriminate on the basis of this information; nevertheless, many dyslexics view this as a request for information that will lead to discrimination. Our anecdotal evidence from our clients, both employers and employees, leaves us in no doubt that this does happen. While it is true that employers need to have the information in order to make appropriate adjustments, it could easily be provided separately after the selection decision has been made. This would be a far more acceptable arrangement for dyslexics, who would in any case not be prevented from disclosing their condition at an earlier stage if they so wished. The only significant problem with this is that adjustments may need to be made to selection procedures, but there are solutions to this problem, some of which are outlined in the next chapter.

MOVING TOWARDS SOCIAL INCLUSION

The government's Department of Work and Pensions have responsibility for amending the Disability Discrimination Act of 1995 to bring it in line with the Framework Directive. At the time of writing, their discussions on this matter are apparently at 'a relatively early stage', and many of the important implications of the Framework Directive for revised legislation here have not yet been 'considered in depth'. Although the revised legislation must reflect the Framework Directive, each member state has room to manoeuvre in terms of adopting the directive into its domestic legislation. Importantly, it is open to the government to go beyond the minimum requirements of implementing the directive. Ministers, have an ideal opportunity to transform the current legislation into a binding code that genuinely offers disabled people protection from disability discrimination.

The Disability Rights Commission continue to pressure the government to introduce the new laws before 2006, and they have made it known that they would like to see certain changes beyond the minimum requirements of the Framework Directive. Whether or not such pressure will make things happen sooner than the set deadlines remains to be seen.

IS DISABILITY ANTI-DISCRIMINATION LEGISLATION THE SOLUTION TO UNFAIR DISABILITY DISCRIMINATION?

The Framework Directive will certainly improve the civil rights of dyslexic people within the European Union, but it does not represent a complete solution to the problems that these people face. Many disability experts and disabled people generally believe that disability discrimination will continue no matter how strong legislation becomes. Barnes & Oliver (1995), cited by Ruebain (2000), probably represent the views of most people involved in this area when they argue that even fully comprehensive and enforceable civil rights legislation will not, in isolation from other measures, solve the problem of disability discrimination. They believe disability discrimination is institutionalised in the very fabric of British society. Legislation is important not so much by virtue of how it improves disabled people's access to justice as by virtue of its role in changing people's behaviour and attitudes towards dyslexia. This view has been expressed by a number of commentators; for example, Ruebain (2000) writes

> I contend that anti-discrimination laws are a necessary part of the ending of oppression— to require the end of exclusion. The ending of exclusion is only the start but a critical one. Accordingly, I believe that without anti-discrimination laws, the process of re-evaluation, of transforming peoples' hearts and minds, cannot begin. Anti-discrimination laws are therefore not the solution but part of the fabric of transformation.

There is a reasonable possibility that the Framework Directive, when fully adopted into United Kingdom legislation, will contribute to transforming 'people's hearts and minds'. Notably, after enforcement of a move away from a legal system that favours the employers, they will not only be more likely to take steps to avoid disability discrimination in the first place and to settle disputes sooner when they do arise (without going to court!), but they will also be forced to look at dyslexia in a new light.

While some people have expressed reservations about a law that requires employers to prove their innocence, the reality is that this requirement is likely to result in less litigation and more consideration by employers for the needs of disabled people. As far as cases that do progress to a full employment tribunal hearing are concerned, although employers will face a more demanding task after the Framework Directive becomes law than they currently face, they will by no means have the complex and daunting task currently faced by disabled employees. The Framework Directive represents a move towards fairness, which most people will probably accept as desirable.

The next chapter examines how employers can take positive action to make workplaces as accessible for dyslexics as for non-dyslexics, and thereby reduce the likelihood that they will gain unwelcome first-hand experience of the legislation described above.

4

Dyslexics in the Workforce: Strengths, Weaknesses and Reasonable Adjustments

INTRODUCTION

In the previous chapter, the concept of reasonable adjustment, as it relates to the provisions of the Disability Discrimination Act of 1995, was outlined and explained. This chapter examines the type and range of workplace adjustments that are appropriate for dyslexic adults. As opposed to focusing on reasonable adjustment as a legal requirement, this chapter examines it as a common-sense measure that employers should take in order to get the best from their employees. The chapter starts with an outline of the benefits, direct and indirect, of having dyslexic people in the workforce. Following this is an outline of how dyslexic work performance can be improved by introducing changes to the physical, social and psychological aspects of the work environment. Details of how human-resource management procedures and systems can be modified to accommodate dyslexic employees are examined in detail. The possible and likely advantages, for the workforce generally, of all the adjustments detailed are discussed.

DYSLEXIC EMPLOYEES: PROBLEMS OR SOLUTIONS?

In focusing on how to make reasonable adjustments for dyslexic employees, there is a danger of reinforcing the false belief that dyslexic employees bring to the workplace nothing more than problems to be solved. The common perception of dyslexia as a condition that creates problems for the individual and all those associated with the person in question is inaccurate and misleading. As we have seen in Chapter 2, many of the problems associated with dyslexia are created by society, and they are not an unavoidable outcome of the condition. It is more constructive to consider dyslexia as being characterised by differences than deficits. This is not to deny that, in general, dyslexics tend to be weaker in some areas than non-dyslexics, but rather to emphasise the fact that they have strengths as well. Most people are not aware of dyslexic strengths, but they are both significant and well established.

An important and common dyslexic strength is the ability to use visual memory, which can be considered as an above-average ability to visualise objects, including complex objects, in three dimensions. It is this skill that has resulted in firms of architects in the United States of America actively encouraging applications from dyslexic adults. In our work we have consistently found that dyslexic adults are very well disposed to developing visual thinking skills. It is not uncommon to find adult dyslexics who have, without any professional guidance, developed their own visual strategies for coping with the demands of their environments—a testimony to their creativity and problem-solving prowess. Our experience of training dyslexic adults has convinced us that they have an above average ability to cope in situations where the available information is incomplete. They have very well developed pattern recognition skills and lateral thinking skills, although sometimes these strengths lie dormant and may need to be activated, e.g., by appropriate training and guidance. West (1997) and Bruce (1999) have argued that dyslexics have strengths in terms of creativity, a view which is consistent with our experience of training adult dyslexics.

While it would be misleading to argue that all dyslexics have a particular strength in visual thinking, the important point is that many do have it. Furthermore, they are more likely than their non-dyslexic peers to have this strength. There are many occupations where a predilection for visual thinking is a highly desirable skill, notably computer science. This particular occupation, and associated technologies, may eventually result in dyslexics being in high demand within the workforce. The future could see a shift of focus from what dyslexics cannot do onto what they can do; they may come to constitute the most 'in-demand' group of workers. Dyslexics may have marked skills in areas other than visual thinking; paradoxically, these include areas that are often considered to be dyslexic weaknesses rather than strengths. This may happen because a weakness may motivate dyslexic individuals to focus so much attention on improving that they end up excelling in that area. For example, dyslexics tend to be fundamentally disorganised. They frequently lose personal items such as keys; they may forget to pick up much needed materials before going to appointments; they may be very untidy, losing tools, misfiling documents, and having untidy desks; they may confuse dates and times, often missing or arriving late for appointments; they may have difficulty with directions; and they may misplace materials they need for their work, causing them to leave tasks unfinished. These failings are particularly damaging in workplaces and can represent a threat to continued employment or progression in employment. The threat can motivate dyslexics to find ways of overcoming their weaknesses.

Many dyslexics are unemployed as a consequence of one or more of the weaknesses listed above, while others, in spite of experiencing the same problems, have avoided being unemployed. Many of this latter group, being aware of their weaknesses, have overcome them by developing compensatory strategies. For example, dyslexic disorganisation is very common, but many dyslexic people who start out being disorganised overcome it by becoming very disciplined in their behaviour. In workplaces, this discipline may emerge as something approaching an obsession with tidiness: dyslexic persons may use colour-coded labels so that all the objects they use in their workplace (papers, tools and equipment) have their clearly marked place. Such persons have gone to an extreme to combat a weakness and turned that weakness into a strength—they become very organised.

A strategy characterised by extremes such as the one described above is often called overcompensation. Overcompensated dyslexics have focused a great deal of effort and energy on developing the skills they lack to the point where they have those skills in abundance. The strategy outlined above is often called overorganisation. Non-dyslexics who live with overorganised dyslexics may find the experience challenging; the very disciplined and strict behaviour of the dyslexic may conflict with the more relaxed behaviour of tolerating a degree of untidiness. In workplaces, however, overcompensated dyslexics may be very efficient workers, as the following case history illustrates.

Patrick's Case History

Patrick, a 31-year-old financial adviser working for a large City firm, decided to seek assessment for dyslexia, following the advice of a lecturer at a college where he was attending evening classes in law. He had approached his tutor for advice on how he could overcome a difficulty he had taking notes in lectures, but after listening to how he employed strategies for doing his work, his tutor felt sure he was dyslexic and referred him to a psychologist for a diagnostic assessment.

The assessment indicated that he had a particularly poor short-term memory—so much so that the psychologist apparently expressed surprise that he had so few problems. Patrick's potential weaknesses were in fact controlled by an armoury of well-developed strategies for overcoming most of the dyslexic difficulties one would expect to see. He had successfully overcompensated in all the areas at risk. For example, he never lost or forgot personal items such as keys, wallet or diary. He was extremely punctual, and he never missed or appeared late for appointments or meetings. His desk was always clear, and his work tasks were invariably completed before any deadline. Furthermore, he was noted by his friends and colleagues for his excellent recall of people's names, telephone numbers and personal details. He could refer back to past events and provide a very detailed summary of what had happened, what was said by whom and what subsequently happened after the event.

In contrast to the above, in relating difficulties he experienced during his school days, he described himself as an extremely disorganised child and adolescent. During his schooling, he had often been reprimanded for lateness, for failing to present his homework, for taking a long time to complete work in class and for not listening in class, for a poor attitude towards learning and for general untidiness.

Although he never bothered to attend to these weaknesses throughout his schooling, they became an issue of great concern to him when he left school and secured his first job as a shop assistant. While he was still on his probationary period of employment, his employer warned him that if he continued to be disorganised, slow in completing tasks and forgetful, he risked losing his job. Patrick's response to this warning was to read about memory improvement. He worked on strategies for remembering numbers, names, directions and facts. He overcame a major difficulty he had, that of losing track of tasks because of interruptions, by developing visual memory techniques that allowed him to be interrupted without losing track of where he was in a task, and so was able to complete his work more efficiently. He was very soon commended by his employer for the improvements he made in a relatively short period of time.

After his success in improving his memory, he started working on improving his organisation skills. He effectively adopted the motto, 'there is a place for everything and everything must be put in its place', as a rule to live by when he was a still a teenager, and he religiously applied it to everything he did in his life. For example, in his work as financial adviser, as soon as he finished using a client file, he replaced it in the filing cabinet, even if he knew he would soon be referring to the same file again. He never allowed himself to have any papers on his desk that he was not actively using at that time. He had materials for organising his desk drawers with sections clearly labelled so that even paper clips, Post-it notes and staples had their place.

Patrick's dyslexia is the reason why he has such a good memory and why he is so organised, reliable and precise, all the qualities that have make him a valued and prized asset to his employer.

Most employers would be very keen to employ someone like Patrick, and his case history illustrates well how dyslexics can develop important employment-related skills. Unfortunately, many very able dyslexics either never gain employment or fail to retain it; all too often, they are rejected because of their weaknesses when they could be accepted because of their strengths.

HOW EMPLOYMENT ATTITUDES AND PRACTICES NEED TO CHANGE

The bottom-line benefit of giving dyslexics an equal chance in employment contexts is that employers will not be exposed to the risk of costly litigation and the bad publicity that goes with it. Employers are not required, either legally or morally, to employ someone who lacks the ability to do the job, whatever their impairment is. However, the law does require employers to ensure that dyslexic persons are not excluded from employment when they are the best candidates for the job. This legal requirement makes sense in terms of what employers want, i.e., the best fit between the skills the job requires and the skills candidates have to offer, but it is frequently not achieved.

Dyslexia is widely misunderstood, and the enormous potential dyslexics have is largely lost because of misunderstandings, prejudices and unreasonable fears. Employers need to resist the inclination to be swayed by the false beliefs that abound in relation to dyslexia. They need to accept that barriers that could easily be removed but that are usually not easy to identify often disable dyslexics. Whereas the problems with visible disabilities usually have obvious solutions—for example, a wheelchair user needs a ramp on the stairs or the blind need instructions in Braille—employers need expert guidance on dyslexia to determine both what the barriers are and how they can be removed.

Employers need to embrace a paradigm shift from the medical to the social model. There is no intention here to suggest that employers should employ dyslexic persons or retain them in employment when they are not competent to do the job. But nor should they reject or dismiss dyslexic persons who are competent simply because they are dyslexic, yet this often happens. Employers need to be aware that they are not compromised by encouraging applications from dyslexic people, nor does employing dyslexic people undermine a firm's market effectiveness. There are no additional risks involved in assessing or employing a dyslexic person as opposed to a non-dyslexic one. There are additional efforts that employers need to make, but to balance this, they stand to make substantial gains by encouraging applications from dyslexic people. Dyslexics are likely to be loyal to an organisation that makes attempts to attract their applications, if only because this is still quite a rare phenomenon. By including them in the recruitment pool and assessing them like anyone else, employers are increasing the chance that they will find an appropriate person for the vacant post.

It is important to put workplace adjustments for dyslexic employees in their proper context. First, not all dyslexics need adjustments and, in many cases, when they are needed they are neither expensive nor disruptive to introduce. Second, when the required adjustments, such as laptop computers and voice-activated software, are expensive, the employer will usually be able to apply for financial assistance under the government's Access to Work scheme. Third, adjustments are simply methods of maximising an employee's performance; i.e., the benefit they represent to employers more than justifies the effort to put them in place. Adjustments for dyslexic employees must, however, be carefully selected to ensure that they are relevant to the needs of the employee. Failure to select them properly can prove both ineffective and costly, typically in terms of lost productivity. Inappropriate adjustments are a particular problem in the context of dyslexia, as the following section highlights.

DYSLEXIA AND ERRORS OF ADJUSTMENT

Attempts to improve employers' understanding of the concept of reasonable adjustment tend to rely on the use of case histories. For example, one government publication lists 13 case studies, including 'a clock repairer with cataracts' who was provided with 'a light on a flexible arm' so he 'could see better', and a person with arthritic hands for whom door handles were changed 'from knob to lever' (Department for Education and Employment, 1997). These examples illustrate and encourage employers to use a simple stimulus-response model in determining reasonable adjustment. A wheelchair user (stimulus) needs ramps installed on the stairs (response).

This stimulus-response model relies on the appropriate reasonable adjustment being an obvious one, as in the case cited. However, while adjustments are very often obvious in the context of visible disabilities, they are usually not obvious in the context of hidden disabilities. It is obvious what to do to if someone at work is unable to stand for long periods of time. It is not at all obvious what to do if people have a range of hidden difficulties that disrupt their work performance. This is reflected in the paucity of relevant advice and guidance on how to solve dyslexia-related problems in the workplace. Information on how dyslexic literacy difficulties can be managed is abundant, but it is frequently of little relevance to the presenting problems. Even when it is relevant, it is usually only a part of the problem and often the part that is easiest to solve. As noted earlier in this book, the relative importance of literacy skills is a key difference between work and education: in the world of education, literacy weaknesses represent an important skill deficit, but in the workplace it is more often the non-literacy-based symptoms of dyslexia that are the obstacles facing dyslexic people.

The non-literacy difficulties that dyslexics experience in their work are almost invariably relegated to the status of 'other problems', implying that they do not warrant serious attention. This tendency is illustrated in an otherwise useful and informative handbook produced by the British Dyslexia Association (1995: p. 116), which acknowledges that 'dyslexic difficulties may range from severe problems with literacy . . . to less obvious difficulties', but which gives very little attention to these 'less obvious difficulties'. It makes no attempt to explore strategies for making reasonable adjustments that would be appropriate for these 'less obvious difficulties'.

The British Dyslexia Association's guide deals with the issue of reasonable adjustment for literacy difficulties by directing employers' attention to a list of nine questions designed to help determine the support a dyslexic employee may require. There is, however, no equivalent list of questions in the handbook for use when the employee's problems are not literacy based. This probably reflects the fact that educationalists, educational psychologists and academics heavily influence the British Dyslexia Association.

The lack of information for employers concerning reasonable adjustment for non-literacy-based dyslexia-related difficulties has important implications for adult dyslexics who are employed. The problem is that the stereotype of a dyslexic struggling to read, write and spell leads employers to make the false assumption that they need only provide assistance with these tasks; when such limited help is provided and fails to produce the expected results, the employer complains. Dyslexics at work can find themselves being blamed for failings that have their origin in their employers' failure to accommodate them appropriately. Dyslexic employees who are not accommodated within the stimulus-response model of reasonable adjustment, i.e., 'dyslexic employees need support with literacy', are often labelled as awkward, lazy, of low ability or incompetent.

Employers in general, through no fault of their own, have insufficient understanding of how dyslexia operates, they are unaware of the extent to which it can disrupt behaviour, and they are largely in the dark concerning the full range of possibilities for reasonable adjustment. A common piece of guidance offered to help employers overcome this difficulty is that they should ask the disabled employees what tasks they have difficulty performing. For example, in its booklet 'Employing disabled people: A good practice guide for managers and employers', the Disability Rights Commission (/drc/Documents/DLE7.doc) comments:

> Good and successful practice is where an employer gives applicants—through standard questions in the job application—the opportunity to say whether any special provisions or facilities are required at interview.
>   Employers can ask applicants on the application form if they are disabled. It can be helpful to ask whether the applicant believes that they will need the employer to make a reasonable adjustment in the selection or interview process, or in the job if the applicant is selected. Sharing this information at an early stage should be to the advantage of both applicant and employer.

This is good advice, and is consistent with the objectives of a social model of disability, but employers need to exercise caution and not place too much reliance on the information they receive in exchanges with dyslexic employees concerning what adjustments are needed. Dyslexics do not necessarily know what all of their needs are. Most dyslexic employees do not have the necessary expertise to identify the full range of their weaknesses and associated needs; some do and can identify strategies for optimising their work performance, but many are unable to produce a comprehensive list of their needs. Dyslexics frequently find articulating their ideas difficult, and while they may know their weaknesses they may not be able to communicate this information effectively. A further complicating factor is that those dyslexics who are able to articulate what their needs are may be disinclined to do so, fearing that it will increase the likelihood of being discriminated against. The stated needs of employees should always be taken into account, but employers should be mindful that there are likely to be areas of need additional to those the individual identifies, and which may be more pertinent to their difficulties than those they identify themselves.

The task of identifying exactly what needs to change in the workplace to support dyslexic workers is not as straightforward as the corresponding tasks of supporting people with visible disabilities. Even in the context of hidden disabilities, dyslexia represents a particularly problematic condition to accommodate in the workplace; there are at least five reasons for this.

First, as discussed in Chapter 1, there is considerable confusion and doubt about dyslexia and how it manifests itself in the workplace. The proliferation of explanations and theories adds to this confusion, leaving employers with no reliable and adequate way of understanding the condition. This vacuum of understanding encourages employers to treat the condition less seriously than they treat other disabilities. If the experts cannot say exactly what dyslexia is and what causes it, it is not surprising that employers come to doubt its existence. Such doubts can easily undermine working relationships between dyslexic employees and their line managers or between dyslexic managers and their employees. The lack of clarity about the nature of dyslexia can predispose people, whether they are managing, or being managed by, dyslexics, to conclude that dyslexia is being used as an excuse for incompetence.

Second, as a consequence of poor definition and misunderstanding of dyslexia, the condition is often hidden from both observers and dyslexics themselves. It is by no means unusual to find cases of adult dyslexics who have experienced difficulties at work for many years before eventually being diagnosed as dyslexic. While the condition is hidden in this way, poor work performance is likely to be interpreted as a lack of ability or competence, not just by observers, such as employers, but by the dyslexic person as well. Adult dyslexics who, because of their lack of awareness of their condition, conclude that they lack ability may give up trying to work, and may sometimes become clinically depressed.

Third, because dyslexia carries with it the quite unjustified stigma of implied low intelligence, dyslexic people, regardless of how supportive their employer may be, often develop strategies for hiding their condition from their employers. These strategies are sometimes very effective; for example, the case history of Patrick that we presented earlier illustrates how strategies can produce the appearance of very able workers in control of their work. However, many strategies are successful in the short term but unsustainable in the long term—for example, the practice of producing work that appears to have been completed in the expected time frame when in fact the employee has taken much longer to complete it. This strategy usually means that dyslexics do significant amounts of their work at home in their own time, although some do it by arriving earlier and/or staying late at their workplaces. This strategy makes the need for adjustments difficult to perceive by the employer and is an example of how dyslexia is often a deliberately hidden disability.

Fourth, many of the dyslexia experts that employers rely on for advice and guidance are teachers, educational psychologists and other academics in the field of education. As was discussed in the previous chapter, although many of these people are very skilled in educational matters, they tend to have insufficient understanding of workplaces and occupational psychology to be able to provide appropriate guidance to employers. Although well intentioned, the advice that is presented to employers by many experts offering adult dyslexia consultancy services is neither as comprehensive as it should be nor targeted on the key areas of need.

Fifth, many employers and potential employers, like the general public, have strongly held false beliefs about dyslexia and the needs of adult dyslexics. Typically, for those employers who attempt to address the problems facing dyslexic employees, it is assumed that the only issues are related to reading, writing and spelling. For employees in office-based jobs, employers may subsequently provide tuition in literacy or, alternatively, computers with voice-activated software. While these interventions have their place, they are often introduced without proper investigation of the presenting problem: it is not unusual to find such adjustments being introduced to support employees whose literacy weaknesses are either not relevant or not significantly relevant to their work-related difficulties. Very often, the provisions and assistance for dyslexic employees in jobs that do not make any demands (or make very few demands) on literacy are poor or non-existent. Dyslexic people employed as truck drivers, builders, manual workers, gardeners, refuse collectors and many other jobs using practical skills are likely to go without support because of the false assumption that their dyslexia does not affect their work. If workplace assessments of such people are carried out, the major obstacles that undermine their work performance are often ignored or subordinated to any problem that remotely involves reading, writing or spelling.

The above factors individually or in combination conspire to make the identification of relevant reasonable adjustment for a dyslexic worker a complex and demanding task. It is nevertheless a task worth doing, not simply because employers have a duty under disability anti-discrimination legislation, but because identifying relevant reasonable adjustments is equivalent to identifying a strategy for maximising returns from an investment in a human resource, i.e., the dyslexic person. Making adjustments is often far more efficient than either struggling on with less than optimal performance or terminating the employee and trying again with a new and unknown quantity.

Introducing inappropriate adjustments is a costly mistake to make. Employers' losses result from several factors that vary according to individual circumstances. Any employee who is not able to work optimally represents a loss, as does any employee who consistently makes errors. Accurately targeted adjustments, what we may call relevant reasonable adjustments, avoid these unnecessary losses. We shall now outline how reasonable adjustments may be identified to ensure they are relevant and how they may be implemented.

IDENTIFYING REASONABLE ADJUSTMENTS BY WORKPLACE ASSESSMENT

The only reliable way of identifying accurate and relevant adjustment is to secure a workplace assessment from a professional who understands both adult dyslexia and the psychology of workplaces. A workplace assessment is a structured procedure for identifying both the needs of a dyslexic employee and the action that an employer should take to meet those needs.

To complete a workplace assessment efficiently, the professional doing the assessment must be able to identify both the potential and the manifest difficulties of the dyslexic employee. Each of these two categories presents difficulties for the assessor. Potential difficulties refer to constitutional weaknesses that are elements of the individual's psychological make-up. They have not developed, i.e., become manifest, because the individual has not been subject to the environment in which they would become manifest. For example, those who are vulnerable to distractions may never realise they have this weakness if they have always worked in quiet environments where there are no distractions. However, they would soon realise they had this weakness if they were moved into a noisy environment. Since many people in this situation would not be able to explain their potential weakness, the assessor must be skilled in methods and techniques for uncovering them. This skill is important because adjustments can involve dyslexic workers changing their organisations or moving to different work environments. Such changes bring the employee into contact with a new set of variables, and the impact of these variables needs to be explored to ensure that the employee is not moving from one set of disabling conditions to another. The most effective way to explore potential difficulties is work sampling, i.e., the employee spends a week or two doing the job, since this will usually uncover many areas of concern.

Manifest difficulties may be directly observed or they may be determined by questioning employees, managers and supervisors. They may, however, be hidden by maladaptive strategies, which may be unconscious and therefore not immediately identifiable by observation or questioning. Effective identification of manifest difficulties that have become obscured by maladaptive strategies requires a specific skill and a body of knowledge about dyslexia. The assessor needs to have detailed knowledge and understanding of all the common dyslexic weaknesses and their associated behaviours. The specific skill is the ability to extract, from the employees, information about their full complement of dyslexic weaknesses. Structured interviewing with tools investigating past events, such as the critical incident technique, a powerful method of collecting personal information first described by Flanagan (1954) and outlined later in Chapter 6, is an effective method for identifying strengths and weaknesses.

The knowledge about dyslexic weaknesses required for completing a workplace assessment can be grouped under three headings: memory, communication and personal management. Dyslexic weaknesses in these three areas and their associated behaviours are listed in Tables 4.1, 4.2 and 4.3. Most people with dyslexia experience only a handful of these difficulties and, as already discussed, there is usually a contextual element to how debilitating the various weaknesses are. Many dyslexics have developed compensatory strategies for dealing with most, or all, of the weaknesses that they experience.

TABLE 4.1 Dyslexic difficulties with memory

Area of difficulty	Typical manifestations
Names, labels, numbers	Taking a longer than average (or failing completely) to learn the names of colleagues, supervisors and managers. Often results in employees avoiding using names and giving a wrong name when making reports that require them to identify people by name.
	Inability to remember, or confusing, dates and times; e.g., appointments and meetings.
	Forgetting telephone numbers to the extent that they cannot be repeated immediately after hearing them, and failing to learn telephone numbers that are used frequently.
	Forgetting door codes, code-using photocopiers, passwords for entering computer systems, standard abbreviations and labels, including the names of common objects.
Sequences	Inability to give accurate directions, or to follow directions given by others; for example, finding rooms in large buildings.
	Retaining instructions given verbally; for example, a list of job tasks given by a manager or supervisor.
	Learning, from written instructions, the sequence of behaviours required for standard procedures.
Reading text	Forgetting what has been read immediately after reading it.
	Taking a long time to extract and retain information when reading material.
Listening	Forgetting what has been said, or most of what has been said immediately after hearing it.
	Losing track of what is being said while listening to it.
Taking messages	Forgetting important parts of the message.
	Confusing or reversing information provided in messages.
Object tracking	Losing personal belongings such as keys, pens, wallet, etc.
	Losing materials, particularly when the employee is working on several sites.

Compensatory strategies for all of the weaknesses outlined in Tables 4.1, 4.2 and 4.3 exist and may be developed either consciously or unconsciously. These strategies may be adaptive, i.e., they can solve the problem effectively without disadvantaging the employee in some other way, or they may be maladaptive i.e., they can solve one problem while creating another. An example of an adaptive strategy is developing visual memory skills to remember people's names. An example of a maladaptive strategy is excessive overwork,

TABLE 4.2 Dyslexic difficulties with communication

Area of difficulty	Typical manifestations
Talking	Talking too much, repeating information and 'going off on tangents'.
	Long pauses in mid-sentence and frequently not being able to find the appropriate word.
	Poor pronunciation, particularly of long words, which may be pronounced with syllables omitted.
Listening	Interrupting people or talking over their speech.
	Failing to demonstrate listening has taken place by giving replies that are not entirely relevant to what the other person has said.
Messages	Giving confusing or garbled messages, sometimes distorting the message because of word-finding difficulties.
Reading, writing and spelling	Reading can be slower than average, and word-decoding difficulties may lead to poor comprehension of what has been read. Dyslexics often rely on guessing the meaning of unknown words from the context, leading to errors of understanding.
	Producing concise and fluent written material is often problematic. Typically, dyslexics' well-organised thoughts become disorganised when they come to write them down.
	Making notes in briefings and taking minutes of meetings are usually areas of weakness.
	Spelling may be bizarre.

which is maladaptive because of the psychological damage it produces through stress and burnout. An important goal of workplace assessment is to determine when maladaptive strategies are operating and to determine how more adaptive strategies can replace them. This, together with other recommendations for appropriate adjustments, should appear in a report of the assessment. The structure of such reports will vary according to the assessor's preferences, but for ease of reference and clarity they should contain separate sections for identifying employee weaknesses and recommended adjustments. An illustrative example of a workplace assessment report showing these sections is provided later in this chapter.

SPECIALIST TRAINING AS REASONABLE ADJUSTMENT FOR ADULT DYSLEXICS

One of the most effective adjustments for dyslexia is to allow the employee to attend specialist training to develop efficient compensatory skills. For example, the best way to ensure that a message or telephone number is accurately recalled, that codes are retained and that abbreviations are learnt is to train dyslexics in memory development and techniques for controlling the flow of information. Specialist training may be the only effective solution

TABLE 4.3 Dyslexic difficulties in organisation and self-management

Area of difficulty	Typical manifestations
Attention	Easily distracted by noise, objects and people. For example, many dyslexics find they cannot continue with a task if other people are having a conversation or if there is any machinery noise; e.g., a photocopier.
Completing unfinished tasks	Dyslexics have difficulty restarting a task—for example, after an interruption—from where they left off. Sometimes they need to start at the beginning again; sometimes they start at the wrong point, which may result in omissions in the completed task.
Time management	Failing to leave enough time to complete journeys and not realising how long a task has taken are very common problems. Failing to meet deadlines is equally common.
Paperwork	General disorganisation, and poor filing and sorting are major problems that lead to a great deal of untidiness. Not getting paperwork done is very common; for example, dyslexics often put off or avoid writing reports, and completing time sheets and expense claim forms.

to some dyslexic problems. For example, this is the case when a dyslexic's listening and verbal communication skills are deficit.

Although potentially a very powerful option, specialist training is ineffective if it requires the very skills that the dyslexic trainee lacks. For example, even though, as explained in Chapter 2, professional skills training programmes tend to be of much higher quality than those offered in colleges and universities, they still fall short of being appropriate learning environments for dyslexic people. This is primarily because they do not, in general, cater sufficiently for the poor memory skills that characterise dyslexia. Specialist training needs to accommodate, in its structure, content and approach, the constitutional differences that characterise dyslexia, such as the preference for visual over verbal presentations, if it is to facilitate the dyslexic trainee's skill development. Details of how to make training appropriate for dyslexics is discussed later in this chapter, and the possible consequences of failing to do so are illustrated in the following case history.

Caroline's Case History

Caroline, a supervisor in a large factory manufacturing machine parts, had management responsibility for six workers. However, she started having difficulties at work after her promotion to a supervisory post after five years of very successful service. Caroline's problems arose because she often gave inaccurate or confusing instructions to those whom she was supervising, and she frequently failed to do all the tasks that her manager asked her to do. She had become the subject of some ridicule by some of the staff she managed because of the spelling errors that she made in their annual appraisal reports. Caroline's line manager was concerned about her failure to do all the tasks he assigned to her, and after a discussion with her, it was agreed that she should be assessed to determine whether she had a condition that could account for her weaknesses.

Caroline was diagnosed as dyslexic, and her assessment report recommended that she should seek help to improve her poor literacy, verbal communication and listening skills. Caroline's employer duly arranged for the recommendations to be implemented: a private dyslexia tutor coached Caroline in literacy, and she attended a standard skill development course in verbal communication. Three months later, although Caroline's spelling had improved slightly, she continued to make the errors related to giving and receiving instructions that had initially raised her employer's concern. Caroline was given a written warning about her poor performance, after which she sought further professional advice from a psychologist specialising in adult dyslexia.

Caroline was referred to a specialist cognitive skills dyslexia-training programme, in which she completed modules on understanding dyslexia, explaining dyslexia, memory development and verbal communication. After this training Caroline was able (after a short period of time practising exercises in her workplace) to function efficiently in her work. Caroline's improved memory functioning strengthened her ability to listen and remember what she heard, as well as her ability to talk fluently and concisely. In her workplace she was able to remember instructions given to her and to present clearly instructions she needed to give to others. In addition, Caroline noticed that her improved memory functioning was helping her literacy development; e.g., she was able to remember sequences, so her spelling improved, and she could more easily remember rules, so her grammar improved.

This case history, insofar as it details the failure of one training course and the success of another, illustrates how organisations (and individuals who are financing their own personal development) can waste time, money and effort by failing to take proper precautions to ensure that training programmes are appropriate for dyslexic people. It also illustrates how making relevant adjustments in terms of training can produce very tangible benefits.

Even courses specifically dealing with memory improvement can fall short of what is required. Many such courses focus on developing memory strategies, but not on how to use memory more efficiently. They provide efficient ways of using an inefficient memory process, which is no solution for communication problems that have their origin in memory weaknesses. General courses designed to improve memory skills may be of some benefit but are not as effective, in the long term, as courses that encourage the acquisition of a more effective way of using memory.

Appropriate specialist training from a competent source will focus on adaptive strategies and may result in dyslexic adults overcoming all their dyslexic weaknesses. When all significant weaknesses have been overcome, the person is known as a 'compensated dyslexic'. In addition to specialist training, there are many other workplace adjustments that can enable dyslexic people to work more effectively. A great deal can be done to work environments and procedures to reduce the negative impact of dyslexic weaknesses once the nature of the dyslexic individual's difficulties has been identified.

SUPPORTING DYSLEXIC WORKERS BY IMPROVING INFORMATION EXCHANGE

In general, modifications to the work environment, as far as information exchange and information processing is concerned, should be designed to achieve two distinct goals. First, access to information should be effortless. Second, information should be available so that demands on memory are kept to a minimum. Below are some specific examples of how to make such modifications with particular reference to the difficulties outlined in Tables 4.1, 4.2 and 4.3.

Discreetly displaying people's names and job titles on doors, desks and office-floor maps is very helpful. It reduces demands on memory and prevents dyslexic employees from wasting time searching for the information and suffering the embarrassment of not knowing names. It allows them, like their colleagues, to use people's names and gives them the opportunity to learn those names over an extended period of time. Using people's names has considerable social significance and is an important element in the development of good social relationships in workplaces. It is therefore important that adjustments are made that allow dyslexic people access to this means of social influence.

The location of offices and rooms should be indicated on maps clearly displayed, and cupboards should be labelled with their contents. Even apparently very trivial modifications may be significant; for example, in some offices, filing cabinets are marked with ranges of the alphabet. Thus, drawers may be labelled A–E, F–K, etc., but this can cause difficulties for dyslexics, many of whom have never learnt the alphabet so well that they can identify exactly which part of it contains the letter they want. A dyslexic is less likely to make filing errors if the markings contain all the letters, so the above labelling should be replaced with labels showing A, B, C, D, E; F, G, H, I, J, K; etc.

All key facts and important information should be displayed where they can easily be seen; the use of pictures, diagrams and colours to highlight key information is highly desirable. For example, displaying year planners clearly indicating when meetings will take place, and providing dyslexic employees with pin boards so they can display information for their own use will help significantly.

Sending reminders of meetings, deadlines and important dates will considerably reduce the likelihood that dyslexic employees miss or be late for these. Confirming verbal instructions in writing—for example, by email—should be standard practice, particularly when more than one instruction has been given verbally. The use of tape recorders and dictaphones should be encouraged as appropriate and with due regard for other people's rights to privacy and their individual preferences. Employers should consider including in policy statements and in briefings that tape recordings are acceptable for use by any employee. Avoiding the use of abbreviations is desirable since these often cause confusion, frustration and errors. Although they are convenient ways of communicating information, when they fail they can cause much confusion; the possible losses arising from abbreviations often outweigh any benefits.

A very commonly occurring dyslexic problem in office or administrative work environments is the incorrect selection of forms from similar looking sets of forms. Colour-coding of either the forms or the containers where the forms are kept is an effective and painless strategy for reducing errors of this type. In many busy work environments, workers frequently need to ask other workers for various types of information, anything from the date of a delivery to the location of a tool; however, remembering who has the information can be a demanding task for a dyslexic employee. Furthermore, dyslexics are likely to seek the same information more times than their non-dyslexic colleagues, who are able to commit the information to memory sooner. Co-workers may find it very annoying to be asked continually for information when they feel the person asking the question should know the answer. This makes appropriate adjustments for this type of dyslexic memory failure particularly important. Some of the suggestions made above deal with this issue, but there is often a need to do more: creating a computer database of information that can be interrogated by any employee or producing a folder containing useful miscellaneous information in a user-friendly format are both adequate solutions. These remedies are usually to the benefit of all employees (Table 4.4).

TABLE 4.4 Example of work-related difficulties and corresponding reasonable accommodations obtained from a workplace assessment

Client: George
Occupation: Technical Representative for——

WORK-RELATED DIFFICULTIES

George's difficulties and his employer's responses (adjustments) to date were identified in this assessment as follows:

1. **Verbal communication in stressful presentations**.
Although George's verbal communication skills are very well developed, he experiences some difficulties in situations where he has had insufficient opportunity to prepare the information that he is required to deliver. These difficulties include slowness in organising information adequately before speaking, resulting in a lack of clear and logical communication and temporary inability to access information that is held in memory. This sometimes results in a failure to construct answers to questions appropriately and/or in real-time. Almost certainly as a consequence of the stress/anxiety produced by these difficulties, George's verbal communication and body language can appear overly defensive. These negative effects are enhanced as he feels the pressure to perform increasing.

2. **Completing work when there are distractions, i.e., noise or activity.**
George explained to me that it often takes him three to four times longer to complete reports if other people distract him by talking or simply walking in and out of his office space. George's line manager commented that he becomes visibly stressed when there is a lot of noise or movement. At present, George has an informal arrangement with the colleague with whom he shares the office, the terms of which allow him currently to complete his work without too many disturbances.

3. **Completing work as fast as peers when working without distractions.**
George explained that his rate of work in ideal conditions, i.e., isolated from noise and visual distractions, is probably 50–100% longer than it should be in relation to usual expectations. He explained to me that the reasons he is slow include the fact that he has difficulty retaining the information that he extracts from the codes of practice files. It appears that the units of information George is able to hold in his working memory are smaller than one would expect of him, with the consequence that he needs to spend more time reading information.

4. **Proofreading.**
George often fails to identify errors he has made in reports and other documents that he has produced.

5. **Organising information when producing documents.**
George requires more time and focus of attention than one could reasonably expect; i.e., he appears to have some difficulty transferring organised thoughts and ideas to paper. It seems most likely that this difficulty is in part due to his inefficiency in working memory, which is exacerbated by the need to use the computer keyboard when producing documents.

6. **General memory tasks.**
George has difficulties remembering alphanumeric codes and needs to check them more often than one would expect, with the obvious consequence of further slowing down his rate of working.

TABLE **4.4** (*continued*)

7. **Filing and organising papers.**

George explained that these tasks are very time-consuming (he estimated that he takes between two and three times longer than his peers in completing such tasks). He explained that although they are relatively trivial tasks he often experiences anxiety in carrying them out.

EXISTING COMPENSATORY COPING STRATEGIES

George is well aware of his difficulties but, to date, he has been unable to overcome them. His key strategy is completing tasks outside his normal working hours, and he accepts that his work intrudes excessively into his private time.

Assessor observations

At present, George copes with his dyslexic memory by preparing for meetings and presentations very thoroughly in advance. He estimates that he spends three to four times longer preparing for important events than do his colleagues. His preparation involves examining relevant information carefully, committing important elements of it to memory, constructing notes on other parts of it, rehearsing what he intends saying and generally making the information easy for him to access in the meeting or presentation; i.e., he organises information in his memory so that he is able to speak fluently and respond efficiently to questions. He does not, however, have an efficient strategy for carrying out this organisation in memory very rapidly in a stressful confrontation with customers; without the careful preparation he has come to rely on, he feels vulnerable and not in control. Although he is able to 'think on his feet' generally, he loses this skill when placed in stressful situations. George does not lack the ability to perform in pressured situations, but his dyslexia masks his ability to perform.

Although in general George's strategies are effective, they are, in the long term, likely to be counter-productive because of the excessive stress they produce. To achieve optimum work efficiency, more appropriate remedies need to be developed for George.

RECOMMENDATIONS

Recommendations with reference to point 1
Specialist training in memory development, verbal communication and stress management, focusing on developing appropriate strategies for rapid organisation of information in memory and verbal presentation, is recommended as a solution in the long term.

In the short term, it is recommended that George be given as much advance notice as possible of the likely nature and content of any meetings/presentations he is required to attend.

Recommendations with reference to point 2
George should be situated in the new open-plan office area with as much protection from distraction as can reasonably be provided. The following action points should be considered:

- The location of George's workspace should take account of his susceptibility to noise and visual distractions; i.e., a corner space away from photocopiers would be ideal since this would reduce the number of people permanently and transiently in close proximity to his workspace.
- Soundproof barriers sufficiently high to provide privacy when he is working at his desk, i.e., to remove visual distractions and reduce sound distractions.
- Additional glass barriers extending the above to the ceiling, thus reducing sound distractions originating from the open-plan area.

continues overleaf

TABLE **4.4**   (*continued*)

- A glass door from floor to ceiling to be provided to allow George's allocated space to be closed when he needs further isolation from noise distractions. A sliding door may be needed, given the dimensions of the workspace available.
- Blinds to be provided on the glass front of the conference rooms in order to ensure that George can remove visual distractions when he is using these rooms.

NB. George's work behaviour is likely to be significantly better if he is provided with a workspace where he can, when necessary, isolate himself from all visual and noise distractions.

Recommendations with reference to points 3 and 4
- Provision of speech-recognition and text-to-speech software to facilitate better organisation of thoughts/information without the need to be so dependent on his working memory.

Speech-recognition software would allow George to work effectively by removing the need for him to use the keyboard, and it would overcome the need for him to know the spelling of the words he uses (Dragon Naturally Speaking Professional Edition v5 is recommended). This software allows the user both to type and speak to the computer, which is the ideal solution since it enables him to use each facility according to his personal preference.

To ensure that George achieves accurate comprehension of material he needs to read and is not disadvantaged by the time it takes, he should be supplied with a package that allows him to continuously scan material into his computer and have that material read back to him. The software should be capable of providing the definition of words so that he is not disadvantaged by any memory-related failure to recognise words. The Kurzweil 3000 (K3000) program (Kurzweil Educational Systems Group) and a flat-bed scanner is recommended.

- Appropriate training on the use of the above software and 12-month telephone support from software suppliers should be provided.
- George should be provided with a printer for his sole use, since this would encourage him to print out information and reduce his reliance on remembering what was on screen; i.e., adult dyslexics tend to use printers more than their non-dyslexic peers.

Recommendations with reference to points 5 and 6
George should receive specialist training designed for adult dyslexics, focusing on improving memory, i.e., strategies for immediate effects, and understanding adult dyslexia.

NB. Memory training provides a more constitutional remedy than the adjustments discussed above; i.e., while the recommendations above should lead to substantial improvements in his work behaviour, they do not impact on the underlying cause of the problem, which is an inefficiency in working memory. Training to understand his condition will enable him to develop appropriate remedies for difficulties as they arise and to anticipate difficulties before they appear, ensuring that he is more efficient. By combining this specialist training with the other recommendations, George's performance is likely to show increasing improvements over time until he reaches the point where he is able to carry out his duties without relying on doing substantial amounts of work in his own time.

Recommendations with reference to point 7
Re-examination of his personal filing system to integrate it with the recommended computer software to reduce demands arising from these tasks. Colour coding and redesign of essential reference papers.

TABLE 4.5 Example of personalised telephone message pad

TODAY'S DATE:	
TIME:	

Message for :	*Message from*:
Andy	*A company name*
Mike	*Another company name*
Jane	*Andy*
Alun	*Mike*
Raymond	*Jane*
	Alun
	Raymond
	Your partner

Message is:	*Dates, times, places, etc.*
Would like to make an appointment for	
Need to produce drawings of	
Call back a.s.a.p. on	
Meeting is at	
Can't meet you on	
Urgently need the report on	
Please contact——urgently	
Needs to speak to you about	

Errors in taking telephone messages can be drastically reduced by designing message pads that allow information to be recorded fast and efficiently, as by ticking boxes or writing single words. For example, if messages are usually for one of a relatively small number of people, and the type of information to be conveyed is largely predictable in terms of its falling into a manageable number of categories, customised message pads are very effective. Table 4.5

TABLE 4.6   Example of personalised memory aid for use when making telephone calls

TODAY'S DATE:
TIME:
CALL TO:
CALL CONCERNING: A meeting to discuss the new arts centre.
1. I'm available on 20 and 23 March and any day in the first week of April.
RESPONSE:
2. Will need to see the new drawings as soon as they are ready. When is that likely to be?
RESPONSE:
3. Who should I contact about the budgetary constraints for the external artwork?
RESPONSE:

illustrates a message pad that was created for one of our clients by her employer and led to marked improvements in her work performance.

The employee prepared a set of these message sheets each evening before going home, filling in the next day's date ready for use as soon as she arrived back at work. It proved so useful that all of her colleagues subsequently used it to take telephone messages.

This type of pad can also be created to help people be more efficient in making telephone calls. It can be used very effectively to overcome typical difficulties such as forgetting what the purpose of the call was, forgetting parts of what was intended to be communicated, repeating information already presented and talking off the point. For example, our client who used the above customised message pad experienced all of the above weaknesses from time to time. Very often, before she started using the pad, she repeated herself to her customers. They would sometimes point out that she had already asked them a question or given them information either in previous telephone conversations or at the start of the current one. Working on her own initiative, she successfully overcame this problem by creating a message pad similar to the one presented in Table 4.6, which, once again, was used to good effect by her colleagues.

Tape recorders or dictaphones can be helpful to remember directions. There are now relatively inexpensive electronic direction finders available that are particularly useful for dyslexic people who spend a lot of time driving. They can help people avoid heavy traffic as well as simply get from A to B.

For problems related to reading and writing, there are very effective solutions in the form of computer software that converts speech to text and text to speech. The software can make life easier for dyslexics because it removes the need for them to use the keyboard to enter information, a task that can be very demanding for dyslexics and one that disrupts their thought processes. Emails and other documents, including letters, articles and books (which can be scanned into a computer), become more accessible because they can be read aloud to the employee directly from the computer. There are programs, such as Kutweil 3000 that read aloud information as it is being scanned, making 'reading' the material reasonably easy and fast.

Where it is not practical to scan material into a computer, the use of coloured overlays can sometimes improve reading speed. Kyd et al. (1992), as well as other researchers, have reported improved reading speeds in children who use these overlays, and our experience is that they can have the same effect in adults. These coloured overlays are technically for overcoming problems related to light sensitivity and the tendency for words to become distorted. These are symptoms not of dyslexia, but of a condition known as scotopic sensitivity syndrome, which was first described by Irlen (1989, 1991). Although often confused with dyslexia, this condition is distinct from it, and in all probability the 'Irlen overlays' would improve most people's reading speed. Dyslexics are simply more likely to notice the benefit and therefore more likely to use them. There are also special software packages that can help people to organise their thoughts, and these make the writing of reports and documents very much easier for dyslexics than they would otherwise be.

Forms and paperwork generally need to be examined by employers for possible restructuring and simplification. Employers should be aware that computer programs can create forms that can then be completed by the above voice-activated software. This can provide a very effective remedy for some dyslexics. Employers should be prepared to make use of colour where practical, since something as simple as having different coloured paper can make tasks easier to perform. There are well-established principles for producing documents, which, if followed, make those documents easier to read by dyslexics. Documents, leaflets, memos and letters should be written in a clear, simple and large typeface and should be structured so that the writing is not too dense on the page. It is often desirable to use double spacing, and, when relevant, sections in documents should be clearly numbered and or marked. Any particularly important information should be highlighted in colour or set in boldface and underlined. Copies of leaflets posted on boards should be made available so people who wish to scan them into a computer can do so and have them read aloud by voice-activated software.

PROBLEMS ASSOCIATED WITH OPEN-PLAN WORKSPACES

In general, modifications to the work environment as far as physical surroundings are concerned should be made so that employees have some choice regarding their immediate social and physical work surroundings. The environment should also be structured so that employees have sufficient physical space to carry out their work tasks.

Open-plan offices (NB: although this discussion refers to open-plan offices, the comments apply to any large, open-plan workspace) are a particular issue in dyslexia. They are currently very popular, particularly in large organisations, where they are generally recognised as cost-effective ways of accommodating workers. Working in open-plan offices presents a range of possible problems for the occupants, the most significant of which are visual and audio distractions. Open-plan offices, by virtue of their function as workplaces for large numbers of employees, have a great deal of noise and movement and a great variety of objects visible. Telephones ringing, photocopiers copying and keypads tapping are all potentially distracting stimuli. Even innocuous objects such as ornaments, pictures and wall charts may become the focus of attention that should be elsewhere.

While the distracting effect of the factors mentioned above can frequently cause an employee's work efficiency to be reduced, their disruptive potential is no match for the extent to which other people can serve as distractions. People represent potentially significant visual and audio distractions to those working in open-plan offices. Whether they are quietly walking through the office, speaking on the telephone, engaged in conversation or simply working at their desks, they have great potential to distract others from their work.

Those trying to work in close proximity to two or more people having a conversation are likely to find that they are unconsciously processing parts of the conversation or even the conversation in its entirety. Our genetic make-up predisposes us to listen to other people talking. When a conversation is in competition for our attention with the processing of almost any other task, it is the former stimulus that is in the stronger position to gain our attention. We are a naturally gregarious species, and the mere presence of other people is in itself sufficient to cause distraction, simply because our genetic make up motivates us to look at and observe others. Even in open-plan offices where partitions are used to create individual spaces, people stand on tiptoe to look over the barriers at what other workers are doing. This practice is so common that the term 'prairie-dogging' has recently entered Collins Concise Dictionary (2001) to describe it.

The factors described above do not always have a disruptive effect on the work behaviour of people in an open-plan workspace. This is simply because, in general, different people react differently to environmental stimulation. For example, Furnham (1997) has described how extraverts, because of their high need for arousal and stimulation, work better in open-plan offices than introverts. The richness of the environment, in terms of having a lot to look at and a lot of noise, improves their work performance. Extraverts and open-plan office environments represent a good person-job fit, with the net result that the task is completed more efficiently.

There is not yet any research comparing the person-job fit between dyslexics and open-plan offices; however, our reasonably extensive anecdotal experience suggests that, in general, it is a very poor fit for most dyslexics. Over the last decade, reports from our clients, concerning the disruptive effect of having to complete tasks in open-plan workspaces has consistently been the most common complaint that we have heard from them. It seems unlikely that an explanation can be found in suggesting that dyslexics have a tendency to be introverts. However, one explanation might lie in arguing that overstimulation disrupts tasks that should be automatic but that are not. The 'automatization deficit' hypothesis, suggested by Nicolson & Fawcett (1990), might offer an explanation here. Essentially, these researchers argue that dyslexia is characterised by a failure to automatise skills fully. This means that the performance of a task can require from dyslexics significantly more conscious resources than it does from non-dyslexics. One outcome of this is that their performance on a task will be adversely affected by any stimulation that directs attention from task performance.

The conscious compensation hypothesis does offer a possible explanation of the greater adverse impact in adults of distractions in open-plan offices. It is an appealing explanation since it implies that dyslexics are different from non-dyslexics only in terms of their threshold level for distractions; i.e., it is much lower than the average. Most people have experienced (or can empathise with) having a greater susceptibility to distractions when they have been involved in tasks demanding a lot of attention; dyslexics are in this position most of the time.

Since attention mechanisms are controlled by working-memory processes, an explanation of dyslexic susceptibility can also be found within the memory model of dyslexia that is the foundation of the material we are presenting in this book; i.e., the definition of dyslexia as an inefficiency in working memory (see Chapter 1). In the framework of the dyslexic working-memory difference, the dyslexic's vulnerability to distractions can be conceptualised as 'distracting', i.e., intrusive and unwanted, information displacing existing information from the working memory. The dyslexic working-memory system, characterised as it is by a smaller than average storage capacity, is more likely to be disrupted by the distracting information. Dyslexics struggling to hold on to information that they need to complete a task will find that anything that catches their attention is likely to push out all, or significant elements of, the information they are holding on to. Losing the key information is disruptive, and they subsequently have difficulty completing the task they were doing when distracted. Once again this explanation is appealing because most people have experienced this effect at some time, i.e., having to start a task from the beginning because a distraction caused them to lose track of what they were doing. Dyslexics simply experience this most of the time; i.e., after a distraction, they are unable to remember exactly what they were doing before being distracted.

The effect of the distractions described above would be much the same whether the distraction was audio or visual. For example, when someone walks past, we are genetically predisposed to look, the looking stimulates a thought and the thought displaces the important task-related information. Curiously, the very fact that people may be moving around unpredictably in open-plan offices could be the reason they are disruptive. A constant stream of people is less of a distraction than a few people passing by infrequently because we learn not to respond to anything that is constant, but we are predisposed to respond to infrequent events. This phenomenon of learning not to respond is called 'habituation', and it applies to both what we hear and what we see.

People habituate to stimuli very quickly; for example, consider what happens in a busy railway station café. Many people who say they are easily distracted can sit during the rush hour reading a newspaper apparently oblivious to the endless stream of people passing by. In quieter periods, however, the same people find themselves distracted by just an occasional passer-by. In the former situation, they learn not to respond, i.e., they habituate, to the people passing by because the environment is constant. In the latter case, the occasional passer-by causes a momentary change to the environment; habituation or learning not to respond to this type of change is either difficult or impossible.

While the above comments apply to all people, they are particularly pertinent to dyslexics. Dyslexic people have a constitutional difference that predisposes them to experience distractions differently from non-dyslexics. Given that people tend to assume that others experience the world more or less as they do, non-dyslexics are often overcritical of dyslexic people for their problems with distractions. Typically, non-dyslexics are dismissive of the dyslexic's vulnerability to distractions, and this may lead to hostility from both sides. General dyslexia-awareness training for all employees is an adjustment that would help avoid this type of situation. If we compare the experience of two people, one dyslexic, one not, who are distracted in the middle of completing a complex task, completion of which requires information to be held in the working memory, such as information about the parts of the task that have already been completed, we will find two quite different sets of results. The effect of the distraction on the non-dyslexic is to stop the task for a short period of time. When the distraction has ended, the person restarts the task from where it was left off. The effect of the distraction on the dyslexic employee is quite different. A distraction causes information to enter their short-term memory store, which is already struggling to hold on to information needed to complete the task, and effectively disrupts the memory process. The new information overwrites the key task-related information, causing a feeling of deep frustration as the dyslexic senses defeat in the struggle to keep hold of the information needed to complete the task. This frustration can become very significant and potentially destructive. It can cause high-ability dyslexics to underperform greatly.

In summary, while non-dyslexic employees are likely to find distractions an annoyance because they take their minds off the task for a short period of time, dyslexic employees are likely to find that distractions are a crisis because once they have been distracted they are effectively back to square one; i.e., they often need to redo part of the task, or even restart the whole task, depending on the task in question and what information has been lost.

Less obvious problems, intrinsic to open-plan offices, which affect dyslexics more severely than non-dyslexics arise from socio-psychological factors. An important one relates to how people make contact with each other when occupying a common space. It is when workers look up from their work and are apparently taking a brief break that other people are likely to make contact by looking, smiling or talking. The 'looking up' behaviour opens a possible channel of communication that is likely to be filled very quickly by others in the space who are looking for a (possibly more substantial) break. When someone is looking for contact with someone else in an open-plan space, anyone who looks up is a very likely target. Dyslexics probably look away from their work more often than average, regardless of distractions. This is a, largely unconscious, strategy for dealing with short-term memory problems, that is, taking many short breaks from a task being completed. The net effect of these two factors is that dyslexics are more likely to make eye contact with other workers and become involved in exchanging information, either directly by talking or in some other way—for example, by having a nonverbal communication, perhaps involving smiles, eyebrow flashes or other facial expressions. It is, then, easy to see why dyslexic people are likely to find open-plan office spaces much more distracting than do their non-dyslexic peers.

A further disadvantage related to open-plan office space arises from another socio-psychological factor known as the audience effect. A well-researched phenomenon, the audience effect arises from the fact that people's work behaviour is affected by the mere presence of other people. In brief, the presence of other people in the same room can cause work behaviour to improve or deteriorate regardless of whether or not the other people are observing the work being done. What determines whether the effect of other people is beneficial or detrimental is how skilled at the task the person working is. If the individual is very skilled, the presence of other people will increase the likelihood of the work's being good; if the worker is someone likely to make mistakes, the presence of others will increase the number of mistakes made. Clearly, then, if dyslexic employees are completing tasks where they are likely to make errors because of the nature of the task, they are more likely to make these errors in open-plan spaces simply because of the presence of others. The key point here is that open-plan spaces may result in dyslexic employees failing to complete tasks accurately when they could complete them accurately in a private space.

Clearly, then, many dyslexic people are potentially disadvantaged when required to work in open-plan offices. There is, however, much that can be done to reduce this disadvantage. Since dyslexics are significantly more vulnerable to distractions than other workers, it is wise to consider whether a relocation of their workstation in the open-plan space would improve the situation. For example, moving them to a quieter corner of the room away from doors, staircases and photocopiers may solve the problem. A solution might well be found in the use of screens, which can range from simple screens placed between desks to larger screens that effectively, and at relatively low cost, create self-contained offices.

Making such efforts to accommodate the needs of dyslexic employees is a very wise investment since open plan spaces can be very distressing for dyslexics. Table 4.4 provides details of a work place assessment that was carried out on one of our clients, a high ability dyslexic who found the experience of working in open offices to be totally debilitating.'

MULTIPLE OCCUPANCY WORKSPACES

Multiple occupancy workspaces include small offices, open spaces such as reception areas and work areas in workshops, warehouses and factories. These workplaces present dyslexics with problems very similar to those that are characteristic of open-plan work spaces but, because smaller numbers of workers are involved there are important differences that should be recognised. In particular if people are working as a team it may be possible to reduce problems, such as the adverse impact of distractions and interruptions, by agreeing how the work is to be completed. For example, workers in a shared office might have equal responsibility for answering telephones or factory workers might have equal responsibility for responding to an alarm indicating that some process is complete and action is needed. In such situations, problems can often arise for dyslexics. There is a tendency for an informal, tacit understanding to emerge in such situations such that the team of workers deals with the common responsibility tasks in rotation, probably because this intuitively appears to be the most equitable way of dividing the work. It would, however, be more efficient to agree on an explicit policy that one or more people have primary responsibility in the morning and another person or persons have primary responsibility in the afternoon. The alternative of people having responsibility between agreed hours or days could be explored. The same principle could be applied to an office environment where workers need to deal with enquiries from people arriving at a reception desk. For dyslexic workers, simply knowing that there are times when interruptions are less likely to occur can enable them to do their work more efficiently. This is likely to be true generally—it just becomes more significant when a dyslexic is part of the team!

ACHIEVING LARGE EFFECTS FROM SMALL CHANGES

Readers may find it difficult to believe that the changes suggested above could make a significant difference to a dyslexic employee's work performance. However, we have personal experience of training clients whose jobs have been under threat because of difficulties that were removed by adjustments such as those listed above. We have also seen many very bright and able dyslexic clients who have lost employment when adjustments such as those outlined above could have been introduced and, if they had been introduced, would, in all probability, have solved their problems.

Dyslexic employees are often reluctant to expose their lack of knowledge because they perceive that they are expected to be able to do 'simple' tasks. If, for example, they cannot listen to and remember three instructions presented orally and others can, they may well not want to disclose this fact, preferring instead to do what they can remember and either guess the rest or deduce, by observing others, what they are expected to do. Such behaviour may seem strange, but it is in fact quite natural, particularly given the school memories that haunt many dyslexic people. The behaviour may seem bizarre to non-dyslexics; for example, hiding a basic lack of knowledge from colleagues, line managers and supervisors may seem counter-productive. Nevertheless, it is common and it is not easy to change, whereas work environments and practices are relatively easy to change; more often than not, the effort needed to make workplace changes is dwarfed by the benefit of those changes. Most of the changes discussed above would improve the overall efficiency of the workforce. Once implemented, there would be little in terms of effort required from employers over and above what would normally be required in terms of managing, updating and replacing systems.

The above discussion has largely focused on general changes that can be introduced into work environments in terms of changing aspects of the physical workspace. This includes introducing aids, practices and procedures that make information processing and recall of information more efficient. These changes would typically be implemented as a result of a workplace assessment completed on the dyslexic worker. This is only a partial solution to dyslexia-related problems in the workplace. Workplace assessments are carried out on individuals who are known to be dyslexic. They do not provide a remedy for the problems arising from dyslexics who are either undiagnosed or diagnosed but not known as dyslexic by their employers. This group is certainly significant in terms of numbers, and it may well constitute the larger group; i.e., there may be more people in this group than in the group of known dyslexic employees. According to the arguments presented in Chapter 1 regarding what happens to literacy-competent and high-ability dyslexics in terms of diagnosis, i.e., they are not diagnosed, it is very likely that most high-ability dyslexics in employment are not known to their employers.

To deal effectively with dyslexia-related issues in the workplace, employers need a system that serves two distinct groups. Those employees who have been, or can be, identified as dyslexic and those that have not been identified. Having a policy of completing workplace assessments on identified dyslexics is the most efficient way of dealing with this group. The challenge for employers is finding a way of accommodating dyslexic employees without needing to know they are dyslexic. Essentially, employers need to make adjustments to their workplaces to reduce the likelihood that they are unwittingly disabling one or more of their employees. In most cases, only a handful of the weaknesses listed in Tables 4.1–4.3 disrupt a dyslexic's work performance. Consequently, only a small proportion of the various adjustments outlined above will arise from a workplace assessment. However, if all or most of the adjustments were introduced, unidentified dyslexics would to a large extent be accommodated, not as effectively as they would be on the basis of a competent workplace assessment, but sufficiently to make them more efficient in their workplaces to the benefit of both employers and themselves.

The approach to making adjustments in anticipation of the dyslexic employees described above can be called proactive adjustment. It might well seem a daunting task, but, in fact, many of the required modifications are relatively simple and inexpensive to introduce. What results from these modifications is a workplace that makes appropriate provision for many dyslexic needs; i.e., proactive adjustments create dyslexia-friendly work environments. The business case for creating dyslexia-friendly work environments will now be presented.

THE CASE FOR MAKING PROACTIVE ADJUSTMENTS FOR DYSLEXICS

Making reasonable adjustment in anticipation of dyslexic employers coming into an organisation or as a method of dealing with unidentified dyslexic people already employed is not a legal requirement. Although proactive adjustments can be more effective than reactive adjustments, i.e., normal reasonable adjustments, there are no sources of external funding for making proactive adjustments. For example, the Employment Service's Access to Work scheme can be used only for identified employees. Nevertheless, creating dyslexia-friendly workplaces by making proactive adjustment makes good business sense.

Creating dyslexia-friendly working environments ensures that general provisions are made, not only for one of the largest single group of disabled people, but also for people with hidden disabilities other than dyslexia. More significantly, however, as will become evident later in this chapter, most of the suggested workplace modifications represent improvements that will translate into improved efficiency generally.

If workplaces are to be dyslexia-friendly, however, and if employers are to operate within the law, every aspect of the work environment, including human-resource management, needs to be examined for possible sources of disability discrimination. Ensuring that all systems are free of disability discrimination automatically makes the workplace dyslexia-friendly.

An important effect of producing dyslexia-friendly workplaces is the motivating effect that it is likely to have on dyslexic employees and others with hidden disabilities. Motivation is a crucially important factor in determining workplace activity, and it requires some attention.

THE IMPORTANCE OF MOTIVATION IN DYSLEXIC WORK SUCCESS

The large number of books and empirical articles that have been written about motivation over the last two decades is a testimony to the perceived importance of the subject. There are many different theories of motivation, no one of which is universally accepted as a full description of the factors that determine work behaviour. However, the thirst for knowledge about the competing theories persists, and its importance can hardly be overestimated. This intense focus of concern on the concept of motivation is by no means difficult to explain; every organisation needs people in order to function, and they need to influence people's behaviour in specific ways in order to ensure that they function effectively. An organisation's effectiveness is determined to a large extent by its ability to influence and guide employees to work towards achieving its goals.

According to Katz & Kahn (1966), organisations must motivate behaviour in at least three ways: first, people must be attracted to join the organisation; second, once employed, they must want to remain in the organisation; and third, while employed, they must dependably perform the tasks for which they were hired. Few would deny the obvious common sense of these three points, yet it is precisely in these areas that organisations often fail to influence behaviour efficiently. This failure is particularly emphatic in the context of motivating certain minority groups, the adult dyslexic population being a notable case in point. Understanding the reasons why organisations fail to cause dyslexics to join, participate and produce gives some insights into how such failure can be reduced and how the consequent loss to both parties can be avoided.

The factors determining whether or not dyslexic people are attracted to join an organisation include all the factors that apply generally, e.g., salary, working conditions, location, benefits, appropriate equal opportunities and anti-discrimination policies, but they will be weighted differently in the minds of dyslexic employees than their peers. In particular working conditions, appropriate equal opportunities and anti-discrimination policies will be more important for dyslexics, and disabled people generally, than for others.

There is an additional factor that is important to dyslexic adults and which employers need to focus on if they are to attract dyslexic applicants. It is the degree to which the organisation appears to potential dyslexic employees to understand and support dyslexics as a distinct group, i.e., as distinct from disabled people generally. While this may appear to be an odd distinction, many dyslexics believe that their condition is misunderstood and that organisations will either not be supportive or provide inadequate support, a fear that is not allayed by advertisements that the employer has an equal opportunities policy relating to disability. These fears are well founded for a number of reasons, the most common being that people with hidden disabilities have historically been, and, many would argue, continue to be, at a higher risk of being discriminated against than people with visible or well-defined disabilities.

Despite the efforts made to cover all disability groups—in terms of disability training of, and awareness raising for, employers—people still tend to associate disability with physical impairment. People either do not think about hidden disabilities at all, or they perceive hidden disabilities as something different from disability. For example, the unfounded belief that certain hidden disabilities, notably dyslexia but also others such as attention deficit disorder and dyspraxia, are related to either mental illness or low intelligence is pervasive and persistent. As most hidden disabilities are poorly understood, in general, employers would probably acknowledge that they do not understand them, with the exception of dyslexia, which would in many cases elicit from employers predictable stereotypical descriptions. The point here is that if employers recognise that they do not understand a condition, they will be more likely to seek expert opinion about what should be done to accommodate people with the condition in the workplace; when employers mistakenly think they know what is needed, they are less likely to seek guidance from experts. The problem facing dyslexics uniquely is that many employers do not understand that they do not understand!

It is not uncommon to find that employers who are prepared to employ dyslexics do so believing either that they know what the solution to their problems is—and that is very rarely the case, or that there is no solution—and that is never the case. Whichever false perception prevails, the dyslexic employee is disadvantaged; i.e., inappropriate adjustments are no more support than no adjustments at all. The belief that an employer is unlikely to understand dyslexia and therefore unlikely to be supportive prevents many potentially excellent candidates from applying for posts, as illustrated in the following case history.

Phillip's Case History

Phillip, a 43-year-old graphic design artist, was successfully working for a television company in Germany, but he wanted to return to England to live and work closer to his family. Although he was a very well-qualified, experienced and valued employee, it had taken him some time to convince his German employer that he was a competent professional: he experienced some considerable difficulties for the first six months after he secured his post, and he almost lost his job because of various mistakes that he made. When he applied for the job, he informed his employer that he was dyslexic, and the managers subsequently assured him that they would make allowances for this in their selection procedures and assessments.

The first hurdle where Phillip had difficulty was the interview, in which he performed very poorly, answering most of the questions inadequately. This was made worse by a less than satisfactory performance in a group exercise, which had gone badly because the candidates had to read information in preparation for the exercise, but he had been unable to remember sufficient detail from what he had read to use in the exercise. Although he had been allowed extra time to read the brief, this had not helped him overcome his problem: he could read fast, but he had difficulty retaining the information. He performed very well in a work sample test that required him to provide written responses to a number of questions. He was given an extra 20 minutes to complete this test, but in the event he finished before the other candidates.

He was appointed largely on both his performance on the work sample test and the examination of his portfolio. His employer supplied him with voice-activated software, which he found useful to some extent, but he had problems that it did not solve. He worked in a room with five other people and would be interrupted in the middle of one task with information about another, disrupting him considerably. He took far longer than expected to complete tasks and often left tasks undone, forgetting them completely until colleagues informed him that the work was needed, usually 'urgently'.

Phillip was fortunate that his colleagues were keen to help, and eventually he established a way of working that allowed him to function efficiently; in effect, he negotiated adjustments with his colleagues and subsequently created a dyslexia-friendly work environment. He was very aware, however, that he had been lucky and that if he moved to another position back in England, he might not achieve the same results. Consequently, although he saw many appropriate positions over the years, he simply never applied, eventually returning to England to work in a self-employed capacity.

The adjustments that Phillip's employer made to accommodate his dyslexia, i.e., extra time in an assessment test and extra time to read material in preparation for a group exercise, will appear very reasonable to many employers. However, they had no impact on his dyslexia-related difficulties, which were tracking information presented orally, remembering information presented in writing, organising his oral communication and speaking succinctly. The result of Phillip's experience was to demotivate him from seeking employment that he was very able to do. This was a loss for him and, given his considerable talents, for his potential employers.

Dyslexics are attracted to join, stay with and progress in a company that they feel is dyslexia-friendly, but there is no way for them to know which companies are and which companies are not dyslexia-friendly. The 'Investor in People' award or the 'Disability Symbol' award gives some indication that policies regarding equal opportunities and disability awareness exist and that the recipient employers are meeting their legal requirements regarding disability. They do not, however, constitute evidence that the organisation is either dyslexia-aware or dyslexia-friendly; as we saw earlier in this chapter, dyslexia is often not perceived as a disability and not catered for in workplaces in the same way visible disabilities are.

There is a pressing need for employers to make efforts to become more accommodating to dyslexic adults and to communicate actively to potential employees that they are doing so. With conservative estimates suggesting that at least 10% of the population are dyslexic, and many experts suggesting the percentage is significantly higher than this, the exclusion of dyslexics from the recruitment pool represents a significant potential loss of talent to employers looking for new employees. It is the perception by dyslexic adults that their needs are not being met, a perception that some, like Phillip in the above case history, have formed on the basis of experience, that needs to be changed if they are to be successfully motivated to apply for employment.

Employers need to communicate openly that they are aware of dyslexic needs and to demonstrate what they have done and are prepared to do to meet such needs. An organisation demonstrating awareness of the condition and a preparedness to accommodate dyslexic needs comprehensively will attract dyslexics. Employers that modify the physical, social, economic and human-resource management aspects of their workplaces to accommodate dyslexics, and that communicate what they have done, will be more likely to attract dyslexic adults into their recruitment pool than employers who either do not make the changes or make them but do not advertise them. This important information could effectively be communicated if there were an award, equivalent to the Disability Symbol, which is currently awarded to employers by the government's Employment Service, that was exclusively to indicate that employers had taken positive steps to make their workplaces dyslexia-friendly. Such an award, which could be given to organisations that met specified criteria for being dyslexia-friendly, would be meaningful to dyslexics, unlike the Disability Symbol, which is general and does not mean a great deal to adult dyslexics.

The special award system proposed could easily be operated by the government through an appropriate department such as the Employment Service, although they would need to take counsel from appropriate experts in developing and monitoring the award. This is not likely to happen, at least in the near future. Nevertheless, individual employers that work towards establishing dyslexia-friendly workplaces are taking positive steps towards creating inclusive societies. This is a powerful and positive corporate image to project, and projecting it should be viewed as good public relations. Employers should advertise the efforts they put into making their work environment dyslexia-friendly. This can be achieved by including the information on websites, in company magazines, in promotional videos and in information sent out to job applicants, such as specially prepared leaflets.

In addition to the positive image that an organisation can project to its customers and potential customers by advertising the efforts that it has made to create a level playing field for dyslexics, there are other benefits to be gained. Adopting such a procedure would, for example, avoid placing dyslexic people in the awkward position of having to choose whether or not to disclose their condition. If adjustments are carefully thought through and presented as improvements in procedures to benefit all people, dyslexic and non-dyslexic alike, then, in all probability, dyslexics who are not predisposed to disclosing their condition, and who may be inclined not to apply would see from the information that their need had been taken into account. They would then be able to apply without concern about disclosing their condition. An additional important benefit is that the possibility of inadvertently discriminating against undiagnosed dyslexics would be much reduced. In terms of adjustments that can in fairness be made available only to dyslexics, such as additional time to complete assessment exercises, it could be made clear that these adjustments are available if required to people who can prove they are dyslexic.

FACTORS INFLUENCING THE RETENTION OF DYSLEXICS IN EMPLOYMENT

Once dyslexics have been employed, the employer needs to ensure that they will stay in the organisation. As with other employees, whether or not dyslexic adults will be retained will be determined to a large extent by how comfortable they feel in the work environment and by the benefits they can expect to receive from staying. When it comes to retaining dyslexic people, what motivates them, like anyone else, are the realities of the organisational culture, customs and practices. An all-encompassing belief in the principle that dyslexic differences, strengths and weaknesses must be respected will certainly help retain dyslexics.

However, the adhesive that will hold them tightly is action; if there is a genuine willingness to create a level playing field and support dyslexics, they are very likely to stay. If there is no evidence that such a philosophy has produced tangible changes, they will leave.

Changes to the physical environment, as outlined in a previous section of this chapter, increase the likelihood that dyslexics will stay in their jobs. However, there is also a need to examine possible improvements to the various human-resource management functions, which will be covered later in this chapter.

Related to ensuring that dyslexic employees remain in organisations is the need to motivate them to do the job and to do it to the best of their ability. There are several important factors here. Ensuring that they have all the necessary knowledge and understanding to do the job is fundamental, yet it is the most common stumbling block, as we shall see later in this chapter. Dyslexics will be motivated if they perceive that they can benefit from training and development programmes. They will also be motivated if they perceive that there is an acceptable psychological contract between the employer and the employee. All of these factors are examined below.

THE IMPORTANCE OF HUMAN-RESOURCE FACTORS IN THE WORKPLACE

Chapter 2 examined how dyslexia experts have neglected human-resource factors in their analysis of adult dyslexic needs in workplaces. The argument presented was that, in general, many of those writing on the subject lacked understanding of the psychology of workplaces. As a consequence of the lack of attention that human-resource factors have received, employers may not be fully aware that the law requires these processes and procedures to be free of discriminatory practices. Human-resource factors in relation to adult dyslexia are referred to briefly by the Disability Rights Commission and are mentioned just as briefly in some textbooks on adult dyslexia. References tend to be made in general terms, and there is little detailed analysis of what constitutes appropriate adjustments of human-resource practices and procedures for dyslexics. The rest of this chapter looks at how key human-resource functions need to change to accommodate dyslexics. Once again, although making such changes provides protection from unnecessary litigation, it is nevertheless simply good business sense to make them.

AVOIDING DISCRIMINATION IN RECRUITMENT

Creating accurate descriptions of what a job entails by specifying key work tasks and the qualities, skills, abilities, knowledge and experience that are required of an acceptable incumbent is the first important step in the process of constructing a dyslexia-friendly workplace. When job and person specifications include irrelevant factors such as requirements for skills or qualifications that are not job relevant, they may result in people who are well equipped to do the job taking themselves out of the recruitment pool. For example, dyslexics with no A level qualifications but all the requisite skills to do a particular job would probably not bother applying for the post if they received a person specification stating that an A level in any subject was required. Employers need to be very confident that what they stipulate as a requirement does relate to what is needed to do the job. Otherwise they risk, at best, losing good candidates and, at worst, becoming involved in litigation with aggrieved potential applicants. The most efficient way an employer can avoid either of these undesirable outcomes is to carry out a job analysis to generate the information that is used to write the job and person specification.

A job analysis is a structured analytical procedure for identifying the key characteristics of a job. A basic job analysis would involve jobholders and their line managers being asked to describe in detail the individual job tasks that make up the job being analysed. It would normally include the tasks most frequently performed, the most difficult tasks and the most important or critical tasks. This information might alternatively be generated by asking employees to keep an activity diary listing what they actually do on an hour-by-hour basis over a set time, such as two or three weeks. Job analysis can also be carried out with structured questionnaires; a popular one is the Position Analysis Questionnaire (McCormick et al., 1972). There are many other ways that a job analysis can be completed; for example, Blum & Naylor (1968) identified nine methods, including questionnaires and checklists administered to workers, interviews with and observations of workers, and work participation: i.e., the job analyst actually does the job. Whatever method of job analysis is used will be an improvement over judgements made on gut instinct and 'common sense'. These are not necessarily wrong, but they are likely to be less accurate and relevant. Job analysis is a technical procedure that should be carried out by a suitably trained person. For small employers who may not have sufficient funds to employ the services of an outside consultant, there are a number of textbooks that describe methods that can be used to do a very basic job analysis. Interested readers can find details in most good textbooks on occupational psychology; for example, *The Psychology of Behaviour at Work* by Furnham (1999) contains an informative section on the subject. There is also much useful information in the book *Job Analysis: A Practical Guide for Managers* by Pearn & Kandola (1990).

In addition to the job and person specification, employers need to ensure that they are not discriminating against dyslexics by any practice related to the way they present information about the job to applicants. Employers also need to be aware that any rules that they impose regarding how applicants should supply information about themselves must not be too stringent without justification. For example, completed application forms that contain spelling errors should not disadvantage applicants, unless there is evidence, as from a job analysis, that spelling proficiency is a valid selection criterion. It is also important to make the application procedure accessible to dyslexic people. In their website, the Disability Rights Commission advise that employers should be prepared to provide vacancy information and receive application responses in different formats, including large print, email and taped material. Although it is common sense that making relevant information easier to access for dyslexics and others will motivate them to apply, it is still a relatively uncommon practice.

AVOIDING DISCRIMINATION IN EMPLOYMENT SELECTION

In spite of legislation to prevent it, few people working in the field of adult dyslexia would doubt that unfair discrimination against dyslexic people persists. At both the point of entry to an organisation and for promotion within it, dyslexic people risk being judged not by their ability but by their condition. While legislation has had a positive effect in reducing direct discrimination, it has had much less of an impact on indirect discrimination, much of which takes place without either the employer or the employee being aware that it has operated. Such discrimination can easily deprive individuals of a job that they were ably equipped to do. This can be a very damaging loss to the individual, and since it can result in an appropriate candidate's not being selected, it can represent a loss to a potential employer as well. It is therefore in the interests of everyone to identify the source of the discrimination and to eliminate it.

A basic principle of good selection is that the measurements made should be directly related to the set of key skills and abilities that the job demands. As indicated in the previous section, this can best be achieved by carrying out some form of job analysis. Employers that follow such principles are immediately less likely to be unfairly discriminating than those that do not follow such principles. While job analysis is an important element in the process of making any selection system fair, relevant and accurately targeted on key skills and abilities, it is particularly important in the case of dyslexics. The reason for this is that dyslexics are more likely to be the victims of indirect discrimination arising from poorly targeted selection instruments than most other groups. This, in turn, arises because many selection procedures require applicants to have higher levels of literacy skills than are required by the job to which the selection relates. Additionally, selection systems may require memory skills that are not necessarily required in the job. The personal view of the employer may be that it is better to employ highly literate people who can remember a lot of information. However, if a selection system has excluded a dyslexic applicant who had sufficient levels of literacy or whose memory was sufficient to do the job, but not to pass the selection assessment, this is a form of indirect discrimination against dyslexic applicants. A job analysis will determine the required levels of literacy, memory and other variables, allowing employers to examine their selection instruments to ensure that they do not require higher levels of those variables than have been identified in the job analysis. The same comments apply to selection for promotion and for redundancy.

Organisations differ substantially in terms of the selection procedures they use to identify the best person for the job. At one end of the scale, there are organisations using assessment centres in which selection may take from one to three days. These usually involve, as a minimum, an interview and some psychometric tests. The longer procedures can involve several interviews, a variety of psychometric tests as well as group exercises, presentations, work sample tests and personality questionnaires. In contrast to the multiple measurements involved in assessment centres at the other end of the scale, some organisations rely on single interviews of a small number of applicants who have been short-listed on the basis either of information provided on their application forms or by personal recommendation. The use of a range of psychometric tests to support the selection interview is growing in popularity, but the single interview is still the most popular way to assess job applicants, particularly in small businesses. There is considerable potential for discrimination across the whole range of possible selection methods, a detailed discussion of which is outside the scope of this text. There are, however, some important general points that need to be noted. Job applicants taking part in selection systems will invariably need to be given instructions about what they are required to do. This is an area where dyslexic adults may be subjected to indirect discrimination. Instructions that require the candidate to remember large amounts of information are likely to discriminate unfairly against dyslexics, as are overcomplicated written instructions. To avoid this, the administration instructions should be made as simple as possible. Testing sessions are more effective when they include practice examples that the administrator can use to ensure that all candidates are clear about what they are expected to do before the assessment starts. Any exercises that involve reading material to be used in later exercises, as is quite common with group exercises and work sample tests, should take account of the fact that dyslexics may need longer to absorb the information than the average person. Unless it can be demonstrated that reading speed is an important job-related skill, a failure to look at this activity would be likely to lead to indirect discrimination. There are many other possible sources of indirect discrimination, many of which are a function of the content of individual selection tools and how assessment centres are structured. This means that employers need to consider possible sources of indirect discrimination at the design stage of assessment centres and take appropriate action to reduce the adverse impact. The two most commonly used selection tools, i.e., psychometric tests and interviews, require some detailed comment.

AVOIDING DISCRIMINATION IN PSYCHOMETRIC TESTING

Psychometric tests are potentially very powerful measurement instruments and can make selection very fair if they are used correctly. But they may also be the source of indirect discrimination, particularly against adult dyslexics. Making specific adjustments to psychological tests is an important factor to consider in the context of reducing sources of indirect discrimination in testing programmes. It is a factor that employers must take seriously. Schools and colleges often make adjustments for dyslexic students by allowing them extra time to complete tests—an extra 15 minutes for every hour of testing. Another, less common adjustment is to allow candidates to have the assistance of a reader and a scribe, so they can have the questions read to them and their responses written down for them. However, although these remedies may appear to be an attractive solution, they are not appropriate in the context of psychometric tests. They should not be used without first establishing that the giving of extra time is valid or that having someone reading aloud and writing responses is valid. Employers using psychometric tests need to give careful attention to all aspects of their testing programme to ensure that it does not discriminate unfairly against dyslexic applicants.

Psychological tests should be purchased only from recognised test developers; alternatively, they may be developed to order by qualified psychologists with sound knowledge of psychometrics. Tests produced 'in-house' can be very good tests, but not unless they are constructed according to established principles of good test construction. This will be evident from the test manual, which should contain information on all aspects of test development and statistical information. Notably, it should explain how the test items were generated and selected, and it should provide statistical information on test reliability and validity. If a test does not have this minimal amount of information, it should not be used. Psychological tests need to be administered, marked and interpreted by competent, trained professionals. For personnel specialists and others, including psychologists, wishing to demonstrate that they are proficient in psychological testing, there is a special qualification, which the British Psychological Society introduced some years ago for the express purpose of improving the use of occupational tests. The qualification is the British Psychological Society's Level A Certificate in Occupational Testing, training for which is provided by many firms of chartered occupational psychologists. This certificate is a nationally recognised indicator of competence in psychometric testing. It is awarded to people who have demonstrated their competence, theoretical and practical, to the satisfaction of a chartered psychologist who is recognised by the British Psychological Society as an expert in this area. It should be considered the minimum requirement for anyone who is making decisions about the use of psychometric tests in selection. Holders of this certificate should be able to carry out all the activities mentioned above including job analysis; i.e., successful applicants for the certificate are required to demonstrate competence in job analysis.

Although it could be argued that the British Psychological Society's Level A Certificate in Occupational Testing did not give sufficient attention to disability issues when it was first introduced. It does now focus on this important area of fairness in testing, and people awarded the certificate from the late 1990's onwards should, in theory, have an appreciation of how to make appropriate adjustments for disabled people taking test. Unfortunately, however, the provisions made for dealing with disabled candidates, in both the training people receive for the 'Level A' certificate and in test distributors' own codes of practice for testing disabled candidates, do not benefit dyslexics as much as other disabled people. The reason for this disparity is the general poor understanding of adult dyslexia. Nevertheless, the situation is better now than it was and it should improve further as understanding of this complex condition improves.

The precautions that are outlined above in the context of using tests in initial employment selection apply to other situations where tests are being used to assess for the purpose of selection, as in assessment centres for promotion or in selection for redundancy.

Sometimes employers are advised to be prepared to waive tests on the grounds that the information can be collected in other ways, but this may not be sound advice. When used properly, psychometric tests are very reliable and valid selectors; they are considerably more reliable than other individual selection methods. They should be used (in preference to other methods) in conjunction with job analysis data and appropriate adjustments. When they are used in this way, employers have a defence against any allegation that they discriminated in the way information was collected. Waiving the test could result in complaints of discrimination from rejected applicants or employees. It would be easy to establish that the alternative method of collecting information was not as valid as the test, and for this reason employers need to exercise caution before dispensing with tests. It is better to follow the codes of practice for testing dyslexic people, which should be available from the test distributor, than arbitrarily to assume that information can be obtained by other methods.

AVOIDING DISCRIMINATION IN SELECTION INTERVIEWS

For numerous reasons, interviews have enormous potential for indirect discrimination against dyslexic employees. One of the main factors making them so vulnerable to unfair discrimination is the amount of information presented in the interview questions.

Compound interview questions, i.e., questions that are made up of several individual questions, are by their nature extremely demanding in terms of what they require of the working memory. Such questions are unfair to dyslexic candidates, who are likely to have difficulty retaining all the points in the question. They are therefore likely to give a response that does not reflect their knowledge or skill. For example, a question such as 'What strengths can you bring to this company, how do you see us using them and what additional strengths do you expect to develop over the next five years if you were employed here?' requires a lot to be remembered. Although the interviewer may well prompt the interviewee, this does not always happen and even when it does, it may undermine the person's confidence. Prompting highlights the fact that interviewees have not answered the question as fully as they should have, a perception which may undermine their self-esteem. One problem is that many interviewers who use compound questions have not prepared them. They simply construct them as the interview progresses, starting a question and adding to it indefinitely. Consequently, the interviewer is unlikely to remember what was asked and therefore cannot help an interviewee who fails to deal with all the points. The discrimination arises when interviewers evaluate interviewees negatively because they perceive that the answers are too brief in relation to the question presented. Non-dyslexics, who can hold more of the question than their dyslexic peers, will give a more impressive response, thus leading the interviewer to discriminate between two candidates not on the basis of ability but on the basis of one interviewee's dyslexia.

Any long, rambling question or any question that presents a lot of facts that need to be retained in memory is a severe disadvantage for a dyslexic interviewee. The remedy to this problem is simple; interview questions should be

- short, concise and clearly worded
- designed to assess specific skills, understanding or areas of knowledge
- structured to focus on only one area
- written down so they can be repeated if required

The only time it may be justified to ask compound or long, detailed questions in interviews is when listening and responding to such questions is a job-related skill that is being measured in the interview, and this is not usually the case.

Closed questions, i.e., questions that require 'yes', 'no' or very brief replies, should be used to check facts presented in interviews. Closed questions are particularly important when interviewing dyslexic adults because they very often give lengthy replies to questions. They can frequently lose the thread of what they intended to say. Interviewers should be aware of this and be prepared to ask closed questions to establish specific relevant facts if these are not clear in the dyslexic's response. An example of how useful this can be comes from the experience of one of our trainees, who attended an interview in which he was asked whether he was prepared to travel abroad as part of the job for which he was applying. He was fully prepared to travel, but, believing that he needed to convince the interviewer, when a simple 'yes' would have sufficed, he gave a lengthy answer, explaining in some detail that he was quite used to travelling and had developed strategies for remembering directions, which had been one of his dyslexic difficulties. He was not appointed, and in the feedback that he received from the interviewer explaining why he had not got the job, he was told it was due to his unwillingness to travel. When he explained that he was very willing to travel, the interviewer responded that he had misunderstood his answer. The interviewer apparently mistook his explanation of how he had developed strategies for remembering directions for an explanation that, because he could not remember directions, he was reluctant to travel. In this case, a closed and very direct question, such as 'Are you saying that you are prepared to travel abroad—yes or no?', would have served both sides very well. Closed questions are most effectively used when they restrict responses to a 'yes' or 'no' but can also be used to establish facts such as dates, names and numbers. Interviewers should be aware that if such questions are used to elicit these facts, dyslexics may make mistakes, as a consequence of memory failure, that misrepresent their true ability. Dates and other factual information should be obtained from application forms, curricula vitae and other relevant documentation.

Selection interviewing is a popular topic for occupational psychologists, and it has been the focus of research for nearly 20 years. However, although the principles for maximising the reliability and validity of interviewing are well established and documented, there is still a very wide range of types of selection interviews carried out in organisations. At one end of the scale are organisations that have used data from job analysis to develop structured interview questions and standardised assessor-marking schemes. As indicated above, each standardised question in a structured interview should be designed to measure a single job-relevant factor, e.g., a candidate's experience of working in multidisciplinary teams, and all candidates should be presented with the same questions. Standardised questions do not exclude the possibility of asking additional questions to establish facts and probe for the required information. The assessor-marking schemes are rating scales that interviewers use to rate responses on each answer given by interviewees. The use of these rating scales is standardised by interviewers agreeing beforehand on how they should rate answers.

Some employers may have reservations about relying on structured interviews, fearing that they would preclude making basic decisions about compatibility. For example, employers frequently want to decide from an interview whether or not they, or their colleagues, could work with or relate to the interviewee in everyday work situations over extended periods of time. This is a legitimate use of interviews, but it is incorrect to assume that questions cannot be structured to measure such factors. If job analysis is carried out competently, it will identify the important factors determining compatibility, allowing questions to be structured to measure this factor in a reliable and valid way as with other important factors.

Overall, the findings from research in occupational psychology provide compelling evidence that structured interviews are, in general, more likely to lead to better selection decisions than unstructured interviews, and employers are therefore well advised to seek appropriate training for personnel involved in interviewing and to include their reliance on such interviews in policy statements.

At the other end of the scale, some employers rely on interviews where neither the questions nor the assessment of interviewee performance is structured or standardised. The latter are interviews that assume, consciously or unconsciously, that the interviewer is an expert. Such interviewers believe, mistakenly, that their gut instinct is sufficient to identify the best candidate from those interviewed. In general, the more experienced the interviewers, the more confidence they have in their decision. The research, however, indicates that gut instinct lacks the reliability and validity that characterises the measurements obtained from interviewers who have been trained in structured interviewing. Furthermore, it is clear from the research findings that the only difference between inexperienced untrained interviewers and experienced untrained interviewers is that the latter group are more confident in their false belief that they are making reliable and valid measurements.

MAKING INDUCTION PROCEDURES EFFECTIVE FOR DYSLEXICS

Employers, prospective employers, career counsellors and other professionals assisting dyslexic adults often perceive them, particularly when they obviously have high ability, as a confusing puzzle. In spite of clear evidence that they should be successfully employed, they have a history of unemployment. Their careers may have failed to develop because they have changed jobs so often that they have never made the progress they should have made. They may be in employment but having difficulties they should not be having. They may be struggling to do tasks that they should by all accounts find easy to perform. Although they have the requisite interest, ability and experience, they may often fail to do the job for which they were hired. Often this is because either they leave undone or unfinished apparently simple or routine tasks or they make basic errors. One solution to this puzzle is that, in terms of becoming competent at performing the tasks expected of them, dyslexics are distinctly disadvantaged by the key strategy that organisations rely on, namely, initial induction training. More often than not, induction is the only strategy used.

Induction training takes place when people join an organisation. It may be very structured and formal or, perhaps more typically, unstructured and informal. It is typically a short period of instruction followed by a longer period of high tolerance of errors or poor performance. Induction training also takes place after organisational changes, such as the introduction of new workplace procedures or demands; after promotion; and when new tasks or procedures are assigned to an employee. For example, the introduction of a new computer program usually involves induction training in the new system. The information required to perform the new job or the new tasks is presented in the induction. For a short period after the induction, there is an expectation that because people are still 'learning the ropes', or 'getting used to the new procedure', they will need to ask questions or be given additional guidance. How long it takes to learn the ropes or get used to the new demands varies according to the job. Usually line managers and colleagues, as well as the employees undergoing induction training, expect that it will take a certain length of time. A period of 2–4 weeks to become proficient is quite common. Those who take significantly longer than this expected time would attract reprimands or negative feedback on their performance.

Once the period of high tolerance of errors after the completion of induction training has passed, employees who still make errors or need guidance will feel pressure from their managers and their co-workers to improve their performance. It is likely that they will start to be judged either incompetent, lazy or poorly motivated, and rather than being given further instruction on what they should do, will be given warnings on what will happen if they do not meet expectations. The assumption underlying this approach to influencing behaviour is that the memory capacity is much the same for everyone. For example, if managers' experience is that most people remember half of what they are told in induction training and that they take a week to learn the rest, these managers will expect everyone to follow this pattern. In reality, a significant minority of people do not follow the pattern; dyslexic employees are one group who are likely to remember less from the induction and have more to learn after it is over than the average non-dyslexic. They will therefore be likely to need longer to 'learn the ropes' than their non-dyslexic peers. Because the period of high tolerance for poor performance expires before they have learnt what they need to learn to meet performance expectations, they are exposed to a hostile learning environment. People who should be accommodating and provide assistance become less amenable, less understanding and less tolerant. They may be explicitly critical and disparaging or quietly so. This hostile environment has the effect of both reducing dyslexic employees' learning efficiency and causing them to hide what they do not know from their peers and their line managers.

The effect of hiding a lack of key knowledge is usually errors that will at some point lead back to the perpetrator. In general, hiding is a short-term solution but is not feasible in the long term. Hiding a lack of competence in key tasks just delays the inevitable. In practice, our experience is that once the errors come to light and are traced back to dyslexic employees, their line managers are usually surprised at how little the employees seem to know about the basic tasks they are supposed to perform. Discovering the extent of the employee's lack of knowledge often serves to reinforce the supervisor's earlier suspicions that the employee is either lazy or incompetent. This may be a strongly held belief that resists attempts to change it. That managers draw such conclusions is quite understandable from both a common-sense and a theoretical perspective.

In many instances, a manager's negative assessment of an employee's ability or motivation is the only logical conclusion from the available information. Psychologists have determined that we all have a need to explain behaviours that we observe in others. In attempting to make sense of what we see, we often jump to obvious but quite false conclusions. Social psychologists have developed a theory to explain this strong, almost unavoidable predisposition to explain behaviour by creating a label based only on the available information; it is called attribution theory.

Attribution theory is not a theory that can be attributed to the work of any individual psychologist or team of psychologists, since it has evolved over time as more has been discovered about human psychology. Many psychologists have, however, explained how it operates, and readers interested to learn more about this phenomenon may consult Baron et al. (1991) and Ross & Nisbett (1991). Smith (1999) provides a very good overview of attribution theory that will help readers understand how important it is in explaining what happens to dyslexic adults. He refers to the work of Ross (1977), who introduced the term 'fundamental attribution error' as a label for what Smith describes as people's strong, pervasive and 'striking tendency to overestimate the role of personal factors and to underestimate the impact of the situation when explaining the behaviour of others'.

Attribution theory suggests that line managers, in the absence of an understanding that dyslexia is characterised by a weakness in the working memory, explain dyslexic failings by concluding that the affected individual is either lazy, stupid, poorly motivated or simply not interested. These 'obvious' conclusions can be dispelled only when all the information is available and the inappropriateness of these labels becomes obvious. An important implication of attribution theory is that in explaining people's behaviour, the behaviour of their peers is used as a yardstick of what is and is not normal. Consequently, in workplaces, the means used to draw conclusions typically includes a comparison of one employee's behaviour with the behaviour of other employees. If one person underperforms on a task on which co-workers perform adequately, that person is assumed to be at fault. This unquestioned assumption leads the line manager to start a search for that individual's failing. Not only is a search for individual failings initiated but also it is guided by a very simplistic analysis that actually ignores evidence. The search for evidence is by no means objective; it fails to acknowledge that the relevant information may well be hidden from view. This process is illustrated in the following two case histories.

Kate's Case History

Kate, a 37-year-old university administrator and diagnosed dyslexic, was referred for a workplace assessment to identify what adjustments the university could make to help her overcome her work-related dyslexic difficulties. One of Kate's key job tasks was to deal with student enrolments, and she was responsible, together with two other administrators, for supplying students and prospective students with enrolment forms. There were three different types of forms; one for new students, one for students changing courses and one for students repeating a year or entering the second or third year of a course. The three different forms looked very similar and were distinguished only by different alphanumeric codes printed on the front cover. Kate remembered that different types of students needed to supply different types of documentation, but she completely forgot that different forms should be used. Incorrectly issued forms were identified further down the system, and as they became more and more numerous, they generated complaints from the staff who were correcting the errors. Eventually, their source was traced back to Kate.

Kate's supervisor expressed disbelief that she could have gone on so long not understanding that the forms issued needed to be selected according to the category of student, but this was only one of many basic facts that Kate had not assimilated into memory from her period of induction. It transpired that Kate's co-workers had labelled her as stupid and expected her to make mistakes simply in the belief that she was unable to do the job. As part of the assessment, Kate was asked to explain how she came to have so many gaps in her knowledge of the job. She replied, 'With the forms I just didn't realise there was more than one. I knew that there were various things I should know that I didn't, but I couldn't ask because people just get annoyed—they expect you to know things and if you don't, they think you're stupid. The more time that passed, the more difficult it was, because people think, "How on earth have you done the job without knowing that?" I found things out by watching and listening to others.' In fact, Kate's concerns about being considered stupid were well founded, since this was what her supervisor and, apparently, some of her co-workers had concluded. Once provided with all the information, her supervisor was able to attribute her behaviour to memory failure and realise that stupidity was not the explanation.

Kate's experience is not untypical, and many dyslexics in employment will empathise with her. Her reluctance to own up to a lack of knowledge and her surreptitious observations of co-workers in order to learn the ropes are common dyslexic strategies. Learning from others and by trial and error may work, but it may just as likely fail; some dyslexics are lucky and others are not! Organisations risk suffering considerable losses, in terms of poor employee performance and the errors that dyslexics make, from their, albeit unknowing, reliance on these learning processes. Kate's story illustrates how disabling a failure of initial induction training may be. A failure of induction training in newly introduced systems for well-established employees may be just as damaging, as the next case history illustrates.

Jane's Case History

Jane, a 25-year-old graduate chemist, was a diagnosed dyslexic employed as a salesperson with a large advertising firm. Jane had never informed her employer that she was dyslexic, fearing it would lead to discrimination. She relied on overworking to acquire the skills she needed to do the job and had never had any complaints from her employer during the three years she had been employed. However, after the introduction of new computer software that she and her colleagues were required to use for a number of purposes, Jane experienced a succession of problems, which were compounded as more new software was introduced. Although her employer had provided training on all the new software, she had failed to benefit from this because it had been presented too fast for her, and key points had been presented orally without a proper demonstration.

Jane became very stressed as a consequence of the errors she was making, adversely affecting other areas of her work, all of which came to the attention of her line manager, Anne. Eventually, on the advice of her doctor, Jane took time off work, the first time she had taken leave for illness since her initial appointment with the firm. Soon after she returned to work, she had a meeting with Anne, who presented her with a catalogue of errors that she had made over the six-week period prior to her sick leave. These errors included failure to use the new software programs as required and other failures unrelated to the new software. When Jane tried to explain that the computer training provided had not been effective, Anne simply pointed out that everyone else had found it adequate.

Anne told Jane that her errors were not related just to the computer software but that she had made errors on work that she had previously completed to a satisfactory standard. Anne clearly considered that this was evidence that it was Jane's attitude and motivation that were at fault, and not any aspect of the training provided. Jane was given an oral warning but failed to improve; she finally resigned to avoid being sacked.

In Jane's case, the line manager formulated a 'theory' based on the available evidence. She probably reasoned that Jane, a bright graduate who had a good work history, did not lack ability, and she therefore excluded low intelligence as an explanation. It seems likely that she considered that the combined facts that Jane's colleagues were using the new software successfully and that Jane had received the same training were sufficient to exclude the possibility that any factor related to the software or the way it was introduced might explain Jane's failings. The line manager inevitably concluded that the explanation was some factor related to Jane. Furthermore, the fact that Jane had made errors not related to the new software probably led Anne to assume that all of Jane's failings had a common origin. On the basis of these rather simplistic assumptions, none of which were scrutinised, Anne went on to find an internal factor to explain what had caused Jane's poor performance. Anne was subsequently happy to use the concept of low motivation; in psychological terms, Anne made an 'internal attribution' of low motivation to explain Jane's failings.

Jane's dyslexia apparently did not influence Anne's thinking in any way, presumably because it is a hidden condition that she simply did not understand. The result was that Jane became a victim of disability discrimination. She was blamed for a failure that was in fact due to the organisation's failure to accommodate her needs. The attribution process will more often lead to discrimination against people with hidden disabilities than those with obvious disabilities. This is because the latter provide more information that line managers can use for constructing theories. Basically, explaining human behaviour with limited knowledge increases the likelihood that the explanation will be false. However, maximising knowledge helps people draw accurate conclusions.

Creating internal attributions to explain the failings of people with hidden disabilities is firmly within the medical model of disability. People with hidden disabilities are much more likely to be subject to this medical model thinking than those with physical disabilities; i.e., they are more likely to be excluded. Internal attribution is simply less likely to take place when impairments can be seen than when they are hidden. For example, managers are unlikely to conclude that a blind employee is of low intellect purely because of inability to read an email. They are unlikely to identify as poorly motivated a wheelchair user who does not come to meetings because they are convened in a room without wheelchair access. Employers need to be aware of how the attribution process works, and they should, as a standard procedure when dealing with employee underperformance, investigate whether the employee has needs arising from dyslexia or some other hidden disability.

The case histories of Kate and Jane illustrate how the attribution process operates to produce discrimination. They also illustrate how important it is for organisations to make adjustments for disabled people in their induction training. Induction is a critical factor determining employee performance, and most organisations need to make significant changes to their induction procedures as part of reasonable adjustments. In general terms, induction training should be longer, more structured and more repetitive, and should be supported by easily accessed information. Information presented should be information that can be reviewed by employees as often as they need to review it. For example, the various problems that Kate experienced would never have arisen if she had been given more support and more time to learn the basics. If all the job tasks expected of her had been demonstrated, if reviews and summaries of what had been presented had been made available and if 'hard copies' of task procedures had existed, she would have learnt more. What she did not know she could easily have found out. In terms of the error described, i.e., not selecting forms, a flow chart of the steps to be followed in enrolling a student, including a decision box leading to one of three forms to be selected, could easily have been produced. A flow chart of the enrolment process would have reduced the likelihood of her making the errors she made. The time and effort involved in creating it would have been insignificant compared to the time and effort expended in solving the various problems that arose from the errors she made. While it may seem onerous to produce documentation for tasks that are performed by workers every day, it is very often time and effort well spent. Employers should bear in mind that improved induction procedures are likely to benefit all employees, not just dyslexics. In this context and many others, the key difference between dyslexics and their non-dyslexic peers is a quantitative, not a qualitative, one. In other words, everyone is likely to miss or forget something from any induction that presents a large volume of information in a short period of time. Dyslexics simply forget more.

Improving induction influences behaviour by ensuring that all workers dependably perform the tasks they were hired to perform. The influence exercised just happens to be more significant for dyslexics. The precise content of an induction programme adapted to accommodate a dyslexic employee will in general be determined by the job in question. It is best determined by a professional job analysis performed by an occupational psychologist who has expertise in adult dyslexia.

IMPROVING PROFESSIONAL TRAINING PROGRAMMES FOR DYSLEXICS

Training courses are the most common ways that employees promote their own professional development. In general, there is a great deal that can be done to improve how training is planned and delivered. Individual cognitive factors, as well as environmental factors, have a bearing on the effectiveness of professional training programmes in the workplace, and there is scope for workplace modifications to both of these. Reid & Kirk (2000) explain that the available research indicates that recognising an individual's learning preferences can enhance learning and success; they suggest that cognitive and environmental aspects of learning in the workplace need to be given careful consideration, pointing out that this will benefit other workers, as well as dyslexic people. They refer to Ingham (1991), who argues that training materials need to be designed to accommodate the preferences of trainees, in terms of their perceptual strengths, which, Ingham suggests, should be assessed by those designing the training. To support this argument, Reid & Kirk (2000) cite a study by Carnevale et al. (1988), completed for the American Society for Training and Development and the United States Department of Labor, which suggests that trainers need to determine, for each employee, the preferred type of sensory stimulus, i.e., visual, auditory or tactile, that helps them learn best. Having determined this learning preference, the trainer is advised to 'design multiple use training that addresses all preferences'. If employers could follow the above advice, it would certainly improve the learning environment for all employees, dyslexic and non-dyslexic alike. In practice, however, it is probably impractical to expect employers to go quite this far. For most employers, carrying out assessments of learning styles and structuring training around them would demand considerably more time, finance and expertise than are likely to be available, and might well be considered an unreasonable burden. In addition, since many dyslexics hide their condition from scrutiny, such attempts to identify trainee needs may not always be successful.

A practical way of making adjustments in training programmes to render them dyslexia-friendly is to design them so that they accommodate the need that most dyslexics have to see the whole task. This involves the content, the goals, the methods and the training materials being presented at the outset. This is in contrast to the more common approach to training, which usually states goals while the content, methods and training materials are revealed as training progresses. This is not problematic for sequential learners, who collect the detail and build a type of detailed cognitive model slowly as the training progresses. Adult dyslexics tend to work better, however, if they are given a cognitive framework at the outset and are then presented with the details to fit into this framework. This dyslexic learning preference is termed a 'global learning preference' by many writers, including Reid & Kirk (2000). Essentially, a global learning preference means that dyslexics process information better when they can see the whole picture; rather than going through a series of steps sequentially, they prefer to see where they are going and how they will get there. Our experience is that many dyslexics do benefit from seeing the purpose of the learning, and from having a preview of how the learning will be achieved, and that they can very ably grasp the overall picture. However, they are not always able to work on several tasks at the same time unless they have developed good visual thinking and problem-solving skills. Similarly, if tasks are presented appropriately, i.e., by visual methods that are designed so that the information presented can be easily remembered, multiprocessing becomes more likely to occur for dyslexic learners.

The desirability of multisensory methods in training is well established and has, for example, been described by Pumfrey & Reason (1991) and McLoughlin Fitzgibbon & Young (1994). The latter authors suggest that the training of dyslexics should also be structured to make it memorable. This can be achieved by repetition of key points, frequent summaries, demonstrations, practical exercises and opportunities for the trainees to be actively involved in the learning process. It is just as important to make full use of pictures, diagrams, models and flow charts. The last-named are a very flexible and powerful tool that can easily be incorporated into training courses to great effect. Douglas & Fitzgibbon (in preparation) have identified a training method called 'layered-image' flow charts that has proved very effective for those whose natural preference is for global learning.

Improving Training for Dyslexics Using Layered Flow Charts

Layered-image flow-charting is appropriate for a wide range of training programmes. It is most effectively used as part of a multisensory programme of training, but it can also be used very effectively as a simple alternative to presenting information as a written set of notes. Material should be carefully prepared for inclusion in a set of layered flow charts as follows:

1. An overview of what the training programme will involve should be created. This should not go into any detail but simply identify the key areas in terms of the sequence in which they will appear and any important relationship between them. A flow chart is then created to present this information—this flow chart is the master chart. The master chart provides the overall picture of what the training programme aims to achieve and how it intends to achieve it.
2. The information to be presented in the key areas identified in no. 1 above is broken down into small manageable units. Depending on the complexity of the training pro-gramme, one or more key areas may need to be broken down into further sub-units, which themselves are broken down further into manageable units.
3. Reference numbers are attached to information boxes on the flow charts, creating links to other flow charts that expand on the points presented.
4. A set of flow charts based on those constructed above is completed, with the written information replaced with images. Dyslexics might prefer to draw their own images, but image sheets should be provided for those who find this difficult.

Complexity should be avoided in both the physical structure of the flow chart and the content of each flow chart element. As a rule of thumb, an individual flow chart should have no more than 10 elements, and the written content of each element should be no more than a short sentence; a single word is acceptable. The presentation of substantial information in an information box produces a new flow chart or several of them as appropriate. The master chart provides an overview of the entire programme and presents the titles of each manageable unit together with a label identifying the number of the flow chart that outlines that unit. Subordinate flow charts work on the same principle; i.e., they present an overview of the unit, with labels on information boxes indicating the number of the linked flow chart that expands that unit of information. Figures 4.1 and 4.2, respectively, illustrate two flow charts (the master flow chart and one of the linked flow charts) for a programme designed to train a dyslexic car mechanic who is being promoted to workshop supervisor in a garage.

In presenting a training programme using layered flow charts, trainers should encourage trainees to find visual representations for each information box. This technique makes the information easier for adult dyslexics (and everyone else) to remember. Layered flow charts are most effective when used in conjunction with other methods, such as exercises, question-and-answer sessions, and models.

Ideally, the training should not involve trainees in any note taking; e.g., a set of layered flow charts, including blanks that the trainees can use to add their own images, should be presented to trainees, possibly backed up with a taped commentary.

Training is often a key to the professional development of employees, and it is therefore important to ensure that dyslexic employees are appropriately accommodated. Manag-ing one's own professional development is sometimes an area of weakness for dyslexic employees. Having had negative learning experiences in school, they may avoid training courses or individual coaching sessions. This will be most likely to happen when dyslex-ics perceive professional training as a repeat of educational experiences that they would rather not repeat. Employers stand to benefit by making their development programmes dyslexia-friendly and advertising them as such. In this way, they will be likely to overcome the reluctance of dyslexic adults to take part voluntarily.

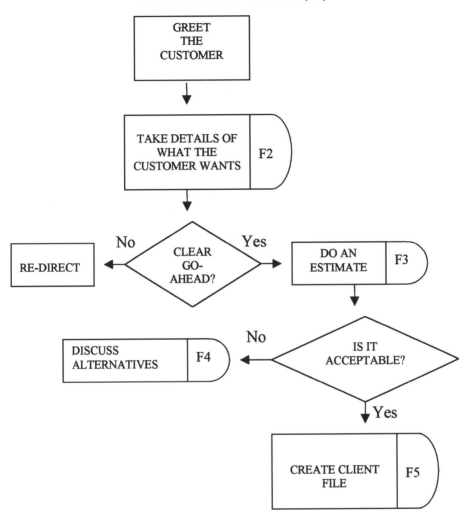

FIGURE 4.1 Example of master flow chart

AVOIDING DYSLEXIA DISCRIMINATION IN PERFORMANCE APPRAISAL

In organisations where staff are subject to annual or any regular performance appraisal, there are a number of issues of which appraisers need to be aware if they are to avoid unfair discrimination against dyslexic employees. It is not our intention to outline how performance appraisal should be carried out in general, since there are many textbooks that do this adequately; for example, the reader will find the subject presented in a clear and informative fashion by *Fletcher & Williams* (*1985*). We are only concerned to identify some important areas where adjustments should be made in order to ensure that dyslexic adults are not subject to discrimination.

LINKED FLOW CHART (F2)

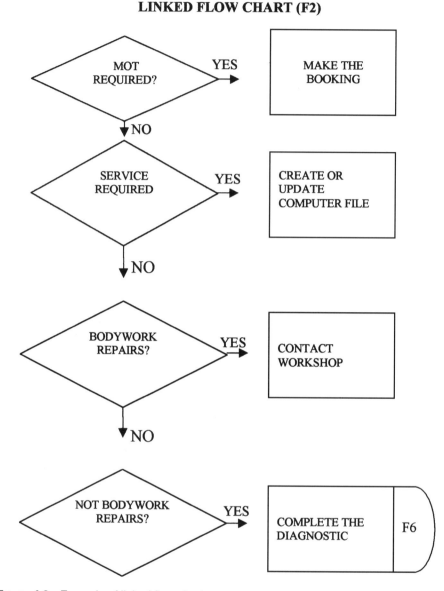

FIGURE 4.2 Example of linked flow chart

The points made in the previous section in relation to assessing dyslexic employees in interviews are very relevant here, and the appraisal interview should similarly take account of all the points outlined in that section. Appraisers should ensure that they appraise the dyslexic employee on the basis of skills that are relevant to the job. They should use the person and job descriptions generated by job analysis. Appraisers should base their appraisal on the employee's performance without reducing ratings because of any adjustments that may have been introduced for the employee.

If an employee is being appraised over a period that includes performance before and after adjustments were introduced, less attention should be paid to the 'before' period. It may also be appropriate to pay less attention to part of the 'after' period when the employee was becoming familiar with an adjustment. For example, if an employee were sent for training to improve memory and organisational skills, it would not be appropriate to assume that there would be immediate improvements. Appraisers should seek expert advice on how to conduct a fair appraisal in such cases. This is particularly important if the appraisal feeds in to decisions about pay or promotion prospects.

If appraisal involves self-appraisal, the appropriate forms should be accompanied by taped versions or presented on computer disks that can be read via voice-activated software. Issues of low self-esteem can lead dyslexic employees to undersell their skills, and this needs to be addressed. It may well be that they need training in self-presentation or a counselling-based intervention (see Chapter 6).

INTRODUCING FLEXIBLE WORKING PRACTICES TO SUPPORT DYSLEXICS

The standard pattern of work that most people follow in terms of working hours, i.e., the '9 till 5', and the fact that they travel to their workplace may often be changed to benefit dyslexic employees without causing any inconvenience to their employers. Such changes do fall into the general definition of reasonable adjustment and may offer almost zero-cost remedies to problems. For example, employees who work in multiple occupancy offices and experience difficulties working because they find other people distracting might benefit from working flexitime. They might prefer to start work earlier or finish later than their colleagues or perhaps both, i.e., starting early and finishing late, in a working pattern typical of many European countries where workers routinely take a three-hour break in the middle of the day.

Some individuals might prefer to work a 'reduced week' i.e., working more hours per day and reducing the number of days per week that they work. Employees varying working hours during the year, working longer at some times and fewer hours/days at other times, but averaging what they should average to meet their contractual commitments is another possibility. Some people may wish to 'bank' their leave, i.e., not take it one year and claim it the next, in order to take extended holidays after long periods of not taking leave.

Employers would need to ensure that any such arrangements do not infring the provisions of the European Working Time Directive, but if the arrangements were legal, operationally neutral or positive in their effect, and if employees could meet their contractual commitments, employers should consider them. Similarly, arrangements that involve job sharing or redistribution of tasks, perhaps two employees agreeing to share their jobs, should be considered as simply sensible methods for optimising the output of employees while improving their job satisfaction and meeting their needs. Another factor worth serious consideration is the extent to which employees could work at home if they wish. In any case, working at home is becoming very popular, with the rapid development of information technology and improved communications. For dyslexics, the option might represent a very significant improvement in their work performance, even if working at home were possible for only a small proportion of the working week.

When the arrangements mentioned above do not compromise the work itself and if there is no operational reason for preventing an employee from working unusual hours, working at home or changing work patterns by, for example, sharing work tasks, an employer should consider these arrangements as possible adjustments. Although initially it may appear impractical to consider reviewing factors as apparently fixed as working hours, place of work and assigned tasks, some employers have discovered that, purely as an organisational change to improve productivity, there is considerable scope for such changes. Many employers would benefit considerably by becoming more flexible in the ways suggested above.

The result of accommodating the needs, desires and preferences of the workforce is a more satisfied workforce and a generally increased worker motivation, which, as we have already acknowledged, are key factors in organisational success. Essentially, the flexibility proposed above is a method of making work easier for employees by taking account of how they work, their needs in relation to work, what they do outside work and how they prefer to organise their non-working time. The idea of taking account of work and leisure activities in deciding how people should work is currently a very popular option, known as the work–life balance; for example, as this book is being prepared, many London borough councils are actively discussing how it can be introduced.

The work–life balance is a concept that is relevant to everyone who works, and getting it right for everyone is a far more effective way of dealing with dyslexia in the workplace than restricting it just to dyslexic employees. Whenever possible, employers should accommodate dyslexics without drawing attention to them as distinct from other workers. One way of achieving this in terms of the work–life balance is by being flexible with every employee; employers have little to lose and much to gain by examining the possibilities outlined above.

The way such changes are introduced and explored is important, and there are some important principles that need to be observed if the enterprise is to be successful. The possibilities should be discussed openly with all staff, and there should be no attempt to force changes on people; i.e., changes should be implemented only with the full agreement of those concerned. Inevitably, there will sometimes be outcomes that could not have been predicted, and employers should therefore introduce changes while making it clear that they are exploratory and subject to cancellation or further change. It may well take time to establish a workable arrangement, but the effort to establish a good work–life balance is an investment worth making.

MAKING CHANGES: A NOTE FOR SMALL EMPLOYERS

As we explained in Chapter 3, from the year 2004, all small employers will be covered by the provisions of the Disability Discrimination Act, and, from 2006 onwards, they will, like all other employers, be in the situation where defending themselves from allegations of unfair discrimination on the grounds of disability will require them to prove their innocence. Although all employers are to be treated the same under the new law, small employers will be most at risk under the terms of this new legislation. Unlike large organisations that have disability specialists and dedicated budgets for dealing with disability issues, small employers often have only their wits and common sense to guide them through the myriad of rules and regulations. While, in theory, the government have a responsibility to ensure that information is disseminated to all small employers about what their responsibilities under the new law will be, in view of past performance, it would be unwise of small employers to rely on this happening. Small employers would be well advised to give very early consideration to how they can ensure that they do not fall foul of the law.

Small employers can take some very basic action immediately. Having up-to-date and relevant information is important, and this can be achieved by making contact and building relationships with relevant organisations and people. Advice on what action should be taken in most situations can be obtained from the Disability Right Commission and from local jobcentre disability employment advisers. In terms of employing disabled people, it is particularly important to seek advice from both of these sources regarding how best to support the affected individuals, but it is also important to involve the disabled persons. As we mentioned earlier, their views on how best they can be supported may need to be supplemented with expert guidance, but their views are nevertheless important, and involving them fully at all points reduces the likelihood of disputes arising and increases the likelihood that any changes made will be acceptable to them.

The Access to Work scheme is of particular importance to small employers since it can be used to finance adjustments that may not otherwise be feasible. As we explained in Chapter 3, the law requires all employers to investigate all sources of funding for reasonable adjustment before excluding them as impractically expensive; therefore, small employers could be exposing themselves to litigation by not exploring the scheme. However, apart from legal requirements, it is just common sense to make use of all available help. Small employers who fail to make use of the Access to Work scheme are missing an opportunity not only to make their workplace dyslexia-friendly but also to maximise the work performance of their dyslexic employees. Small employers are primarily at risk because of lack of knowledge; by being proactive and finding out what they can and should do, they can remove the risk.

TAKING ACCOUNT OF PRIMARY AND SECONDARY DYSLEXIC WEAKNESSES

This chapter has examined how individual dyslexic employees can be supported directly, i.e., by providing adjustments to meet their specific needs, and indirectly by proactive adjustments designed to create dyslexia-friendly workplaces to support dyslexic employees whose condition is not known to their employers. The focus of attention has been adjustments to accommodate what McLoughlin, Fitzgibbon & Young (1994: p. 48) call the primary dyslexic symptoms, which are 'difficulties remembering facts, figures, sequences of instructions, messages, names and almost anything that places a heavy demand on [the working memory]'. Chapters 5 and 6 focus on strategies for managing and overcoming the secondary symptoms, which are 'poor motivation, low self-esteem...lack of confidence...stress disorders and depression'. Secondary symptoms are best accommodated by positive management practices, which are the subject of the next chapter, and various forms of counselling, which are the subject of Chapter 6.

5

MANAGING ADULT DYSLEXIA
IN THE WORKPLACE

INTRODUCTION

There are a remarkable number of theories of how best to manage people at work, but no one model occupies a dominant position in the hearts and minds of management scientists. Nor is there reason for optimism that a consensus will ever be reached regarding exactly what bewildered managers should do to bring out the best in those they manage. As far as managing people with dyslexia is concerned, the philosophies that managers subscribe to, in terms of schools of thought on how they should best perform their job, are not as important as having an awareness and understanding of dyslexia.

Managing effectively the needs of dyslexic workers enables them to realise their potential, and it avoids dyslexics at work becoming disabled by a system that makes false assumptions that fail to recognise and value their strengths. Dyslexic needs in the context of employment refer to differences that generally distinguish dyslexics from non-dyslexics, and that manifest themselves in the workplace as weaknesses. The most common such 'weakness' is a reduced capacity to hold verbal information in the working memory. One direct effect of this, as we discussed in Chapter 1, is that dyslexic workers are less likely than non-dyslexic colleagues to retain the content of a conversation; consequently, workplaces that rely on workers remembering verbal information disable dyslexics. Many other examples of how dyslexic weaknesses lead to dyslexics being disabled in workplaces and remedies for those problems were discussed in Chapter 4. In this chapter, we look at potential areas of weaknesses in management practices that can disable dyslexics and how they can be remedied.

This chapter starts by examining the manager's role in the identification of dyslexia in the workplace. The important issue of how to approach the subject of dyslexia with an employee when there is cause for concern is also examined. Following this is a discussion of how dyslexia may be implicated in workplace stress and what action managers can take both to reduce the stress risks and alleviate the symptoms of stress.

IDENTIFYING DYSLEXIA: THE MANAGER'S ROLE

In the previous chapter, we discussed the benefits of making workplaces dyslexia-friendly by making proactive adjustments and how such measures contribute to improving the performance of undiagnosed dyslexics. Proactive adjustments represent all that can reasonably be done for employees with dyslexia when for some reason they have not been identified to the employer. This very general support offers substantial benefits to both sides since in many cases it translates into a user-friendlier environment for the employee and consequent increased productivity for the employer. For some employees with dyslexia, proactive adjustments will be sufficient for them to realise their full potential. Others, however, will feel some benefit but will need support specific to their needs in order to maximise their work performance. Such support might be needed in the form of further adjustments to the physical environment or in terms of specific management interventions.

When employees are known to be dyslexic, the action required from a manager is straightforward. A workplace assessment should be carried out, recommendations for adjustments implemented, the effects of the adjustments monitored and the situation managed to ensure that the employees are not disadvantaged by any part of the process. For example, if an adjustment involves training, it may be necessary for a manager to reschedule work tasks to ensure that the employees do not become overburdened by work and that they have sufficient time to consolidate the training in the workplace. There are two important points that need to be addressed in this situation. First, the workload should be reduced by 20% in recognition of the fact that trainee employees are physically available for only 80% of the time they would normally be available to work. Second, since the translation of strategies acquired in specialist training to the workplace usually involves an initial slowness, as is the case for any newly acquired skill, managers should be prepared to show a high tolerance of reduced work performance and errors during the time the employee is being trained. In reassigning tasks to accommodate the above factors, managers must be careful not to create hostility to the employees among their co-workers, who might feel they are being asked to do the dyslexic employees' work. The following case history illustrates how training can be either undermined or assisted by the nature of management support for employees.

Anita's Case History

Anita, a diagnosed dyslexic, was employed as a senior organiser by a small but busy firm that organised national and international conferences. She had difficulties with a number of key tasks that she was expected to perform. These included recording accurately the requirements of people who telephoned her to secure places at conferences, making hotel bookings on behalf of clients and producing speaker schedules for her conferences.

Anita was referred for specialist adult dyslexia training to develop her memory, verbal communication and organisational skills in a programme that involved attendance for training one day each week for 16 weeks. Her manager organised cover for her one-day per week absence by employing a temp, who was simply required to take over all of Anita's duties in her absence. Anita's manager, once he had arranged cover for her absence, took very much a back seat, leaving Anita's colleagues to support the temp and deal with any questions she had. The temp was not able to work as fast as she was expected to, and Anita's co-workers found that they were doing a lot of the temp's work as well as their own, in spite of which some of the tasks were still left undone. Anita found that she was working extra hard on the four days she was at work, and to add to her difficulties, she found that she had problems to solve arising from errors made by the temp, which her co-workers were routinely leaving for her to solve, because they felt it was her responsibility. Anita's workload actually increased while she was attending her training programme.

Anita was trained in specific strategies for completing a number of her work tasks; however, because of the work pressure she was under and the increased workload, she never had the opportunity to practise them in her workplace. Negotiations with her manager were amicable but failed to produce any significant change. Anita's performance improved only slightly after she completed training and, frustrated by her continued problems with her work, she resigned her post only months after completing her training.

Anita next gained employment in the personnel department of a large organisation, where her manager took account of her dyslexia, allowing her time off to do further training; this was an extended induction training to ensure that she had mastered the main job tasks and to support her in putting into operation the strategies that she had acquired from specialist dyslexia training. In addition, Anita's manager organised team meetings regularly to ensure that anything affecting her colleagues was discussed and that acceptable remedies were found. Anita progressed well in her new employment, eventually becoming able to perform her tasks as effectively as her colleagues.

HOW MANAGERS CAN IDENTIFY DYSLEXIA IN THEIR WORKERS

Managers need to be skilled in both recognising dyslexia in employees and knowing what to do with this information. Employees may be aware of their dyslexia but choose not to disclose it, or they may be unaware that they have the condition. In both cases, the manager who has become aware that dyslexia might be the issue may benefit from an awareness that the employees could respond in any one of a number of extreme ways. Approaches to dealing with the various responses that employees may make when a manager raises the issue of dyslexia are examined in Chapter 6, where the role of counselling skills is outlined. We shall now describe the other skill a manager needs to have, i.e., that of identifying when dyslexia might account for an employee's poor work performance.

ADULT DYSLEXIA SCREENING

Accurate identification of dyslexia is possible only through a structured diagnostic proce- dure, usually involving personal interviewing, psychometric testing and clinical judgement, all of which need to be conducted by, or under the supervision of, a chartered occupational psychologist. Prior to this procedure, however, individuals must be identified for referral to the psychologist for the formal assessment, and here managers and supervisors can play a key role. Managers need to have in their armoury of skills the ability to screen employees for dyslexia.

Dyslexia screening may be done by various methods ranging from those using standard tests, developed specifically for that purpose, to checklists that require only 'yes' or 'no' re- sponses. Caution needs to be exercised in selecting from among the various screening tools available, since many have been designed for use with children or in education and should not be used out of that context. Furthermore, some tools promoted as appropriate for workplaces are often just modifications of those procedures designed for children. They are inappro- priate for adults because they retain an educational or child orientation that, among other faults, may adversely affect the way adults respond to the screening questions and exercises.

Screening tests that are commercially available and designed for adults include the Dyslexia Adult Screening Test (DAST) developed by Fawcett & Nicolson (1998), which is easy to administer, taking about 30 minutes to complete, and provides a substantial amount of information. It is not diagnostic, but it can provide a very good indication of whether or not an individual should be referred for diagnostic assessment. Another tool for deciding whether an individual should be referred for formal assessment is the Bangor Dyslexia Test developed by Miles (1991). This is also short and easy to administer. It generates information that can be used in discussion with individuals to investigate their difficulties, but it is arguably not as comprehensive as the Dyslexia Adult Screening Test and not as useful for detecting dyslexia in adults.

Although professionally constructed screening tools such as the above may be useful, they are not always attractive options. For example, some people find the idea of formal testing of any type intimidating, while others perceive it as invasive and are reluctant to take part in it for that reason. The same people will often willingly take part in meetings with their personnel managers if all they are required to do is respond to a list of questions and be advised appropriately after some discussion of their answers.

Checklists are an attractive option for many people, and they can be useful if they are used appropriately. As far as managers are concerned, we believe that checklists, as part of a structured procedure involving sensitive interviewing or consultation of the employee, are often feasible in situations where other approaches are not.

The dyslexia-screening procedure presented below, which uses a dyslexia checklist, is one that we have developed in the context of our work as psychologists offering adult dyslexia services to organisations. It is a practical and pragmatic procedure designed for the world of work and intended to be accessible to managers with minimal requirements in terms of specialist training. The procedure requires from the user:

- an understanding of adult dyslexia in the world of work
- a basic skill in counselling and interviewing
- an ability to interpret the collected information.

The material in this book provides an understanding of dyslexia in a work context, an understanding which, if supplemented by appropriate training, is adequate for conducting effective screening. Counselling and interviewing skills are largely practical skills that are acquired by appropriate training and, ideally, developed with practice under supervision. Some managers and supervisors have good counselling and interviewing skills, as well as relevant understanding of adult dyslexia, and are therefore in a position to use the screening procedure when they have absorbed and understood the information presented below. Managers and supervisors who have not been trained in these skills should consider such training i.e., counselling and dyslexia awareness training. Such training is not only relevant to the context of dyslexia screening but is generally useful for any professional who has a human-resource function.

A DYSLEXIA-SCREENING PROCEDURE FOR THE WORKPLACE

The next section outlines how to use a screening procedure that we designed for use by human-resource personnel, line managers, trainers and counsellors, as well as individuals who wish to self-screen for dyslexia. Our own informal investigations of this tool have consistently demonstrated that it can very effectively distinguish dyslexic adults, including high-ability compensated dyslexics, from other adults who do not have the condition. It is, however, important to emphasise to potential users of this procedure that, while it may be very effective in identifying dyslexic people, it does not diagnose the condition. It simply indicates whether there is cause for concern and whether there is some justification for further investigation by, or under the supervision of, a chartered psychologist.

The screening procedure involves three steps:

1. administration of the Adult Dyslexia Checklist
2. calculating the scores
3. interpretation and conclusion.

Step 1

Complete the checklist in Table 5.1 for the person being screened.

Step 2

Count the number of ticks in the positive indicator boxes. Count the number of ticks in the compensation indicator box.

TABLE 5.1 An adult dyslexia screening checklist

Checklist Administration Instructions

FIRST ADMINISTRATION

- For each item on the checklist, the question, '*Is this person significantly weaker than average compared to peers*?', is investigated (see supplementary note 1).
- If the answer is 'no', the item is marked as FALSE.
- If the answer is 'yes', before marking the item TRUE, possible reasons for the weakness must be investigated (see supplementary note 2). If there is a reason for the weakness, the item is marked FALSE; if there is not, it is marked TRUE.

SECOND ADMINISTRATION

On the second administration, all those items marked TRUE or FALSE are re-examined (items marked DON'T KNOW are not examined in the second administration).

For each item marked TRUE, the question, '*Is this weakness incongruous with the person's behaviour*?', is investigated (see supplementary note 3).

- If the answer is 'yes', tick the positive indicator box for this item.
- If the answer is 'no', put a cross in positive indicator box for this item.
- Put a cross in the compensation indicator box for this item.

For each item marked FALSE, we consider the question, '*Was there ever a time when the person being screened would have had this item as a weakness*?' (see supplementary note 4).

- If the answer is 'yes', put a tick in the positive indicator box for this item and put a tick in the compensation indicator box.
- If the answer is 'no', put a cross in the positive indicator box and put a cross in the compensation indicator box.

continues overleaf

TABLE 5.1   (*continued*)

The Checklist Items

1. Confusing dates, days and times (for example, arriving for meetings on the wrong day or date or at the wrong time).

TRUE	FALSE	UNSURE/DON'T KNOW
	The positive indicator box	
	The compensation indicator box	

2. Underestimating how long it takes to complete journeys (for example, arriving late for appointments because travelling takes longer than estimated).

TRUE	FALSE	UNSURE/DON'T KNOW
	The positive indicator box	
	The compensation indicator box	

3. Arriving very early for meetings or appointments (for example, arriving an hour or more early for appointments as a strategy for not being late).

TRUE	FALSE	UNSURE/DON'T KNOW
	The positive indicator box	
	The compensation indicator box	

4. Taking too long to finish tasks (for example, regularly taking work home to complete when other people doing the same or similar tasks finish it in working hours).

TRUE	FALSE	UNSURE/DON'T KNOW
	The positive indicator box	
	The compensation indicator box	

5. Difficulty keeping track of what is said in conversations (for example, asking people a question that they have already answered).

TRUE	FALSE	UNSURE/DON'T KNOW
	The positive indicator box	
	The compensation indicator box	

TABLE 5.1 (*continued*)

6. Slow reading, particularly when a lot of detail needs to be remembered.

TRUE	FALSE	UNSURE/DON'T KNOW

The positive indicator box

The compensation indicator box

7. Poor spelling (for example, avoiding spelling by using words that can be spelt rather than more appropriate words that can't).

TRUE	FALSE	UNSURE/DON'T KNOW

The positive indicator box

The compensation indicator box

8. Difficulty taking notes in training courses or meetings (for example, writing notes that don't make sense because important facts have been left out).

TRUE	FALSE	UNSURE/DON'T KNOW

The positive indicator box

The compensation indicator box

9. Excessive talking and often not allowing others to speak (for example, giving too many examples to illustrate points and going off on tangents in conversations).

TRUE	FALSE	UNSURE/DON'T KNOW

The positive indicator box

The compensation indicator box

10. Forgetting messages or important facts, as in telephone conversations.

TRUE	FALSE	UNSURE/DON'T KNOW

The positive indicator box

The compensation indicator box

11. Difficulty remembering numbers (for example, forgetting 'pin' numbers or not remembering telephone numbers long enough to write them down).

TRUE	FALSE	UNSURE/DON'T KNOW

The positive indicator box

The compensation indicator box

continues overleaf

TABLE 5.1 (*continued*)

12. Writing numbers in the wrong order (for example, mistakenly writing the number *57* for *75*).

TRUE	FALSE	UNSURE/DON'T KNOW
	The positive indicator box	
	The compensation indicator box	

13. Forgetting people's names (for example, avoiding using people's names as a strategy for hiding the fact that the name is not known).

TRUE	FALSE	UNSURE/DON'T KNOW
	The positive indicator box	
	The compensation indicator box	

14. Word-finding difficulty (for example, leaving long gaps in conversations because the word has gone, or struggling to remember the names of common objects).

TRUE	FALSE	UNSURE/DON'T KNOW
	The positive indicator box	
	The compensation indicator box	

15. Forgetting information very soon after reading it (for example, forgetting a page of writing immediately after it has been read).

TRUE	FALSE	UNSURE/DON'T KNOW
	The positive indicator box	
	The compensation indicator box	

16. Difficulty completing tasks and following interruptions (for example, needing to start a task from the beginning after an interruption).

TRUE	FALSE	UNSURE/DON'T KNOW
	The positive indicator box	
	The compensation indicator box	

17. Interrupting people inappropriately in conversations (for example, stopping someone in mid-sentence with an irrelevant remark, question or comment).

TRUE	FALSE	UNSURE/DON'T KNOW
	The positive indicator box	
	The compensation indicator box	

TABLE 5.1 (*continued*)

18. Missing out details when doing tasks (for example, not filling in all the information requested on a form).

TRUE	FALSE	UNSURE/DON'T KNOW
The positive indicator box		
The compensation indicator box		

19. Poor organisational ability (for example, having a very untidy desk or creating piles of papers without ever attending to them).

TRUE	FALSE	UNSURE/DON'T KNOW
The positive indicator box		
The compensation indicator box		

20. Losing track of objects (for example, forgetting to pick up keys, pens, bags or papers).

TRUE	FALSE	UNSURE/DON'T KNOW
The positive indicator box		
The compensation indicator box		

21. Poor attention (for example, being easily distracted in open-plan offices by other people's conversations).

TRUE	FALSE	UNSURE/DON'T KNOW
The positive indicator box		
The compensation indicator box		

22. Forgetting or confusing items in sequences or lists (for example, failing to complete one or more job tasks from a list of tasks to do).

TRUE	FALSE	UNSURE/DON'T KNOW
The positive indicator box		
The compensation indicator box		

Step 3

Decide whether the results can be meaningfully interpreted by looking at the number of 'don't know' scores (see supplementary note 5).

The higher the positive indicator score, the more evidence there is of dyslexia and the more justification to refer the employee for a formal assessment. There is no hard and fast rule that can be applied, but, in general, we have found that most dyslexics obtain positive indicator scores of 8 or above; therefore, we believe it reasonable to refer someone with such a score. However, a lower score might also lead to referral for formal assessment if the weaknesses identified are very important to the work the person being screened is doing; i.e., the tool is designed to help focus attention on areas of concern that can be discussed, and the discussion is often more important than the positive indicator score obtained.

The compensation indicator score provides a measure of how much the person has compensated for their dyslexia, i.e., the larger the score the more the person has compensated. It is useful because it enables a discussion about strategies that the individual being screened may be using. Determining whether or not such strategies are effective in both the long and short term or only in the short term is important to determine whether strategies are likely to create problems in the future. Such an investigation may not take place until after a formal assessment but will still be useful since replacing maladaptive strategies is an important way to avoid the negative impact of dyslexia.

UNDERSTANDING THE SCREENING PROCEDURE

The effectiveness of the procedure is dependent on its being used as it was intended, and an understanding of the logic behind its design increases the likelihood that it will be used appropriately. Accordingly, some supplementary notes are provided in Table 5.2.

TABLE 5.2 Supplementary notes for the adult dyslexia screening checklist

1. How to answer the checklist items

- In using the checklist, the items should be marked according to the person's current situation.
- An item should produce a 'TRUE' response only if the person being screened shows the behaviour significantly more than colleagues or peers do. Alternatively, if there is no suitable comparator, the person needs to exhibit the behaviour more than could be considered reasonable. There needs to be evidence that the behaviour is persistent.
- A 'TRUE' score should not be based on a single event; for example, with reference to item 10, to mark this item TRUE, it is not sufficient that the person has forgotten telephone messages on only one or two occasions. Only when the subject has persistently done this over a long period of time should it be marked 'TRUE'.

2. Looking for explanations

- With the items marked TRUE, investigate why they are true.
- *Example 1.* With reference to point 13 on the checklist, if someone with a hearing impairment had this point marked 'TRUE', consideration would need to be given to whether he or she was forgetting names or just not hearing them.
- *Example 2.* With reference to point 7, if it emerges that the person attended very little school for reasons of illness, this, although a weakness, is not a positive indicator of dyslexia.
- *Example 3.* With reference to point 15, if the person has been under particular pressure or is stressed—for example, because of a marital breakdown—this might explain the weakness.

3. The concept of incongruity

- Dyslexia screening is not simply about determining whether certain behaviours are present or absent; it is about investigating the gaps between ability and performance and whether or not such gaps are incongruous with reference to all the available information about the individual being screened.

TABLE 5.2 (*continued*)

- Incongruity in an individual's behaviour is arguably the most significant indicator of dyslexia, and it is an important concept to grasp if the screening procedure is to be effective. In the workplace, dyslexic behaviours may often be very puzzling to observers, particularly when an apparently very able individual has difficulty doing relatively simple tasks. The examples below illustrate the incongruous behaviours of some adult dyslexics who attended a specialist adult dyslexia training course.
  —A chartered engineer who was respected for his practical engineering skills but known for his inability to extract any information from lectures or training courses that his colleagues and subordinates found easy to digest.
  —A business systems analyst who was able to remember large amounts of computer codes and related information, but who couldn't track even brief conversations.
  —A well-qualified and articulate solicitor who had difficulty following simple directions for getting from one building to another.
  —A successful scientist who couldn't spell most of the words he used in writing his papers for publication.
- All of the four examples above involve marked incongruity, i.e., weaknesses that are not predictable from the obvious talents of the people in question—such incongruities are strong indicators of dyslexia.

4. How strategies can hide dyslexia

- Many dyslexics expend considerable energy on developing strategies to deal with their dyslexia; consequently, although their dyslexia has created constitutional weaknesses, their weaknesses are not apparent. 'FALSE' responses to items may reflect the energy the person has put into developing strategies for overcoming fundamental dyslexic weaknesses.
- In-depth interviewing is sometimes required, with careful investigation of problems and difficulties subjects had in the past that they no longer have.
- *Example 1.* A person who attended memory training may have no difficulty recalling people's names but may have been motivated to attend the training because of forgetting names.
- *Example 2.* A person who reads fast may have developed speed-reading techniques because of particularly slow reading.

5. The significance of DON'T KNOW scores

- The higher the 'DON'T KNOW' score, the less knowledge the person completing the checklist has about the person being screened. This usually indicates that in-depth interviewing and careful questioning of the person being screened are required.
- If most items, more than about 15, produce 'DON'T KNOW' responses, there is usually little that can be concluded from the screening procedure.

MAKING DECISIONS ABOUT DYSLEXIA SCREENING

The screening procedure described above may be effectively used in situations where employees acknowledge that they are having problems and seek guidance from their managers or supervisors. The employees should then be fully informed about the purpose of the procedure, which may then be completed with the their informed consent. Sensitive exploration with the employees of the positive indicators from the checklist; i.e., step 2 in the above procedure, may be very helpful to both sides whether or not the result suggests the presence of dyslexia. This is because such discussion can bring to the surface explanations of why the employee exhibits the behaviour in question, which may be caused by reasons other than dyslexia. This is illustrated in the following case history.

Raj's Case History

Raj, a 22-year-old office assistant in a further education college, was responsible, along with other office staff, for dealing with telephone and face-to-face enquiries from prospective students. Soon after he took the job, his officer manager explained that a number of people had complained that he failed to provide some people who had telephoned for information about courses with all the information they had requested, and that some others had received the wrong information.

In addition to the above errors, his office manager pointed out to him that he was also forgetful in responding to requests from lecturers, and that he was extremely weak in spelling. This latter weakness resulted in the office manager's arranging for an assessment for dyslexia. Raj was not diagnosed as dyslexic, and in the interview it became apparent that he had very poor hearing. It was an impairment that he was aware of but embarrassed about. He had been told by his doctor that he needed a hearing aid, but he had not pursued this because he was unwilling, for reasons of personal vanity, to consider using one. It also transpired in the interview that his schooling had been very disrupted, as a consequence of both his hearing deficit and his childhood illnesses, which had kept him off school for long periods.

Raj provided the information about his schooling history and his hearing difficulty freely. Although he was embarrassed by his poor hearing, he was nevertheless quite willing, in a confidential setting, both to discuss it and to reconsider the hearing aid option; for example, as something he would use sparingly just in his workplace.

Raj revealed that during the assessment he had been anxious and worried that he might be labelled as stupid if he was found to be dyslexic; he was very relieved to discover that he was not. His anxiety was an unnecessary experience that could have been avoided if his manager had been able to use a screening procedure such as that described above. In all probability, the information that came out in the assessment would have been generated in a screening procedure, and action could then have been taken to help him perform his duties without the need for the formal assessment and the stress and anxiety it caused.

Of course, dyslexia screening is not a necessary precursor to referral for a psychologist's assessment, but it is an attractive alternative to such referral in a number of situations, most obviously when there is no past history of dyslexia's being diagnosed, but either the employee or the manager considers that it may offer an explanation of difficulties experienced, perhaps because of information obtained from books or media coverage of the subject. It may also be useful when employees are for some reason reluctant to undergo formal assessment; since it might raise their awareness of what the condition involves, it may make employees feel more comfortable with the idea of formal assessment.

DYSLEXIA SCREENING: THE IMPORTANCE OF TRUST AND CONFIDENTIALITY

In the context of employees being screened by their manager, the screening procedure described above is not an intrusive procedure and is, largely, merely a framework for organising information that the manager will typically already have (or can easily access) about the employees. Nevertheless, it should be used only with the informed consent of the person being screened. Managers can use it as a guide to understanding problems while relying only on observation of an employee's work behaviour. This is a reasonable course where a manager is simply trying to understand the possible causes of an employee's difficulties, but no conclusions could or should be drawn without involving the employee in the process. Managers who use it to interpret behaviours they have observed and conclude that the employee may be dyslexic must have the necessary skills to approach the subject with the employee and investigate the matter further; i.e., managers need to have appropriate counselling skills. It is important that managers acknowledge the individual's rights, as discussed in the next section.

DYSLEXIA SCREENING: RESPECTING THE INDIVIDUAL'S RIGHTS

Managers should take care to ensure that dyslexia-screening procedures do not lead to any deterioration in the way a line manager or supervisor treats the employee. An employer should exercise extreme caution when using information obtained from a screening procedure, whether the employee is interviewed or not. The information used and the conclusions drawn should be treated as confidential and should not be provided to, or shared with, others in the organisation without the (written) informed consent of the individual. In any case, information should be shared with others only if there is a justifiable purpose—for example, if it is being used as part of a procedure being developed by managers and supervisors to design adjustments, perhaps for an employee who wants neither an assessment nor a discussion about the possibility of being dyslexic.

A person's co-workers should never be given access to information about, or conclusions drawn from, any dyslexia-screening or assessment procedure without the fully informed consent of the person screened. When sharing information with a subject's co-workers, managers should ensure that no more than the essential information for the intended and agreed purpose is provided to them.

Positive screening should not be considered an end in itself and should never be confused with positive diagnosis. Employers need to be aware that many people find emotionally traumatic even the suggestion that they are dyslexic, and employers should be on their guard against making assertions about an employee's supposed dyslexia on the basis of positive screening alone. The purpose of a screening procedure should be to determine whether there is justification for referring the employee for formal assessment by a chartered occupational psychologist, assuming the employee agrees to this. Employers should be mindful that while screening may result in the eventual diagnosis of dyslexia, it is not necessary to identify the condition in order to make appropriate workplace adjustments for it, a topic that was discussed in detail in the previous chapter.

WORKPLACE STRESS AND DYSLEXIA: THE EMPLOYER'S RESPONSIBILITIES

Occupational stress is a topic that has produced sharp divisions of opinion between professional psychologists. Some believe the term is so poorly defined that it is meaningless, while others identify it as a major cause of illness-related absence in the workforce. Whatever the pros and cons of the arguments that stress is non-damaging, it would be unwise for organisations to ignore the topic. Stress is a recognised hazard in workplaces and employers have a statutory duty to carry out stress risk assessments under both the Health and Safety at Work Act 1974 and the Management of Health and Safety at Work Regulations 1992. The significance of stress as a workplace hazard became obvious at the end of the 1980's when a former employee of Northumberland County Council became the first person in British legal history to be awarded compensation for psychiatric damage caused by work-related stress. The employee in question was awarded £200 000 in compensation, although, he later settled 'out of court' for a payment of £175 000. There have been a number of cases since this one, in which people have been awarded similar 6-figure sums in compensation for injury arising from occupational stress. Inevitably, as law firms become more aggressive in their marketing and employees become more aware of how they can seek redress for the way their employment has harmed their health; more employees will turn to the courts for solutions. However, the high profile court cases, where individuals are awarded large amounts of compensation, do not cost industry as much as the day-to-day negative effects of stress on productivity. Arnold et al. (1998: p. 242), well-respected researchers in this field, state, on the basis of sound research, that

> Stress at work is costing industry a great deal of money. It has been estimated that nearly 10 per cent of the UK's Gross National Product is lost each year due to job generated stress in the form of sickness absence, high labour turnover, lost productive value, increased recruitment and selection costs and medical expenses.

These researchers have investigated workplace factors that are causally linked to stress, and they have identified five major categories, i.e., intrinsic job factors, role in the organisation, work relationships, career factors and the nature of the organisation, under each of which they present subcategories with explanations of how these mediate stress. Although all the observations that Arnold et al. (1998) make are relevant to adult dyslexics, two factors are particularly important in the context of dyslexia: stress from working long hours and stress from poor relationships at work. These two factors are frequently responsible for excessive stress in dyslexic workers, as we shall now explain.

THE DAMAGE CAUSED BY WORKING LONG HOURS

Arnold et al. (1998) explain how it is generally accepted that anyone working more than 40 hours per week is at risk of developing ill health through stress. They also point out that having too much work to do and having work that is too difficult lead to stress, in part, because these factors lead to long working hours. These findings are relevant to adult dyslexics because this group very often resort to working long hours as a strategy for coping with their work when appropriate reasonable adjustments for them have not been implemented.

Dyslexics in workplaces where they are disabled by the absence of appropriate adjustments may spend considerably more time working than they should just to keep up with others doing the same job. The practice of starting work early, finishing late and/or consistently relying on completing work tasks at home may be viewed in some quarters as the visible evidence of a dedicated and loyal employee. In the long term, however, such behaviour is damaging to the individual, to the company and to the economy. Psychological studies consistently indicate that this type of work behaviour causes high levels of stress and illness, disrupts relationships and causes burnout.

It is of course true that many non-dyslexics fall into this category of worker, i.e., one that overworks, and therefore the question arises, 'How is it a dyslexic issue?' The answer is that adult dyslexics who have not compensated for their memory inefficiency always need to do more than their peers in order to maintain an acceptable work output unless the employer has made appropriate reasonable adjustments. It is not that dyslexics are any more susceptible to stress than non-dyslexics—any employer following a punishing schedule of overwork would experience burnout—but rather that dyslexics are likely to enter the 'at risk of burnout' category sooner than non-dyslexics because workplaces are less accommodating for them than for their non-dyslexic peers.

Many very able dyslexic adults take up employment that is well within their ability, only to find that inadequacies in the organisational structure disable them. They face jobs where they have too much to do and where the tasks are too difficult for them to do because they do not have access to the appropriate tools, knowledge or flexibility that they need to do the work to the expected standard. The lack of appropriate adjustments effectively disables such people and exposes them to the dangers of stress. Long hours, too much work and work that is too difficult to complete are generally outcomes that employees face when they have irresponsible employers. Although such employers may be content to ignore the overwork, it is worth noting that this might not protect them from litigation since the law does not accept ignorance as a defence when relevant knowledge about the dyslexia could have been obtained.

Dyslexic employees, however, may find that they face the risk of stress even if their employer is very responsible and has implemented policies designed to avoid stress in the workforce. Effective selection procedures, adequate induction training, good personnel support and an explicit policy of discouraging employees from working longer hours than they contracted to work are procedures that should reduce stress. However, such policies are usually developed without due attention being given to adjustments for people with dyslexia (see Chapter 4) and are therefore not as effective with dyslexics as they are with their peers. Dyslexics often hide their overtime working by taking work home and so become susceptible to stress from this practice. Dyslexics exposed to the stress risk associated with working long hours often hide their behaviour from scrutiny because of beliefs, sometimes well founded, that they will be judged as failing if they are open about their need to work long hours.

HOW POOR RELATIONSHIPS AT WORK CONTRIBUTE TO STRESS

Hans Selye (1974), an influential researcher in the field of stress, argued that learning to live with other people is one of the most stressful aspects of life. More recently, Makin et al. (1996) made similar observations but pointed out that other people may be a source of support as well as a source of stress. Arnold et al. (1998) comment that little research has been done on this positive effect, but, with reference to relationships between workers and managers, they report that there is much support from doctors and clinical psychologists for the idea that problems of emotional disability result when there are poor relationships between managers and those they manage. With reference to relationships with colleagues, they report that, because people spend such a large amount of time at work, relationships 'can be a huge source of stress'.

Although dyslexics are not more likely to develop stress than other people, they are more likely to find themselves in stress-inducing situations. In the context of work relationships, as we discussed in Chapter 3, dyslexic workers often find that they are isolated because their fellow workers misunderstand their behaviour. For example, some dyslexics avoid all social contact while working on a task, as a strategy for preventing distractions from taking them off track, because they are unable to restart tasks efficiently if they are distracted. In this sense they are more likely to experience stress arising from poor relationships. Other factors conspire to undermine relationships at work; for example, when a dyslexic employee under-performs, it naturally leads to a discussion with the line manager, and this may be good or it may lead to deterioration in the relationship. The manager who has an awareness of dyslexia may well be able to assist the employee, but, more typically, the discussion leads to an impasse, with neither party knowing why the problems have arisen. The explanations by the employee may include that the induction training was inadequate, that other training had not been effective or that the instructions given were simply forgotten. However, such explanations are often dismissed or lead to false conclusions concerning the employee's intellectual ability. The outcome may be a marked deterioration in the relationship, with the employee feeling that the manager lacks understanding or concern, and the manager judging the employee lazy, incompetent or disruptive. Both parties feel the stress, but the employee is usually more affected. In a similar fashion, co-workers often make negative judgements about dyslexic employees. Errors or any failure by employees to work at the same rate as their co-workers is likely to cause resentment, as are concessions given without appropriate explanations to dyslexic employees by the manager.

If stress is to be minimised, organisations need to take positive action to combat it. Being aware of how dyslexia manifests itself in the workplace, and working to create dyslexia-friendly environments, as described in Chapter 4, are powerful weapons. Dyslexia-awareness training that presents the condition within the context of a social model and explains what organisations can do is highly desirable. For example, advising adult dyslexics that, because of their disability, they should be prepared to work longer hours than they are paid to work is not an acceptable position for an employer to take. It is similar to advising disabled employees with mobility restrictions that they should work an hour longer each day to make up for the fact that they are slow in getting around their workplace.

Awareness of dyslexia among people in workplaces would reduce the likelihood of stress arising from deterioration in workplace relationships; such awareness is a key to ensuring that stress between co-workers is avoided. Managers need to control actively the way perceptions of dyslexia develop in the workforce, and one way of promoting this is to make dyslexia awareness training available to the entire workforce. Dyslexia-awareness training, supported with ongoing monitoring, and explicit and high-profile policies of non-discrimination against dyslexics, reduces the likelihood of the stressful breakdown of relationships at work. This type of action is particularly desirable in situations where dyslexic workers might otherwise face hostility from their work colleagues. As well as the obvious common-sense reasons for taking appropriate action, managers have a responsibility under the Disability Discrimination Act of 1995 to take such action. Under the act, employees can initiate legal proceedings against their employer based on the actions of another employee, and it is not a defence for employers to show the action took place without their knowledge or approval. It does, however, contribute to a legal defence against allegations of disability discrimination if employers can demonstrate that they took reasonably practicable steps to prevent their employees from indulging in discriminatory behaviour. The Disability Rights Commission (DDA, Section 4.56) have given the following advice on how employers should deal with this issue:

> Employers should communicate to their employees and agents any policy they may have on disability matters, and any other policies which have elements relevant to disabled employees (such as health, absenteeism or equal opportunities). All staff should be made aware that it is unlawful to discriminate against disabled people, and be familiar with the policies and practices adopted by their employer to ensure compliance with the law. Employers should provide guidance on non-discriminatory practices for all employees, so they will be aware what they should do and how to deal with disabled colleagues and disabled applicants for vacancies in the organisation, and should ensure so far as possible that these policies and practices are implemented.

Employers need to exercise caution in informing some or all of their employees about a dyslexic worker's condition, but informing workers is sometimes unavoidable. If an adjustment is introduced that is highly visible—for example, assigning some workers less work than their colleagues—it is usually more productive to inform those other workers. If they are kept in the dark, it may lead to deterioration in relationships, with all the damaging stress this entails. The Disability Rights Commission (DDA, Section 4.59) has given the following advice on this issue:

> It may be necessary to tell one or more of a disabled person's colleagues (in confidence) about a disability which is not obvious and/or whether any special assistance is required. This may be limited to the person's supervisor, or it may be necessary to involve other colleagues, depending on the nature of the disability and the reason they need to know about it.

Revealing personal information is a delicate subject that should be managed with sensitivity, and there are important legal implications about which employers would be wise to make themselves aware. Once again the Disability Rights Commission (DDA, Section 4.60) have given advice on this.

> The extent to which an employer is entitled to let other staff know about an employee's disability will depend at least in part on the terms of employment. An employer could be held to be discriminating in revealing such information about a disabled employee if the employer would not reveal similar information about another person for an equally legitimate management purpose; or if the employer revealed such information without consulting the individual, whereas the employer's usual practice would be to talk to an employee before revealing personal information about him.

DYSLEXIA AS A SOURCE OF STRESS IN NON-DYSLEXIC EMPLOYEES

Employers' failure to respond effectively to the needs of their dyslexic employees may have enormous implications not just for these employees but also for others in the organisation. Non-dyslexic employees are at risk of their workload's being increased or obstructed whenever an employer fails either to make adjustments or take full account of adjustments made. A common scenario is that employees find they are required to work considerably harder or longer than they should reasonably be expected to work because they have been reassigned tasks that have been taken away from a dyslexic employee. This represents a poor management decision since, rather than solving a problem, it simply displaces it. A reasonable adjustment that enables one employee represents little gain if it disables another. Management decisions that have a less obvious potential to lead to stress reactions include failing to investigate the impact a dyslexic employee may have on co-workers who are responsible for, or dependent on, tasks that must be completed by the dyslexic. This is illustrated in the following case history.

Karen's Case History

Karen, a personnel officer in a large retail company, had, in addition to her normal duties, special responsibility for mentoring newer members of staff. She was also a National Vocational Qualifications assessor for other employees in the organisation.

When Karen was mentoring programmes or overseeing someone working for a National Vocational Qualification, she was given an agreed number of hours to do this. However, when Jonathan, a diagnosed dyslexic, joined her team and started working towards his National Vocational Qualifications, Karen discovered that he was significantly different from other staff she had worked with in the past. Because of his dyslexia, Jonathan was completely incapable of organising the considerable amounts of documents, and related record keeping, for his National Vocational Qualifications. He was quite bewildered by the various tables and charts that he was required to complete, and he was overwhelmed by the quantity of reading and paperwork generally. The onus of responsibility for ensuring that this work was completed devolved on Karen, who was keen to assist him. While Karen's workload took account of the time and effort she was expected to dedicate to her duties as National Vocational Qualifications assessor, it took no account of what an assessor would need to do for a dyslexic candidate such as Jonathan.

Karen became progressively more tired as she struggled to cope with the excessive demands that her employer was making of her, albeit inadvertently, by failing to acknowledge that dyslexic trainees require more support than their non-dyslexic peers. She raised her concerns with her line manager, but he did not accept her argument that her workload was greater because of her colleague's dyslexia, and she was forced to continue in this very stressful environment. With the support of her trade union, however, she forced her employer to make appropriate changes, but not before her stress had caused ill health and a lowering of her work performance.

Karen's case history shows how a failure to manage dyslexia effectively may expose people who are not dyslexic to the psychological injury, e.g., clinical depression, which may be caused by stress. Although no legal action against the employer was taken in the case described above, Karen arguably had a strong since she had clearly been exposed to health risks, made her employer aware of the fact and received no support.

Employers who fail to manage dyslexia effectively are exposing themselves to the threat of legal action, not just under the Disability Discrimination Act of 1995, but also under Health and Safety legislation. The Health and Safety Executive recognise work-related stress as a hazard that may cause psychological injury. As stated above, there have already been successful legal actions by employees against their employers, the basis of which was that they sustained psychological injury as a result of employment-generated stress. In the example outlined above, in which employment-related stress was produced in non-dyslexic employees as a consequence of their employer's failure to take proper account of a dyslexic employee's needs, the employer could be seen to be failing in the duty of care to provide a safe working environment for all workers. Whether or not an employee would have a case in circumstances such as those described above will become clear only if and when such a case reaches the courts. What is clear now is that the employer stands to lose by not taking action to avoid such eventualities. Making reasonable adjustments is important, but it needs to be accompanied by effective management that takes full account of the impact that dyslexia has on organisations, including its potential for producing stress-related disorders.

The implications of not taking full account of dyslexia in the workplace may be devastating in both psychological and financial terms. If, however, organisations do take account of dyslexia—for example, by ensuring that they manage diversity in the workforce—dyslexia is unlikely to be a source of problems, and this is clearly the common-sense solution. At present, common sense is not making the impact it should, with the result that many dyslexics are exposed to stressful environments; some of these people will need counselling to survive the experience, a topic that is discussed in the next chapter.

6

COUNSELLING ADULT DYSLEXICS

INTRODUCTION

While the differences between psychotherapy and counselling may be debated, we shall not be concerning ourselves with that debate. We shall use the term 'counselling' to refer to any procedure that focuses on helping clients solve a specific personal, or work-related, problem or to make progress in their personal development. The key aspects of the therapeutic exchange discussed here, which are specific to dyslexics, still remain pertinent to both counselling and psychotherapy. We are defining 'psychotherapy' loosely as any intervention that aims to facilitate major changes affecting the whole person, by thinking, talking, listening and reflecting.

Miles (1988) draws a distinction between 'generalist' and 'specialist' counselling expertise. The former he describes as being common to all forms of counselling, including the ability to be a good listener, show empathy and be non-judgemental. The 'specialist' expertise refers to skills that are required for specific areas of concern in relation to individual conditions. According to Miles, counsellors with specialist expertise are those who have a 'technical knowledge over and above their ability to listen and discuss'.

This chapter will focus on the specialist expertise that we have concluded is both relevant to and required for effective support, training and counselling of dyslexic adults. Our conclusions are based on more than 25 years of combined experience in providing services to adult dyslexics in employment. Although generalist skills are not examined in this chapter in any significant detail, the underlying assumption is that anyone providing support services to adult dyslexics will have these skills as well as other appropriate qualifications.

The chapter starts by examining some important general issues that counsellors and therapists need to understand if they are to provide effective interventions for adult dyslexics. Those areas where counsellors need to use mostly generalist skills are outlined, and this is followed by a discussion of dyslexic issues that require specialist skills. The role and benefits of Internet counselling, or 'cybercounselling', are discussed, and the chapter concludes with some brief comments on psychotherapy and the possible applications of the Internet as a psychotherapeutic tool for adult dyslexics.

APPROPRIATE COUNSELLING FOR ADULT DYSLEXICS

There are many theoretical approaches to counselling that have relevance to helping adult dyslexics overcome their emotional, personal and related problems. Rogers' client-centred therapy (Rogers, 1961) is an effective generalist counselling that, if part of a counsellor's armoury, is also an adequate tool for dealing with many of the general problems that dyslexics face. The principle of 'unconditional positive regard', i.e., complete and unqualified acceptance of a client's feelings and actions, which is central to client-centred therapy, is a powerful concept that is particularly appropriate for dyslexics. Although it may be argued that unconditional acceptance is not entirely achievable, it offers many dyslexics an entirely new and very positive experience. Unconditional positive regard is particularly welcomed by those whose childhood involved constant criticism of their actions and very little in terms of significant others acknowledging their feelings. The central goal of client-centred therapy, to support the client in a journey to become a fully functioning (mature) person, is very appropriate for adult dyslexics.

It is important to emphasise that client-centred counselling is not, in itself, sufficient to solve many of the common problems that lay siege to adult dyslexics. An integrative approach is required, where client-centred counselling is part of a flexible intervention structure that is responsive to the changing priorities and psychological state of the client. For example, dyslexic persons' understanding of the nature of their difficulties is pivotal in enabling them to address those difficulties, and when this is legitimate business, the 'cognitive restructuring' approaches to interventions, discussed below, are more appropriate and successful in moving this group towards their goals than is client-centred counselling. There is no doubt, however, that when clients are struggling to cope with emotionally draining thoughts about their early life, client-centred counselling has a great deal to offer.

Cognitive restructuring therapies are 'directive', in contrast to client-centred counselling, which is 'non-directive'. A directive approach to counselling is one that effectively proposes solutions to problems or suggests actions that the client might consider taking to cope with personal difficulties. The benefit of directive approaches for dyslexics is that they involve less open-ended talking by the client. Exchanges between client and counsellor involve clear, unambiguous statements, questions and assertions. For example, rational emotive therapy, which was developed by Ellis (1962), is a directive counselling approach that has a great deal to offer to adult dyslexics, because many dyslexics are blocked in their personal development by maladaptive thoughts and feelings. They have acquired behaviours that undermine the development of their potential, and they need the practical advice on action to overcome this barrier that rational emotive therapy can provide.

Rational emotive therapy assumes that maladaptive feelings are caused by irrational beliefs. Ellis argues that, through mistaken assumptions, people make excessive demands upon themselves. For example, the adult dyslexics who assume, incorrectly, that most people are very skilled in spelling, and who consequently think that their own spelling skills are much worse than they really are, are typical of those who make excessive demands of themselves. Rational emotive therapy challenges such assumptions. It operates in what is known as an 'ABC' framework.

- 'A' is the activating event—for example, the fact that Jack has failed to get promoted.
- 'B' is the beliefs Jack held about the activating event A; for example, Jack may believe that his failure is evidence that he is worthless.

- 'C' is the behavioural reaction arising from 'B', which Jack mistakenly thinks is directly related to 'A'; for example, Jack might feel depressed and never bother trying for promotion in the future.

Rational emotive therapy focuses on changing Jack's beliefs, making them rational and tied to what happens outside the person rather than tied to individual failings constructed inside the person.

Another similar example of cognitive restructuring is the work of Beck et al. (1979), which attributes numerous psychological problems to the negative patterns in which individuals think about themselves. This approach involves questioning clients so that they can discover for themselves the distortions in their thinking and can then make changes that are more consistent with reality. This approach is illustrated later in this chapter.

COUNSELLING ADULT DYSLEXICS: PERCEPTIONS, FALSEHOODS AND PREJUDICES

It is crucially important that any counsellor or therapist working with dyslexic clients is aware of the various external influences that operate and have operated in the dyslexic person's past. There is a great deal of general misunderstanding about the nature of dyslexia; the ability and potential of affected persons are often underestimated. Extreme prejudice and false beliefs abound, and they can, and frequently do, determine who the dyslexic person becomes.

The fact that, until relatively recently, dyslexia was perceived as a childhood malady that somehow disappeared in adulthood is a key to understanding the psychology of ignorance that persists about adult dyslexia. The fact that dyslexia is still largely conceptualised as a purely educational issue is just as important, since most employed dyslexics are disabled by deficits, unrelated to literacy and learning, in the provisions available to them in the workplace.

Although adult dyslexia is now a recognised condition, the framework in which most researchers attempt to explain it is an educational, as opposed to an occupational, one. This framework distorts considerably the nature of the difficulties that dyslexic people experience. This distortion exists as much in the minds of dyslexics themselves as it does in the minds of their employers, work colleagues, friends and family. Counsellors should be mindful of these distortions and misrepresentations, and seek to determine, by careful inquiry with all clients, the context in which their dyslexia operates. They need to determine the specificity of each dyslexic condition and what interventions will best progress their clients towards a less troubled existence. Counsellors will need to work with their dyslexic clients without being dominated by the stereotyping of the dyslexic personality portrayed in the media and elsewhere.

WHAT COUNSELLORS CAN ACHIEVE

Many of the difficulties that dyslexics have are the consequence of a medical-model orientation towards disability, i.e., a conceptualisation of dyslexia as an illness and personal tragedy (see Chapter 2). Dyslexic people are different from non-dyslexic people in that they have a pattern of strengths and weaknesses that differs from that of non-dyslexics. Society, however, construes this difference as an illness, together with the idea that somewhere there is a cure. Consequently, many dyslexics are on a wild goose chase; there is no illness, and therefore no cure may be found, but seeking the elusive cure becomes for some dyslexics an obsession. There is a great deal of potential in interventions that focus on realigning perceptions that dyslexics have of themselves as ill within a social model framework so that the concept of illness as the cause of their difficulties may be replaced with one of failure by society as the cause.

There is an important distinction to be made between solving dyslexic problems and 'solving dyslexia'; the latter is a futile enterprise while the former may be a rewarding activity for client and counsellor alike. Many clients look for a utopian kind of cure, which will not be forthcoming; counsellors have an important role in empowering their clients to confront and modify this type of self-defeating behaviour. In identifying failures of society as the cause of problems facing their dyslexic clients, counsellors clearly risk promoting in those clients negative and defeatist attitudes; however, counsellors have methods they can use to combat this tendency. For example, interventions structured around rational emotive therapy can give clear guidance about how to cope with such failures of society and how to avoid being a victim of them. In this sense, rational emotive therapy represents a challenge to the medical model of disability, and it can promote attitudes consistent with a social-model orientation. Counsellors may decide that such a change is one that offers their clients the most benefits, in which case they will be promoting changes in society that are much needed for dyslexics generally.

Although substantial progress towards the social model of disability has been made both nationally and within the European Union in the last 10 years, it has had far less impact on dyslexia and hidden disabilities generally than on visible disabilities. In spite of significant progress in Europe towards social inclusion for disabled people, dyslexics are still largely the victims of a medical model of 'normalisation', i.e., a model that classifies dyslexia as an illness and dyslexics as abnormal. Dismantling belief systems that have their origins in these assumptions represents a considerable challenge to counsellors, but success has many rewards. Once the burden of medical-model thinking has been lifted from their shoulders, dyslexics can start to move forward to take control of their lives.

THE IMPACT OF LABELLING ON ADULT DYSLEXICS

Many of the psychological difficulties that dyslexic people experience have their origins in the stigma associated with the term 'dyslexia'. The stigma comes not only from the condition's being classed as an abnormality but also from the other labels that are used to describe dyslexics, labels such as 'learning disabled', 'specific learning difficulties' and 'slow readers'. These labels are all the product of convenient medical-model explanations, and for the most part they are misleading, yet they powerfully determine attitudes and undermine dyslexic people's confidence. Many dyslexics need to express their feelings and responses to the labels that they have been given, a need which has obvious implications for counselling objectives.

Dyslexic clients who are aware of their condition have usually had it confirmed by a psychologist's assessment. This may have provided them with a convenient explanation in the form of a medical or academic definition of dyslexia but little in terms of person-oriented descriptions and conceptualisations. The clients may therefore need assistance in developing their own way of describing and defining their experience of being dyslexic. The process of developing acceptance and understanding of how dyslexia has affected their life requires insight and self-knowledge, which are, for the dyslexic client, both particularly important and very hard to achieve. Understanding is unlikely to result in significant progress for dyslexic persons if it is limited to the nature of their dyslexic difficulties. Counsellors may wish to promote in their clients a better understanding of their sense of identity, their emotional experiences, their intellectual life and their interpersonal relationships, all of which contribute to who they are as persons. From an early age, most dyslexic clients have experienced a lack of contact with these important structural elements of human existence, and this will usually have compromised the development of their self-esteem and self-image. As already mentioned above, various interventions, such as the cognitive restructuring approaches to counselling, may be used to assist clients in challenging such areas of weakness. Substantial progress may be achieved by employing methods that best enable clients to 'reframe' and interpret their experiences positively. Dyslexics stand to benefit considerably by reinterpreting negative past experiences as learning experiences to draw upon in overcoming present problems; this can help them to plan a successful future.

Dyslexics often have difficulties that are a consequence of people's prejudice towards them. This can take the form of explicit assaults on their self-concept—for example, derogatory remarks such as 'thick', 'slow', 'lazy', 'retarded' or 'stupid'. Such prejudice may also be implicit in the way other people treat them, as by being condescending or dismissive. The outcome of this is that the clients may intellectually understand their dyslexia and its causal relationship to who they have become, but may still retain underlying negative attitudes and beliefs about being dyslexic. The person's fundamental sense of being at fault because of dyslexia is a perception that may need to be challenged; without such a challenge, any progression in counselling or therapy towards health may well be much slower than it might be. Improvements at a conscious level will be affected by the unconscious negative beliefs. Self-acceptance, at both the conscious and unconscious levels, may assist dyslexic persons to reach a position of being and feeling fundamentally integrated as fully accepted and acceptable members of society. Self-knowledge of the pattern of dyslexia may be important because it may help the persons to understand their strengths and natural talents. This may in turn inform them of what needs to be done, what difficulties need to be overcome and how they may be assisted by therapeutic counselling. This proactive approach to self-acceptance is likely to be more dynamic than unconditional positive regard.

HOW DYSLEXIC SELF-PERCEPTIONS DETERMINE EXPERIENCES

Looking more closely at the issues of stereotyping and labels relates to what advocates for the disabled have deemed to be the preferred terms. 'People with dyslexia' is generally preferred to the term 'dyslexic people'. However, use of the latter term is preferred in terms of the social model of dyslexia; the term conveys a more useful message to therapists and counsellors than does the former. To view a client as someone who has dyslexia is to adopt a reductionist medical-model perspective. Identifying someone as a person with dyslexia promotes an understanding of dyslexia as a discrete entity that is separate from the individual. Such an orientation is likely to expose clients to the danger of identifying parts of themselves as being non-dyslexic and therefore 'healthy', while believing that their dyslexic traits are unhealthy and that they need treatment for their dyslexic illness. The view of dyslexia as an unhealthy part of the person undermines what is probably the most potent intervention that can be provided to dyslexic adults, a strategy that we may call 'positive reframing'. This intervention focuses on changing negative perceptions of dyslexia as a problem to be solved into positive perceptions of dyslexia as a solution to problems. For example, appropriate counselling can transform the belief that dyslexic weaknesses such as poor memory and lack of verbal fluency are barriers to employment into the belief that dyslexic strengths, such as good visualisation skills and lateral thinking ability, are highly relevant employment-related skills. Dyslexics can come to realise that many of their strengths are in demand in workplaces, that their strengths and potential strengths may in fact make them strong candidates for employment, not infrequently giving them an edge over their non-dyslexic peers.

The point being stressed here is that dyslexic persons will generally find it more constructive to come to terms with the difficulty dyslexia creates if they are supported in the process of accepting themselves as a whole. It is more appropriate for clients to view their dyslexia as the fabric from which they are made rather than a disease they have caught. It is important to understand the negative impact that dyslexia has in the development of the individual, but this should not be confused with the conclusion that it has only negative impacts. The counsellor who both strives to ameliorate the negative impacts of dyslexia and enhance the positive aspects is developing the client. For many dyslexics, the key requirement from the counselling environment is an approach that honours and supports difference instead of one that constrains the dyslexic client into an uncomfortable and unhealthy conformity.

UNDERSTANDING DYSLEXIC STRENGTHS AND WEAKNESSES

It is very useful for counsellors to have a detailed understanding of how the constitutional differences between dyslexics and non-dyslexics make certain tasks more difficult for dyslexics than for non-dyslexics. It is particularly useful to keep in mind that dyslexia is characterised by an inefficiency in working memory, as discussed in Chapter 2. Knowing how this memory difference affects dyslexic people's behaviour is an important element in creating an empathic relationship with the client. Being able to work with the memory difference that characterises dyslexia is a key skill that counsellors should have in their repertoire of 'specialist' skills for counselling dyslexic clients. Counsellors who wish to attract dyslexic clients should explore what adjustments they can make to ensure that dyslexic people can easily access their services. This would certainly involve giving some thought to dyslexic memory differences and related dyslexic strengths and weaknesses. For example, giving consideration to counselling by telephone, fax and email may prove fruitful, but each option requires specific skills if it is to be successful. For example, telephone counselling requires sensitivity to dyslexic memory weaknesses.

A direct consequence of the inefficiency in working memory that characterises dyslexia is that a dyslexic person needs to expend more energy and effort acquiring certain skills than does a non-dyslexic person. Notably, dyslexics have difficulty remembering facts, figures, messages, names and sequences of instructions. They also have weaknesses in organisational skills and timekeeping that are due to difficulty with the concept of time.

Adult dyslexics have difficulty tracking conversations, expressing themselves succinctly and keeping in mind what they intend to say. Finally, as we have seen in Chapter 1, dyslexics take longer to develop literacy skills, often working much harder than do their non-dyslexic peers simply to keep up with them in the learning process. All of these difficulties, which are a direct consequence of the dyslexic inefficiency in working memory, have been termed the 'primary symptoms' of dyslexia by McLoughlin et al. (1994).

In contrast to the primary symptoms are the indirect consequences of dyslexia, which McLoughlin, Fitzgibbon & Young call the 'secondary' symptoms. Secondary symptoms are psychological conditions and disorders, ranging from mild to severe. There is a lack of certainty regarding the level of such disorders in the dyslexic population, but, according to Prosser (1999), it is highly likely that most of these conditions remain undiagnosed. Our experience is entirely consistent with what Prosser claims to be the case; i.e., a large proportion of the dyslexic clients we have seen have had undiagnosed psychological problems and disorders.

SECONDARY DYSLEXIC SYMPTOMS: THE PSYCHOLOGICAL PROBLEMS OF DYSLEXICS

The secondary symptoms of dyslexia include anxiety, low self-esteem, lack of confidence and depression. These factors typically have multiple origins, some of which are obvious, such as continual negative feedback during schooling, and some less obvious, such as lack of positive expectations. In the vast majority of cases when dyslexics have serious psychological disorders because of their dyslexia, these can be traced back to childhood experiences. Continual negative feedback from teachers is a common childhood experience for many dyslexics and a cause of many problems in adulthood. The effect of negative feedback is very often to demotivate children; it does this by communicating to them that nothing they can do will lead to success. Children often develop a condition known as 'learned helplessness', as described by Seligman (1975); it is a state characterised by the strong belief of affected people that no action that they could take to solve their personal problems would solve those problems. Learned helplessness is a state that leads to low self-esteem, depression and other significant problems of living.

Lack of positive expectations of children by their parents and teachers is another important factor, related to the negative feedback factor discussed above, that leads to psychological disorders in adult dyslexics. Low expectations lead to a range of maladaptive and dysfunctional cognitions in the child that serve to undermine the development of adaptive coping mechanisms. Many dyslexics simply fail to develop coping skills to deal with emotional difficulties, and their lack of experience in coping effectively determines that they will go on failing to develop relevant coping strategies (Lindsay et al., 1998).

THE COMPLEXITY OF DYSLEXIC SYMPTOMS

It is important to understand how distinct dyslexic weaknesses and symptoms may be related, how they interact to produce additional difficulties in the person's life and how they mediate a range of maladaptive behaviours. The complex interaction of the psychological difficulties and the constitutional weaknesses (primary and secondary symptoms) of dyslexics is very fruitful material for examination in counselling contexts. If counsellors can help their clients gain insights into these complex relationships between their various weaknesses, those clients can start to exercise more control over their own lives and thus make progress towards the goal of becoming fully functioning members of society.

It is instructive to map how one symptom of dyslexia can lead to a complex of problems. For example, if we look at the most obvious primary symptoms, which are literacy weaknesses, we can examine the process. The need to learn in a prescribed way, as well as the dominance of written communication, results in children with literacy weaknesses having a great deal of difficulty keeping up with their peers. Medical-model thinking conceptualises this as an individual failing, and the highly inefficient and inflexible school system, with its refusal to accommodate diversity, disables the dyslexic child by not providing an appropriate learning environment. The children grow up believing that they are failures.

The dominance of medical-model thinking not only obscures people's understanding of how problems could be solved but also causes the development of strongly negative attitudes and prejudices. As we discussed in Chapter 1, the medical-model orientation towards dyslexia leads to damaging discriminating behaviours towards some dyslexic children by significant others. The hostile environment, which is inextricably tied to the medical-model thinking, serves to undermine the confidence of many dyslexic children and contributes to the development in those children of significant low self-esteem and negative self-image. The disruption of the normal development of these basic psychological structures, self-esteem and self-image, is exacerbated if, as often happens, the children's peers, family members and teachers, dismiss them as having low intelligence because of their low skill-acquisition rate. A direct consequence of low self-esteem, poor self-image and lack of confidence is the reduction of the child's motivation to do anything, a result which people interpret as further evidence of low ability. Being assessed as failing in this way often leads dyslexic children to be isolated and excluded from those activities where they would normally acquire the social skills to function effectively in social groupings, further increasing their isolation. If, in childhood, dyslexics are unfortunate enough to be the victims of the processes described above, then, as adults they are, as a consequence of the conditions developed in their childhood, vulnerable to the development of various disorders, notably learned helplessness, anxiety and depression. Counsellors can most effectively deal with these interrelated disorders by appreciating their origin and development; interventions will usually focus on past as well as current experiences.

THE FOUR LEVELS OF DYSLEXIC FUNCTIONING: A FRAMEWORK DETERMINING INTERVENTION

As we have seen, the primary and secondary difficulties outlined above generally interact, creating complex problems for the dyslexic individual. Training and counselling can ameliorate some of these problems by increasing dyslexic persons' control of their social and work environments. Increasing control is the route to success for dyslexics and a factor that distinguishes successful from unsuccessful dyslexics. Gerber et al. (1992) have outlined how control is the determinant of concrete life experiences such as academic and occupational success. Control can be achieved by facilitating the development of self-awareness, understanding of dyslexia and knowledge of individual strengths and weaknesses. The key to this development is the implementation of compensatory strategies. That is to say that compensation is a prerequisite for dyslexic people to gain control over their lives. Compensation may be conscious or unconscious but is most effective when it is conscious. Conscious compensation allows people to create, tailor and fine-tune their compensatory strategies to their lifestyle and environment. McLoughlin, Fitzgibbon & Young (1994) combined these two dimensions, i.e., consciousness and compensation, to identify four levels of social and psychological functioning of the dyslexic client, each of which is described below.

- At level 1 are dyslexic people who are not aware of their weaknesses and have not developed any strategies to overcome them. Adult dyslexics at this level have learned to live with their particular difficulties and weaknesses. They are unaware that they are less able than their peers; they accept that there are certain tasks they cannot do and they live with that reality. Individuals at this level have made no effort, consciously or unconsciously, to compensate for their poor skill development.
- At level 2 are dyslexic people who are aware of their weaknesses but have not developed strategies to overcome them. These people may be unaware that their weaknesses are due to dyslexia. While realising that they have specific weaknesses, they have not developed compensatory strategies for dealing with them. When challenged about their predicament, they may suggest that the cause is poor education, low motivation or other external factors. The difficulties that they are most concerned with are likely to be reading, writing and spelling. People at this level have accepted their limitations or may have, in disillusionment, learned to live with their difficulties.
- At level 3 are dyslexic people who are aware of their weaknesses and have acquired compensatory strategies but unconsciously. Dyslexics at this stage of awareness have similarities to the preceding group, as they acknowledge their difficulties, but they differ in terms of their response; e.g., they try to achieve things that people at level 2 believe to be unachievable.
- At level 4 are dyslexic people who are aware of their weaknesses and have consciously developed strategies to overcome them, although they may still not be aware that they are dyslexic. Dyslexics at this level are exercising considerable control over their lives and tend to be the most successful of the four groups. The difference between people in this group and those at level 3 is that, in developing strategies, they are fully aware that they are involved in a process of making themselves more effective in terms of their lives.

We shall now examine the application of these levels in determining the delivery of counselling and training for dyslexic people. The starting point for working with a dyslexic is to determine at which level the client is functioning, since this determines the intervention strategy. Without this evaluation, there is the danger that genuine differences in need will go unnoticed and standard interventions will be applied as if adult dyslexics were a homogeneous group. Understanding the likely responses of each group to counselling interventions and why they may exhibit these responses is important.

THE CHARACTERISTICS OF DYSLEXICS AT THE FOUR LEVELS

The shortcomings for those at level 1, i.e., lack of self-awareness and failure to develop compensatory strategies, are frequently the product of a school and home environment that has focused on weaknesses rather than strengths. These people may have natural abilities that remain hidden or undeveloped because they have never been stretched emotionally, intellectually or academically. Dyslexics who might achieve a great deal but who have only ever been expected to achieve a little may never risk pushing their abilities to test themselves. By definition, people at level 1 do not seek help to improve their situation. There are, however, a number of ways in which such people may be identified. For example, a change in personal or working life increases the likelihood of dyslexia's coming to light. Whatever precipitates the identification of dyslexia in someone at level 1, the response from the person identified will usually be a mixture of shock, denial, fear, withdrawal and anxiety.

The reaction of someone at level 1 contrasts with the probable reaction of a person at level 2; in this case, the typical response is a mixture of relief, anger and happiness. People at this level have frequently experienced great frustration because of their inability to deal with basic tasks; for example, they may have experienced constant problems remembering instructions given to them verbally by their supervisor. As children, their teachers, peers and family may well have dismissed them, implicitly or explicitly, as worthless, lacking intelligence or potential, and unlikely to repay any investment made. After extensive exposure throughout their schooling to these persistent messages of ubiquitous inferiority, they come to accept this status. The identification of their dyslexia may result from the same set of circumstances as for people at level 1, but those at level 2 are more likely to be identified because they have sought help to improve their weaknesses. On finding that there is a less pejorative explanation for their experiences than simply that they are lacking intellect, they are often elated and relieved, although they may also display anger.

In general, these two distinct groups (levels 1 and 2) of adults respond differently to the information that they are dyslexic; however, there are also some common reactions. People at both levels may be confused and disoriented when given a diagnosis; some will simply not believe what they are being told, perhaps because of a reluctance to believe that their schools could have failed them so significantly.

Adult dyslexics at level 3, although they have developed some compensatory strategies to overcome weaknesses, may have to contend with similar emotions to those described at levels 1 and 2. The information that there are ways of improving performance is sometimes interpreted as a failure by society to implement action that could have made a significant difference to their lives, an interpretation which may result in a range of emotional responses, notably anger and sadness. Although they are aware of the origins of their difficulties and have developed coping strategies, dyslexia has served to reduce their ability to determine their position in life. Since these people are likely to be of reasonably high ability, they often respond to interventions with enthusiasm and sometimes want to go much faster than is practical in terms of personal development.

It is often the secondary symptoms of people who are at level 4 that are the significant issues. They have dealt with all of the primary problems but are left with problems of low self-esteem and lack of confidence. The approach for the counsellor in this situation is weighted in favour of 'generalist' expertise. Feelings of embarrassment, self-deprecation and helplessness are often the problems presented by people at level 4. They frequently report that they are living in fear that at any time they might be 'found out', and they anticipate the cringing embarrassment that this revelation would cause. It is sometimes purely generalist skills, such as those of the Rogerian counsellor, that people at this level seek. They are often very high-ability dyslexics who in their workplaces are suffering psychologically from 'problems with living'. There may be scope for improving their strategies, but if, as sometimes happens, they do not want anyone 'meddling' in their ways of coping with work demands, then, in recognition of their right to choose, the conclusion must be that generalist counselling is all that is required for these people.

There is, however, a need to examine the way dyslexics at level 4 are compensating, if they agree to such exploration. This intervention is to ensure that their coping mechanisms are efficient, and it requires specialist counselling and training skills. This may be a very sensitive topic; dyslexics at level 4 may be working hard to maintain their coping mechanisms, and they may be offended and very defensive in response to suggestions that they could improve their strategies. The most effective intervention here is to assist them to gain insight into their cognitive functioning so that they can assess for themselves whether what they do is maximally effective and whether it could be improved on. One approach to doing this is to use role-play methods with visualisation, as by encouraging clients to outline how they have responded to their most recent demands, to visualise what happened while describing it and then to role-play similar situations but with relevant changes to external demands. Guiding clients to explore for themselves how they respond to various situations and to allow them to test, in a safe environment, alternative strategies or variations of their existing strategies may result in their gaining insights into improvements to their strategies. Exploration of existing strategies and the possibilities for transferring them to other situations and tasks is an appropriate starting point for an intervention with a 'compensated' dyslexic; such an intervention is, in effect, training.

THE IMPORTANCE OF INFORMED CONSENT

Vivienne Young (2001, personal communication) suggests a useful distinction between two groups at level 4: level 4a comprises those dyslexics who have compensated but would benefit from reassessing their strategies and others who have good strategies in place but experience secondary difficulties that need resolving. Level 4b comprises the fully compensated dyslexics who have efficient strategies and no significant secondary difficulties. Ostensibly, it would appear that progressing clients to level 4b should be the goal of all interventions, but this is not always desirable, practical or achievable. Dyslexic people vary considerably, most notably in terms of their ability to understand their dyslexia and to compensate for the weaknesses it has caused them. The aim of interventions should be to enable dyslexics to function effectively in all the contexts that they consider are important to them. The assumption that they should be progressed to level 4b is not always a valid one. For example, progression to this point may disrupt relationships that the client has with significant others. In a relationship in which the partner of a dyslexic client has adopted the role of helper, the dyslexic adult may not wish to usurp the power of the partner in their relationship. The partners may be unaware of both the fact that they are involved in a relationship that involves this power distribution and that counselling might disrupt it. Many counsellors feel it inappropriate to make value judgements in such cases, preferring instead to explore with clients what they find to be acceptable goals of the intervention. There may be a need for the counsellor and client to see and understand the appropriateness of an intervention before it is implemented; counsellors obviously have a duty not to expose their clients to unnecessary risks. At the outset, many counsellors want to feel confident that the client has the psychological resources to deal with the changes that may occur. There are often consequences which neither client nor counsellor could anticipate, but this need not prevent a discussion of possible outcomes. Counsellors have an obligation to ensure that they have their client's informed consent before introducing interventions that may produce significant changes in their client, and therefore it is important to be aware of the above issues.

THE IMPACT ON THE INDIVIDUAL OF A POSITIVE DYSLEXIA DIAGNOSIS

The provision and availability of counselling or longer-term therapy as a support and a 'fail-safe' mechanism are advised in some form in all circumstances. This is an extremely important point that should be considered in all interventions, including diagnosis, which is often underestimated in terms of its potential to create a range of responses in clients. Accurate identification is the first step in the process of understanding, but diagnosis, in itself, does not convey much understanding of what the individual faces. Furthermore, the effect of being diagnosed dyslexic in adulthood is often a traumatic experience, particularly when the diagnosis is not accompanied by useful advice and guidance.

People who discover that they are dyslexic in their adulthood very often experience strong emotions. They may feel confused and disoriented. Anger and frustration, often directed at an educational system that failed to detect their dyslexia in spite of the evidence, is the most typical emotion displayed in these situations. It is not just the people who have obviously suffered who react strongly. Many people who have achieved considerable success may feel let down by a school system that failed to detect and respond to their condition appropriately. Many adult dyslexics who have been diagnosed in adulthood report hardship and loss of opportunity that they feel could have been avoided if their dyslexia had been identified earlier. It is not surprising to find such reactions from successful dyslexics. The consequences of success in the workplace are, for the undiagnosed adult dyslexic, often at the expense of personal social success and emotional stability. The lack of awareness and understanding of their condition often forces them to make choices they need not have made. As we have already seen in Chapter 5, success may also have a cost in terms of stress and burnout.

Many dyslexic people experience secondary symptoms as a consequence of not receiving counselling support after positive diagnoses. When dyslexics become aware of their difficulties and lack access to appropriate support to help them cope with those difficulties, there is the risk that they will suffer unnecessarily. The lowest level of support in terms of diagnosis, which is often not provided, is feedback to the client. As a minimum, this should involve an explanation of what dyslexia is, what action clients can take to further their goals, where and how they can access support should they feel they need it and an opportunity to ask their own questions about the diagnosis. In relation to clients asking questions about their diagnosis, it is preferable to provide them with an opportunity to present questions after they have had time to absorb the information presented in their diagnostic report. If arranging a face-to-face feedback session is not possible, alternatives such as telephone feedback or emailing questions and answers should be considered. A diagnosis that fails to indicate to clients how they can acquire insights to overcome their difficulties and gain control of their environment may cause unnecessary distress, serious psychological problems and, in extreme cases, even mental breakdown. It is essential that counsellors and trainers always acknowledge the risks of inappropriate intervention and strive to avoid them.

A COUNSELLING INTERVENTION PROGRAMME FOR ADULT DYSLEXICS

Determining the level at which an individual is functioning is generally straightforward and is a useful first step in the process of designing a counselling intervention programme for an adult dyslexic. If a competent dyslexia assessment has been completed on the individual, the level of functioning will have been identified in the report, although not necessarily explicitly so; i.e., the report will contain all the requisite information to determine the level of functioning. When no assessment has been completed, one should ideally be completed; however, if this is not possible, the screening procedure outlined in Chapter 5 of this book may be used to determine the level of functioning. Alternatively, structured interviewing can achieve the required determination of the dyslexic level of functioning.

As we have seen, dyslexics in general require interventions that involve a mixture of generalist and specialist counselling skills. The mixture tends to change from one that is dominated by specialist skills to one dominated by generalist skills, as we move from level 1 to level 4. There are, however, great variations in individual requirements, and the combination of generalist and specialist counselling skills is a function of the individual client's needs, which may change considerably in the course of a programme.

For assisting our dyslexic clients to overcome personal problems and to facilitate their personal development, we have been using a method that we designed and have been developing for some years. The 'dyslexia change-intervention programme' is appropriate for clients at any level, and it includes an ongoing assessment of need as part of its structure. The dyslexia change-intervention programme is a tool that has been developed in response to client needs on an on-going basis for some years. It has been influenced by various approaches to counselling, training and problem solving, including methods devised by Lindsay & Olley (1998), which were themselves the result of modifications to elements of Beck's cognitive therapy (Beck et al., 1979). The dyslexia change-intervention programme is a powerful procedure because it is flexible, pragmatic and responsive to the specific needs of this client group. For example, at any of the 'procedural states', a wide variety of tools may be employed to complete the activities according to the skills and experience of the facilitator and the preferences of the client. The counsellor and client engage in a procedure that starts with 'agenda setting and communication mode decisions' and then progresses to any of the six procedures, according to individual client needs and circumstances. Although some programmes would involve all the procedures in the order presented in Table 6.1, it is not necessary for them to take place in that order; some procedural states may be visited only once while others may be visited several times. It is very important that the procedure involves and is controlled by the client rather than the facilitator, who should provide guidance and encourage the client to take control of the process. The following case history illustrates the flexibility of the programme and the fact that clients are in control of it.

TABLE 6.1 A seven-step procedure for counselling adult dyslexics

Step	Activities
1. Agenda setting and communication mode decisions	A discussion to determine realistic goals and outcomes of the programme
	An exploration of possibilities for exchanging information and relevant training requirements if any; for example, face-to-face, telephone, fax, email, use of mental visualisation, drawings, specialised computer software programs
2. Skill development and programme preparation	Cognitive skills development
	Cognitive restructuring through relaxation and skill development to reduce negative emotions such as anger
3. Assessments	Determination of client strengths, weaknesses and personality factors
4. Establishing the extent of dyslexia-related problems	Examination of possible cause-effect relationship between areas of client concern and dyslexia
5. Raising awareness of internal activities	Exercises to reveal how unconscious beliefs, attitudes and thoughts operate to maintain client problems
6. Client-monitoring procedures	Exercises to collect personal data on internal activities, skill development and changing pattern of client needs
7. Change and development	Implementation of agreed activities arising from analysis of change-monitoring procedures; for example, training in cognitive skills, client-centred counselling, rational emotive therapy, reality testing and procedures to challenge maladaptive strategies and behaviours

Martha's Case History

Martha, a 24-year-old civil servant, was aware of her dyslexia and had a number of strategies for coping with its manifestations, although none were very well developed or effective (she was effectively a dyslexic between levels 3 and 4).

Martha was unhappy in her employment; she reported finding the work unchallenging and, apparently because of mistakes she had made, she had alienated co-workers. Furthermore, she felt she was being treated very poorly by her line manager. She was suffering from depression and high levels of stress when she presented for help, ostensibly to deal with her dyslexia.

In an initial orientation session to agree the agenda for her programme, Martha stated that she wanted to give up her employment and study medicine. One of five children, she explained that her two elder sisters and two younger brothers were doing very well academically and professionally. Martha believed that her parents had few expectations of her and that they would never support her in her ambition to become a doctor. She had never discussed this with them, but, apparently, once when she had mentioned leaving her employment to return to study, there had been a family row, with both her parents and sisters arguing that she should keep her job. Martha expressed a variety of emotions in the initial session, including anger at her sisters.

It was agreed that Martha's programme should initially focus on reducing and controlling her stress and her anger. It was also agreed that Martha's programme would progress by telephone and email contacts as well as face-to-face sessions. Martha's programme started with face-to-face sessions and continued with mainly telephone contacts, although it also involved occasional emails. She was initially trained in stress management techniques and assertiveness, which she used from early in her programme both to control her stress and manage her anger.

After some weeks, Martha stated that she was feeling more in control and that she would like to look again at what the objectives of her programme should be, and it was agreed that sessions would take place to help her improve her confidence and self-esteem. In face-to-face sessions, she discussed how she had failed to achieve academically what her parents expected of her and that, although dyslexia was an issue, she believed that she was not as bright as her sisters. In telephone sessions, the degree to which her parents' unreasonable expectations were responsible for her failure was explored.

In exercises looking at some of Martha's key past experiences with techniques from rational emotive therapy, Martha was able to grasp that her beliefs about events were invariably negative. Typically, she would make suggestions to her parents about her intentions, and when her parents questioned how well she had thought these suggestions through, she would interpret their response as rejecting her. When she examined exchanges she had had with her parents, she was able to see an alternative explanation; not that they were rejecting her but that they were keen that she did not take on too much and sacrifice what she already had.

Martha again returned to procedural step 1 to redefine her objectives, and it was decided that she would benefit from completing a personality inventory and assessment of strengths. After completion of the assessments, Martha undertook some training in memory development and verbal communication with the goal of improving self-presentation. Cognitive skill-training sessions took place alongside Rogerian-based counselling face-to-face, in which she discussed her emotions and fears related to her self-concept, personal goals and relationships with family and friends.

Martha took advantage of emails, writing substantial amounts of often apparently unrelated information about feelings, emotions, desires and daily events. The various questions she posed in her emails were responded to by return emails and telephone calls.

Martha made progress in many ways, and her relationships with her parents became much less stressful. She became particularly skilled in using visual memory strategies to keep large amounts of information in memory. The information she kept included the progress that she was making in gaining control of her environment, such as reducing the errors she was making at work, improving relationships with co-workers and talking with her sisters.

Martha's sessions became much less frequent after an initial period of some three months when she was making contact regularly (two to four times each week), eventually ending with very occasional telephone contacts in which she used to discuss specific issues that she needed to resolve. By the end of the programme, Martha no longer wanted to train as a doctor; instead, she decided to train as a nurse with the full support of her family. She was advanced in terms of her memory development and was working on developing strategies for dealing effectively with her future nursing studies.

This counselling structure is appropriate for major personal development programmes and individual problem solving, either personal or work related. The latter is discussed below under 'Brief Intervention Counselling for Dyslexics'. When used in the context of personal development, the procedural states are usually recursive; i.e., each one may be operated several times. An important element of this programme, when used in personal development, is procedural step 6, since client-monitoring procedures are generally central to personal development programmes for adult dyslexics. When memory differences or deficits in literacy skills make client-monitoring procedures too demanding without support, there are a number of alternatives. Training in memory skills is one option and the most adaptive one. Other options include use of pictures, drawings and diagrams (including representations of emotions) with selected clients. The use of voice-activated software on a laptop or desktop computer is another option. A further possibility is the use of various specialist computer programs; for example, the Widget program offers exciting possibilities. This is a system that can create individualised pictorial or iconic communications that assist understanding and the ability to complete records. Counsellors must be careful to ensure that any option chosen is appropriate for the client.

METHODS OF COLLECTING DATA FROM DYSLEXIC CLIENTS

Client-monitoring procedures can involve a wide range of methods, and the more techniques counsellors have, the more effective they will be in using the structure outlined above. The use of self-report techniques is a powerful method for investigating emotional experiences. They are particularly useful when clients are not effective communicators and have few insights into their personal psychology, but some caution is required. Historically, it was thought that the impoverished cognitive and linguistic capacities of dyslexic people create major difficulties in using self-report techniques. As a consequence, researchers have in the past interviewed relatives or significant people in the client's life. An extensive literature has developed on the identification of the emotional problems of clients by standard interviews and symptom checklists filled out by significant others. It may therefore seem valid to use significant others as a source of information; it might even be the case that the client recommends such action, but it is not generally recommended. Nadarajah et al. (1995) demonstrated that clients may have very different perceptions from those of the significant others in their lives, who may misunderstand the significance of events in the client's life—e.g., misconstrue or misunderstanding their meanings. These researchers found that direct, semistructured interviewing is an effective method to identify non-verbal cues of emotion. Developments in assessment techniques have found more reliable and systematic methods of asking clients to judge the nature of their cognitive and emotional difficulties. While there is some indication that dyslexics have difficulties with some approaches—for example, reporting results from the administration of the Zung self-rating anxiety scale and self-rating depression scale (Zung, 1965, 1971)—Lindsay & Michie (1988) found that standard presentations produced very low reliability scores. However, by simplifying the language, the concepts used and the response choices, they found that respondents could use the assessments with a high degree of reliability. These findings emphasise that if therapists take due care, reliable and valid assessments of the feelings and thoughts of dyslexic people can be gathered directly. While it is common to find people assuming that dyslexic people are a population with a less stable cognitive system than the non-dyslexic population, this is, arguably, unfounded (Lindsay et al., 1998).

An alternative to self-report techniques that we have found to be a very flexible and powerful method of information collection, particularly for use with people at levels 3 and 4, involves interviewing with a simplification of the critical incidents technique (Flanagan 1954). This technique is a well-established method of job analysis. Our simplification requires clients to provide anecdotes or examples of events that they were involved in and which resulted in either success or failure. For example, the event might be a job interview in which they performed very well or a social event that did not go well for them. The clients first describe the event, then their feelings about the event at the time and then their feelings about the event now. They then use visualisation to change aspects of the event to identify reasons for the success or failure. The information that emerges may give insights into the client's strengths, weaknesses, strategies and development needs, from which appropriate interventions can be developed. These might include personal development through counselling approaches such as client-centred therapy or specialist training.

SOME IMPORTANT SPECIALIST COUNSELLING SKILLS

In using the counselling procedure that was introduced and discussed above, there are a number of areas where the counsellor will need specific specialist skills as indicated below.

Developing Dyslexics' Self-Esteem, Self-Image and Confidence

There are several distinct routes to facilitating the development of self-esteem, self-image and confidence. Training in memory development and verbal communication often results in marked improvements as clients receive self-feedback showing that they can match and exceed the performance of others in the prized assets of recall and articulation.

More direct methods are available, and we have seen significant and rapid improvements, which have proved to be constant over time, resulting from the use of affirmations, such as positive statements about taking control of the consequences of dyslexia and about the positive outcomes related to the condition. By making a commitment to the regular use of affirmations, dyslexic people can greatly enhance their self-esteem. It is generally recognised that visualisation, which is a strength of dyslexics, is also a powerful tool that, when used in the cognitive rehearsal of intended behaviours, can improve social performance. This often leads to objective evidence of improvements in the dyslexic's self-esteem in the form of desirable changes in behaviour and reduction in self-effacing comments. The use of visualisation for the anticipation of problems can provide a range of possible solutions, the successful application of which may increase the dyslexic's success in all elements of life. In the long term, this success feeds into further positive changes in self-esteem, self-image and confidence.

Stress Reduction and Management for Dyslexics

Counsellors who provide stress-related services to dyslexics need a variety of methods for combating stress. It is generally important to facilitate an understanding of the major stress triggers related to dyslexia. The counsellor should be able to detail their likely consequences and to specify the range of defensive and offensive techniques that may be deployed by organisations and utilised by individuals to address these stress triggers. Clients are encouraged to create visualisations, according to individual preference, which they associate with the stress triggers (trigger pictures). These visualisations correspond to their felt-experiences of stress. Client are then encouraged to control these visualisations so that they gain control over their perceptions of environmental stressors. Self-instructions, regarding responses to stress triggers, in terms of how they will invoke visualisations, are built in to a mental routine that is practised to promote its becoming an automatic response. What this means is that clients may reach a point where they can invoke, at will, visualisations to help them manage stressful events. The acquisition of coping skills is a key element in progressing a dyslexic adult towards success. The variety of possible coping skills and the areas in which they are needed is very large, and counselling interventions must be tailored to individual client circumstances, including ability, education and personality. An important overarching principle is that whatever the coping mechanism is that serves the coping system, it must exist on three levels: an attitude, a thought and an action. The counsellor-trainer must address each of these levels and may do so by employing visualisation techniques in cognitive rehearsal of intended behaviours, thoughts and attitudes.

BRIEF INTERVENTION COUNSELLING FOR DYSLEXICS

Apart from comprehensive programmes of personal development, which was the main concern above, dyslexic clients often present counsellors with a specific concern or problem to be solved. Many dyslexics present problems that need solutions rapidly; for example, they need to take action to keep their employment when under threat of being sacked because of dyslexia-related difficulties. This problem often arises, and it frequently involves counsellors advising clients on how they should disclose their dyslexia. In addition to this type of very practical problem, there are also relationship problems that may present the need for rapid action. While such problems might well lead to a full personal development programme, they do not necessarily do so. Counsellors are therefore often required to provide strategies for solving specific problems without involving their clients in long periods of counselling.

We have developed an intervention for helping dyslexics to deal with this type of situation; our brief intervention counselling involves using the 'dyslexia change-intervention programme' described above. Steps 1–6 are visited briefly, but most time is spent on step 7, which usually involves visualisation, supported by cognitive rehearsal and self-instructional training. The latter technique involves developing internal dialogues to help overcome performance difficulties and social anxieties, and to supplant self-criticism or self-doubt with self-reinforcement (Meichenbaum, 1977).

USING THE INTERNET FOR DYSLEXIC COUNSELLING

The Internet offers some interesting possibilities vis-à-vis counselling for adult dyslexics. The fact that there are now programs making it possible to talk to a computer and to have documents, such as emails, read aloud from the computer, combined with the fact that this method offers total anonymity to the client, makes Internet counselling a very attractive option for the conduct of counselling. Other software programs that can be used to structure people's thoughts, ideas and concerns into coherent and concise documents further enhance its attractiveness. As already mentioned, dyslexic clients have a fundamental problem with both expressing their feelings clearly and understanding what the counsellor is saying to them. These problems may be unrelated to any possible intellectual deficits, but they may be a consequence of the dyslexic inefficiency in working memory. As we have already seen, dyslexic adults have a range of difficulties, of which literacy is the most obvious, but not the most significant. These various problems may pose obstacles to the provision of the traditional therapies that are based on complex and subtle linguistic understandings. The speed with which oral or written communications are delivered and processed by dyslexic adults is typically slower than that of their non-dyslexic peers.

To understand in more detail what is happening, we need to look at the dyslexic population, which is made up of those who have compensated for their dyslexia, and those who have not. In general, the non-compensated dyslexics are those who can neither express themselves effectively nor follow efficiently what the counsellor is saying. They face very significant difficulties because they cannot track and recall the content of questions and observations made by the counsellor when the input is purely verbal. Nor can they, when left to their own devices, articulate, in a fully meaningful way, how they are feeling, what they are thinking or what they require in order to gain peace of mind.

Compensated dyslexics have strategies for understanding what they read. They usually comprehend written sources of information by relying on semantic reading, i.e., a method of reading that many dyslexics develop, which bypasses silent speech. They follow verbal exchanges by relying on acquired skills in controlling conversations so they can track efficiently what is being said. While many can express themselves very well verbally, in general, they are able to do this only if they have time to prepare in some way what they intend to say. Even very high-ability dyslexics find that they need to have preparation time if they are going to answer questions or talk generally. They find talking very difficult when they have not prepared, particularly when they are in high-stress situations. Dyslexics tend to be very ineffective in situations where they need to express their feelings in response to immediate situations presented to them. In employment, this weakness may lead to prejudiced views that dyslexics lack social skills or openness. This lowering of efficient verbal communication is emphatically the case when the material in question is highly charged emotionally. Consequently, compensated dyslexics in a counselling context are at a distinct disadvantage; they may be able to follow what the counsellor is saying, but significant self-expression is undermined by their condition. Furthermore, as far as following what the counsellor is saying, although it may not be apparent to the counsellor, taking in material to be remembered may be a demanding task for even high-ability dyslexics. The dyslexic's effort to assimilate what is being said detracts from the understanding that the counsellor may expect from the client. Compensated dyslexics will, however, be able very efficiently to describe their emotions, feelings and thoughts if they have time to prepare them and record them on paper, as by using voice-activated software.

Thus, compensated dyslexics, although more able to benefit from face-to-face counselling than their non-compensated counterparts, are likely to have more difficulties speaking of their feelings directly to a counsellor than they would have either typing or using voice-activated software to express their feelings. Of course, the option of speaking to a computer is one that opens up effective counselling opportunities for the non-compensated dyslexic as well.

Counselling over the net, by swapping emails between counsellor and client, is potentially the solution to many of the problems associated with talking therapies in the context of dyslexia. 'Cybercounselling', as we may call it, offers an opportunity for dyslexics to overcome the communication difficulties that they have in face-to-face situations, and that are a consequence of working-memory deficits. Dyslexic clients would need access to software that allows them to speak directly to the computer in order to compose emails and other software that would read aloud the counsellor's responses. If clients are allowed to absorb what is being communicated by reading and rereading (or listening and 're-listening') to that communication as often as they need, they are more likely to benefit from it. Rereading what is received over the net does not disrupt the feeling of immediacy of interaction that would be lost if the counsellor simply gave a hard copy to the client after a session. In counselling where the only mode of communication is written communication, the writing needs to be carefully constructed—it is a dynamic process and very different from what would usually be written in a hard copy presented, after a verbal exchange, for the purpose of recording the key features of that exchange. The latter is a summary of what has transpired while the former is a dynamic, interactive process. This is a very important point: when writing or typing (including producing text by voice-activated software) is the only communication, it must contain much more information than do summaries. The dyslexics are not likely to lose key information, as they could in a verbal exchange. Similarly, being able to prepare an explanation of feelings and transmit it is preferable to having to utter something that needs to be modified by what may be very lengthy and confusing explanations.

A significant feature of this cybercounselling for dyslexia is that it provides time and space for the client to reflect on the issues being examined in the therapeutic exchange. For a dyslexic, this feature represents a valuable gain since it is the pressure to respond that, for dyslexics, is often the barrier to the benefits of counselling or therapy. This may well have important implications for the broader context of therapy on the Internet in general, since time to reflect may be an important element in people overcoming their difficulties. The net is a mainstream device for worldwide communications, and the focus is on the product, not the way it was constructed. In using the net, dyslexics are not being distinguished from other communicators. It does not matter how long it takes to absorb what is received or to construct what is sent—this is an empowering experience. We have seen clients for whom cybercounselling has proved to be this empowering experience. We have encountered a predictable problem in evaluating the effectiveness of this counselling because of difficulties identifying what produces this positive outcome; it may well be the empowering effect of using the net that produces the observed positive changes (as opposed to what the counsellor is doing). However, to pragmatists, uncertainty about the 'real' cause of desirable change is not important; i.e., whatever is in fact responsible for the positive changes is not as important as the fact that there are positive changes.

THE INTERNET AS PSYCHOTHERAPY FOR ADULT DYSLEXICS

The provision of psychotherapy is an area in which there is little literature specific to the requirements of the dyslexic clients. A notable exception is the psychotherapeutic approach practised by Alfred A. Tomatis (1978), who developed an approach to the psychotherapy and treatment of dyslexia and learning problems in the early 1960s. He maintains that dyslexia stems from impaired listening and argues that the ear plays a fundamental role in language development. Tomatis's psychotherapy is mainly focused on retraining people to hear sounds by the therapeutic use of music and sound generators. However, he appears to support this process by assisting dyslexic clients to identify and analyse the response they have to their 'dyslexified world', which is the label he gives to the dyslexic experience of being isolated from and poorly understood by others. This is an interesting approach that warrants further attention, along with many other issues related to psychotherapy for dyslexic adults.

As we mentioned earlier, the distinction between counselling and psychotherapy is not well established. Some authors, e.g., Truax & Carkhuff (1967), use the terms interchangeably, while others make various distinctions. Here we shall use the term 'psychotherapy' to refer to a long-term process to change fundamental personality features that have developed as a consequence of the life experiences of dyslexics.

Psychotherapy tends to require people to be very articulate in a spontaneous fashion i.e., the efficacy of the procedures is lost if clients cannot cope without preparing what they want to say. The Internet may offer dyslexics access to psychotherapy by removing this barrier. For over a hundred years, the 'physical reality' world, in contrast to the 'virtual reality' world of computers, has been exposed to the theories and techniques of psychoanalysis and psychotherapy. All of these therapies are based on, or are a reaction to, the methods and concepts created by Freud and those theorists who followed him, extending and modifying his original recognition of the conscious and unconscious elements of the mind. The Internet potentially opens up these areas to adult dyslexics who would otherwise effectively be denied access. The key word is 'potentially'; the concept of psychotherapy over the net is very new and it needs to be tested. In particular, key psychodynamic concepts, such as transference, counter-transference and projection, need to be re-examined within this new medium. The Internet is now ubiquitous and evolving almost beyond imagination; for the moment, it is beyond the control of political and corporate power. It is bringing together very disparate groups of people into a community that is intangible, a community in cyberspace. This cybercommunity offers people who are disabled by the societies they live in an opportunity for inclusion and an opportunity to resolve some of the problems that exclusion has created. One of those problems is perceived equality; dyslexics often feel that society has relegated them to the status of 'less important than non-dyslexics'. The cybercommunity may be one society where, because of the fundamental nature of that society, dyslexics can lose this negative self-perception; i.e., becoming a part of cybersociety may have psychotherapeutic effects for dyslexics. The work of Deleuze & Guattari (1987) offers a contemporary way of conceptualising the Internet for therapeutic interventions with dyslexics. Their concept of the rhizome is the key to understanding this. They define (p. 21) 'rhizome' as a state whose key aspects are 'an acentered, nonhierarchical, nonsignifying system without a general and without an organising memory or central automation, defined solely by a circulation of states'.

The Internet can be conceptualised as a rhizomatic system: essentially, this means that it is a system of social order characterised by active encounter rather than objectification. According to Deleuze & Guattari, the rhizome is not hierarchical in structure, but anti-hierarchical. No point must come before another, no specific point must be connected to another point, but all points are and must be connected. This may be viewed as a description of the emerging Internet society, which is pioneering a system, based on a form of communication, wherein both dyslexic and non-dyslexic persons may be more nearly equal. Whether or not the Internet proves to be the ultimate non-discriminating society remains to be seen; it does, however, appear to offer dyslexics an alternative to Tomatis's 'dyslexified world'. This is an area that we, as practitioners, are exploring, with the long-term goal of providing comprehensive, effective and efficient therapeutic support to dyslexic people.

APPENDIX: USEFUL ORGANISATIONS

ORGANISATIONS OFFERING SERVICES IN ADULT DYSLEXIA

Fitzgibbon Associates

39–41 North Road, London N7 9DP, UK
Tel: 020 7609 7809
Fax: 020 7609 8205
Email: fae@fitzgibbonassociates.co.uk
Websites: www.adultdyslexia.co.uk
            www.fitzgibbonassociates.co.uk

A firm of occupational psychologists offering comprehensive services in the areas of adult dyslexia, stress risk assessment, stress management and creativity in organisations.

Employers' Forum on Disability

Nutmeg House, 60 Gainsford Street, London SE1 2NY
Tel: 020 7403 3020
Fax: 020 7403 0404

An organisation concerned with the employment and training of people with disabilities.

European Dyslexia Association

12 Goldington Avenue, Bedford MK40 3BY
Email: eurodysass@kbnet.co.uk
Website: http://www2.soutron.com/eda

An organisation that offers support to dyslexic groups and promotes links between groups.

Dyslexia Institute

133 Gresham Road, Staines, Middlesex TW18 2AJ
Tel: 01784 463 851
Fax: 01784 460 747
Email: dyslexia-inst@connect.bt.com
Website: http://www.dyslexia-inst.org.uk

A registered educational charity with centres throughout the United Kingdom Provides psychological assessment and tuition (for those they assess).

British Dyslexia Association

98 London Road, Reading RG1 5AU
Helpline: 0118 966 8217
Administration: 0118 966 2677
Fax: 0118 935 1927
Email: helpline@bda-dyslexia.demon.co.uk
Website: http://www.bda-dyslexia.org.uk

A national charity organisation representing dyslexia organisations, support groups and corporate members. Provides national support network. Publishes a magazine, *Dyslexia Contact*, an annual *Dyslexia Handbook* and (in collaboration with John Wiley and Sons, publishers) an international research journal, *Dyslexia*.

Adult Dyslexia Organisation

336 Brixton Road, London SW9 7AA
Helpline: 020 7924 9559
Administration: 020 7737 7646
Email: dyslexia.hq@dial.pipex.com
Website: http://www.futurenet.co.uk/charity/ado/index.html

A national charitable organisation that offers advice about dyslexia assessments and provides a range of pamphlets and videos.

COMPUTING SUPPORT FOR ADULT DYSLEXICS

Computer Centre for People with Disabilities

University of Westminster, 72 Great Portland Street, London W1N 5AL
Tel: 020 7911 5000
Fax: 020 7911 5162
Website: http://www.wmin.ac.uk/ccpd/

Computer Information and Advice Service

98 London Road, Reading RG1 5AU
Tel: 0118 966 2677
Email: admin@bda-dyslexia

Hands Free Computing Ltd

Enterprise House, Old London Road, Hickstead, West Sussex, RH17 5LZ
Tel: 01444 880 880
Email: sales@hands-free.co.uk

OTHER RELEVANT ORGANISATIONS

The British Psychological Society

St Andrews House, 48 Princess Road East, Leicester LE1 7DR

Department for Education and Employment

Sanctuary Buildings, Great Smith Street, Westminster, London SW1P 3BT
Tel: 020 7925 5000
Fax: 020 7925 6000
Website: http://www.dfee.gov.uk

A UK government department that provides advice to the government on education and employment issues.

REFERENCES

Aiken, L.R. (1985) Psychological Testing and Assessment. Allyn and Bacon: MA. Newton

Arnold, J., Cooper, C.L., & Robertson, I.T. (1998) Work Psychology: Understanding Human Behaviour in the Workplace (3rd Edn). Pearson Education Limited: Edinburgh.

Baddeley, A.D. (1986) Working Memory. Oxford University Press: London.

Baddeley, A.D., & Hitch, G.J. (1974) Working memory. In Bower, G. (Ed.), Recent Advances in Learning and Motivation (Vol. 8, pp. 47–90). Academic Press: New York.

Baron, R.M., Graziano, W.G., & Stangor, C. (1991) Social Perception and Social Cognition. In Baron, R.M., Graziano, W.G., & Stangor, C.R. (Eds.), Social Psychology (pp. 108–159). Holt, Rinehart & Winston: Fort Worth, TX.

Bartlett, D., & Moody, S. (2000) Dyslexia in the Workplace. Whurr: London.

Beck, A., Rush, S., Smith, D., & Emery, G. (1979) Cognitive Therapy of Depression. Guilford Press: New York.

Blum, M., & Naylor, J. (1968) Industrial Psychology. Harper & Row: New York.

British Dyslexia Association (1995) Dyslexia: Signposts to Success, A Guide for Dyslexic Adults and Their Employers. British Dyslexia Association: Reading.

British Psychological Society (1993) Codes of Conduct, Ethical Principles and Guidelines. British Psychological Society: Leicester.

British Psychological Society (2001) The Directory of Chartered Psychologists. Codes of Conduct, Ethical Principles and Guidelines. British Psychological Society: Leicester.

British Psychological Society (1999) Dyslexia, Literacy and Psychological Assessments. British Psychological Society: Leicester.

Campbell, J. (2001) Valuing diversity—the disability agenda. We've only just begun. Lecture presented at Bristol University, Bristol, UK on 9 November 2001.

Carnevale, A.P., Gainer, L.J., & Meltzer, A.S. (1988) Workplace Basics. The Skills Employers Want. American Society for Training and Development: Alexandria, VA.

Casey, D., Gerry, R., Reed, M.T., & Schenk, F. (n.d.) Employment Law. Obtained from the website at http://www.cglaw.com/text_version/employment.htm.

Collins Concise Dictionary (2001) 21st Century Edition. Harper Collins Publishers. Glasgow.

Critical Analysis of the Disability Discrimination Act (n.d.). Obtained from the website at http://www.freespace.virgin.net/steven.jacklin/ddacrit.html1.

Deleuze, G., & Guattari, F. (1987) A Thousand Plateaux. University of Minneapolis Press: Minneapolis, MN.

Disability Discrimination Act (1995): The Employment Provisions and Small Employers: A Review. (1997) DfEE. London.

Disability Rights Commission. Information obtained from the website at http://www.drc-gb.org.

Douglas, S., & Fitzgibbon, G. Strategies for training adult dyslexics (in preparation).

Drake, R.F. (1999) Understanding Disability Policies. Macmillan Press: London.

Ellis, A. (1962) Reason and Emotion in Psychotherapy. Lyal Stuart: New York.

Fawcett, A.J. and Nicolson, R.I. (1998) Dyslexia Adult Screening Test. London: The Psychological Corporation.

Fitzgibbon, G. Improving Dyslexic Performance by Developing Visual Memory Skills (in preparation).

Flanagan, J.C. (1954) The critical incident technique. Psychological Bulletin, 51, 327–358.

Frith, U. (1997) Brain, mind and behaviour in dyslexia. In Hulme C., & Snowling M. (Eds), Dyslexia: Biology, Cognition and Intervention (pp. 1–20). Whurr: London.

Furnham, A. (1997) The Psychology of Behaviour at Work: The Individual in the Organisation. Psychology Press: Hove.

Future of Social Policy (1994) HMSO: London.

Gerber, P.J., Ginsberg, R., & Reiff, H. (1992) Identifying alterable patterns in employment success for highly successful adults with learning disabilities. Journal of Learning Disabilities, 25 (8), 475–487.

Goss, N. (2000) Jobs Worth: Disability in Small Business. RADAR. London.

Ingham, J. (1991) Matching instruction with employee perceptual preference significantly increases training effectiveness. Human Resource Development Quarterly, 2 (1; Spring), 53–64.

Irlen, H.L. (1989) Scotopic Sensitivity Syndrome Screening Manual (3rd Ed). Perceptual Development Corporation. Long Beach: California. USA.

Irlen, H.L. (1991) Reading by the Colors: Overcoming Dyslexia and other Reading Disabilities Through the Irlen Method. Avenbury Publications: New York.

Katz, D., & Kahn, R. (1966) The Social Psychology of Organisations. Wiley: New York.

Kyd, L., Sutherland, G., & McGettrick, P. (1992) A preliminary appraisal of the Irlen screening process for scotopic sensitivity syndrome and the effect of Irlen coloured overlays on reading. British Orthothalmic Journal, 49, 25–30.

Lester, A. (1994) Hansard, 22 May 1994. Obtained from the website at http://www.freespace. virgin.net/steven.jacklin/ddacrit.html1.

Lindsay, W., & Olley, S. (1998) Psychological treatment for anxiety and depression for people with learning disabilities. In Fraser, W., Sines, D., & Kerr, M. (Eds), The Care of People with Intellectual Disabilities. (9th Edn). Butterworth Heinemann: Oxford.

Lindsay, W., Overend, H., Allan, R., Williams, C., & Black, L. (1998) Using specific approaches for individual problems in the management of anger and aggression. British Journal of Learning Disabilities, 26, 44–50.

Lindsay, W., & Michie, A. (1988) Adaptation of the Zung self-rating anxiety scale for people with a mental handicap. Journal of Mental Deficiency Research, 32, 485–490.

Makin, P., Cooper, C.L. and Cox, C. (1996) Organisations and the Psychological Contract. Leicester: British Psychological Society.

McCormick, E.P., Jeanneret, R., & Mecham, R. (1972) A study of job characteristics and job dimensions as based on the position analysis questionnaire. Journal of Applied Psychology, 56, 367–368.

McGuiness, D. (1998) Why Children Can't Read. Penguin Books: London.

McLoughlin, D., Fitzgibbon, G., & Young, V. (1994) Adult Dyslexia: Assessment Counselling and Training. Whurr: London.

Meichenbaum, D. (1977) Cognitive Behavior Modification: An Integrative approach. Plenum Press: New York.

Miles, M., & Huberman, M. (1984) Qualitative Data Analysis: A Source Book for New Methods. Sage: Thousand Oaks, CA.

Miles, T., (1988) Counselling in dyslexia. Counselling Psychology Quarterly, 1, 97–107.

Miles, T. (2001) Reflections and research. In Hunter-Carsch, M. (Ed.), Dyslexia: A Psychosocial Perspective (pp. 32–38). Whurr: London.

Miles, T.R. (1991) Bangor Dyslexia Test. Learning Development Aids: Cambridge.

Miles, T.R. (1994) Towards a rationale for diagnosis (pgs 101–108). In Hales. G. (Ed). Dyslexia Matters. London: Whurr Publishers.

Moustakas, C. (1994) Phenomenological Research Methods. Sage: London.

Nadarajah, J., Roy, A., Harris, T., & Corbett, J. (1995) Methodological aspects of life events research in people with a learning disability. Journal of Intellectual Disability Research, 39, 47–56.

Nicolson, R.I., & Fawcett, A.J. (1990) Automaticity: A new framework for dyslexia research? Cognition, 35, 159–182.

Novaco, R. (1986) Anger as a clinical and social problem. In Blanchard, R. & Blanchard, C. (Eds), Advance in the Study of Aggression (vol. 2). Academic Press: New York.

Patton, J.R., & Polloway, E.A. (1992) Learning disabilities: The challenges of adulthood. Journal of Learning Disabilities, 25, 410–415.

Paulesu, E., Demonet, J.-F., Fazio, F., McCrory, E., Chanoine, V., Brunswick, N., Cappa, S.F., Cossu, G., Habib, M., Frith, C.D., & Frith, U. (2001) Dyslexia: Cultural diversity and biological unity. Science, 291(5511), 2165.

Pearn, M., & Kandola, R. (1990) Job Analysis: A Practical Guide for Managers. Institute of Personnel Management: London.

Prosser, P. (1999) Anxiety and learning difficulties. The Psychologist, 12 (5), 215–217.

Pumfrey, P.D., & Reason, R. (Eds.) (1991) Specific Learning Difficulties (Dyslexia): Challenges and Responses. NFER-Nelson Publishing: London.

Rack, J. (1994) Dyslexia: The phonological deficit hypothesis. In Nicolson, R.I., & Fawcett, A.J. (Eds), Dyslexia in Children: Multidisciplinary Perspectives (pp. 5–37). Harvester Wheatsheaf: Hemel Hempstead.

Reid, G., & Kirk, J. (2000) Dyslexia in Adults: Education and Employment. Wiley: Chichester.

Rogers, C.R. (1961) On Becoming a Person. Houghton Mifflin: Boston.

Ross, L. (1977) The intuitive psychologist and his shortcomings: Distortions in the attribution process. In Berkowitz, L. (Ed.), Advances in Experimental Social Psychology (vol. 10, pp. 173–220). Academic Press: New York.

Ross, L., & Nisbett, R.E. (1991) The Person and the Situation: Perspectives of Social Psychology. McGraw-Hill: New York.

Ruebain, D. (2000) What is prejudice as it relates to disability anti-discrimination law? Obtained from the website at http://www.disabilityworld.org/10-12_00/news/symposium.htm.

Seligman, M.E.P. (1975) Helplessness: On Depression, Development and Death. Freeman: San Francisco, CA.

Selye, H. (1976) The Stress of Life (Rev. Edn.). McGraw-Hill: New York.

Smith, R.E. (1999) Psychology. West Publishing Company: MN: St. Paul.

Taylor Brown, V.Y. (1998) Dyslexia and Affect. Unpublished dissertation.

Thomson, M. (2001) The Psychology of Dyslexia: A Handbook for Teachers. Whurr: London.

Thomson, M.E., & Watkins, E.J. (1990) Dyslexia: A Teaching Handbook. Whurr: London.

Tomatis, A. (1978) Education and Dsylexia. Association-Internationale d'Audio-psycho-Phonologie: Switzerland. Fribourg.

Truax, C.R., & Carkhuff, R.R. (1967) Towards Effective Counselling and Psychotherapy. Aldine: Chicago.

Turner, M. (1977) Psychological Assessment of Dyslexia. Whurr: London.

Wechsler, D. (1999) Wechsler Adult Intelligence Test (WAIS-III). The Psychological Corporation: New York.

Wechsler, D. (1992) Wechsler Intelligence Scale for Children (3rd Edn) (WISC-III). The Psychological Corporation: New York.

West, T.G. (1997) In the Mind's Eye: Visual Thinkers, Gifted People with Learning Difficulties, Computer Images and the Ironies of Creativity. Prometheus: Buffalo, NY.

West, T.G. (1999) The future is with dyslexics. Paper presented at Dyslexia and Employment, Now and the Future Conference. Adult Dyslexia Organisation: London.

Zola, I. (1972) Medicine as an institution of social control. The Sociological Review, 20(4), 487–504.

Zung, W. (1965) A self-rating depression scale. Archives of General Psychiatry, 12, 63–70.

Zung, W. (1971) A rating instrument for anxiety disorders. Psychosomatics, 12, 371–379.

INDEX

Added to page number 't' refers to a table.

Index compiled by Siona Smith